Penguin Books
POISONED REIGN

Bengt Danielsson was born in 1921 at Krokek,
Sweden. He holds a Ph.D. in anthropology, was
formerly director of the National Museum of
Ethnography of Sweden, and is presently Honorary
Associate in Anthropology in the Bernice P. Bishop
Museum, Honolulu. He has done most of his
anthropological field work in Eastern Polynesia, but
also in the Amazonas and Australia. He first came
to French Polynesia as a member of Thor
Heyerdahl's famous Kon-Tiki raft expedition in
1947.

Marie-Thérèse Danielsson was born in 1923 at
Vosges, France, and married Bengt in 1948.
During their lifelong residency in French
Polynesia, she has been active in local politics,
women's organizations and associations for the
protection of nature. Since 1977 an elected town
councillor in Paea, on the west coast of Tahiti,
where the Danielssons have their home.

The Danielssons have published a number of
popular books which have been widely translated,
including *Raroia, The Happy Island* (1951), *Love in
the South Seas* (1954), *What Happened on the
Bounty* (1962) and a six-volume history of French
Polynesia, *Le Mémorial Polynésian* (1976-80).

Bengt Danielsson
and Marie-Thérèse Danielsson

POISONED REIGN

*French nuclear colonialism in
the Pacific*

Penguin Books

Penguin Books Australia Ltd,
487 Maroondah Highway, P.O. Box 257
Ringwood, Victoria 3134, Australia
Penguin Books Ltd,
Harmondsworth, Middlesex, England
Penguin Books,
40 West 23rd Street, New York, N.Y. 10010, U.S.A.
Penguin Books Canada Ltd,
2801 John Street, Markham, Ontario, Canada L3R 1B4
Penguin Books (N.Z.) Ltd,
182–190 Wairau Road, Auckland 10, New Zealand
First published by Stock, Paris 1974, under the title Moruroa Mon Amour
Revised English language edition published by Penguin Books 1977
Second revised edition published by Penguin Books 1986

Typeset in Monophoto Plantin
Made and printed in Australia by The Dominion Press–Hedges & Bell, Victoria

CIP

Danielsson, Bengt, 1921–
Poisoned reign.

Rev. ed.
ISBN 0 14 008130 5.

1. Nuclear weapons – Testing. 2. French Polynesia –
Politics and government. I. Danielsson, Marie-Thérèse,
1923– . II. Danielsson, Bengt, 1921– . Moruroa,
mon amour. III. Title. IV. Title: Moruroa, mon amour.

320.996´2

CONTENTS

ABBREVIATIONS

BRGM   *Bureau de Recherches Géologiques et Minières*
(Agency for Geological Studies and Mining
Explorations)

CEA   *Commissariat à l'Energie Atomique*
(Atomic Energy Commission)

CEP   *Centre d'Expérimentation du Pacifique*
(Centre for Experiments in the Pacific)

LMS   London Missionary Society

MIRV   Multiple Independently Targetable Re-entry
Vehicle

ORSTOM   *Office de Recherche Scientifique et Technique
d'Outre-mer*
(Agency for Scientific and Technical Researches
Overseas)

ORTF   *Office de Radiodiffusion Télévision Française*
(French Radio and Television System)

RDPT   *Rassemblement Démocratique des Populations
Tahitiennes*
(Democratic Party of the Tahitian Population)

SCPRI   *Service Central de Protection contre les
Rayonnements Ionisants*
(Central Agency for the Protection against
Atomic Radiation)

SMSR   *Service Mixte de sécurité Radiologique*
(Amalgamated Radiological Safety Service)

UDR   *Union des Démocrates pour la Ve République*
(Union of Democrats for the Fifth Republic) or
Union pour la Défense de la République
(Union for the Defence of the Republic), the
successive names of the Gaullist party since
1968

UNR   *Union pour la Nouvelle République*
(Union for the New Republic); the name of the
Gaullist party from 1958 to 1967.

FOREWORD

On 10 July 1985, the French exploded two more bombs in the South Pacific. These explosions, in Auckland Harbour, New Zealand, were nowhere near as powerful as the 150 kilotonne test the French had conducted two months earlier at Moruroa. However, the Auckland explosions were to emit a much larger shock wave.

The Greenpeace protest ship *Rainbow Warrior* had sailed into nuclear free New Zealand on 7 July, in preparation for another Moruroa campaign later in the year. It was tied up at Marsden Wharf in the heart of Auckland. While members of the Greenpeace crew were celebrating a birthday three nights later, on 10 July, at least one French agent, using sophisticated rebreather diving apparatus, attached powerful limpet mines to the hull of the *Warrior*.

The first explosion tore a hole the size of a garage door in the side of the ship. Such was the force of the blast that a freighter on the other side of the wharf was punched five metres sideways. The dazed crew climbed onto the wharf. It was only minutes to midnight. The photographer, Fernando Pereira, remembering his expensive camera gear, returned to his cabin in the stern.

That first explosion had been placed to sink the ship. A second, attached to the ship's spine, near the propeller, was designed to cripple it. It was probably the shock wave from this second blast which killed Pereira.

The French agents escaped into the night, no doubt confident they would not have to face the consequences of their crime. They were doing a job, commissioned by their own government – and after all this was New Zealand, a country unconditioned to terrorism.

I arrived in Auckland two days later. I had been sent by 'Four Corners', and Australian Broadcasting Corporation television current affairs programme, to cover the bombing. There is nothing unique about terrorism, even in the South Pacific, but this bombing was unusual. We had never heard of a peace ship being sunk, let alone in nuclear-free New Zealand, which is about as far from a war zone as you can possibly get. In New Zealand, the papers were speculating about a lunatic Vietnam veteran. The police were tight-lipped and Greenpeace members had that dazed look which follows in the wake of tragedy. In their cramped offices, a single burner kerosene stove was heating lunch. There were bicycles in the hallway. They hardly seemed likely targets for terrorists.

The French Secret Service, however, had certainly taken them seriously. These Auckland offices had been penetrated earlier in the year by a DGSE (Direction Générale de Sécurité Extérieure) agent, Christine Huguette Cabon. Calling herself Frédérique Bon-lieu, she had attached herself to the trusting Greenpeace, and learned something of their Moruroa tactics.

Greenpeace had had reason to suspect that recent tests had opened a crack in the atoll, causing a dangerous radiation leak. They were planning their most sophisticated assault so far. The *Rainbow Warrior* and other protest boats would launch Zodiac inflatable speedboats from just outside the twelve-mile exclusion zone. They would attempt to avoid the security screen and land on the atoll. Approximately a dozen Zodiacs would carry Greenpeace members of many different nationalities. They knew from experience the French would be forced to arrest the Greenpeace protesters and then face the embarrassing prospect of having to deport each of them to their home countries. In Europe, the USA, Australia, in fact all over the world stories about the tests would appear in the press, assisted by photographs sent via the sophisticated transmission equipment aboard the *Rainbow Warrior*.

Aware of Greenpeace plans and uncomfortable in the face of such publicity, the French chose to stop the *Rainbow Warrior* before it got anywhere near Moruroa. Top level meetings took place at DGSE headquarters in Paris and the Elysée Palace. Elaborate plans were drawn up. A team of combat divers, trained at Corsica's Aspretto Diving School began preparing for the operation. One purchased a Zodiac raft and an outboard motor in London. Another flew to New Calendonia and organized the hire of an 11-metre yacht, *Ouvea*.

They produced a ridiculously complicated plot. The Zodiac and outboard were shipped to New Caledonia. The bombs and diving gear were acquired there and hidden on board the *Ouvea*. Four men, posing as tourists on a diving holiday, sailed from

Noumea on 14 June. The fact they were heading for stormy New Zealand in the middle of winter was not supposed to arouse suspicion. Presumably, their dangerous and illegal entry into Parangarenga harbour in New Zealand's north was also not meant to be noticed.

The reverse effect was achieved. New Zealand is something of a village. People are nosy, but nosy in the nicest way. They welcomed these uncommonly tidy young sailors, reported their presence and mildly chided them for evading customs. On the very day the *Ouvea* illegally entered New Zealand, 22 June, a second team of agents arrived in Auckland after a long flight from London. They posed as a pair of Swiss tourists. Yet another DGSE operative arrived to supervise.

Over the next few weeks they played out something of a French farce. The teams made numerous attempts to connect with one another, leaving their distinctly Gallic footprints all over New Zealand. The *Ouvea* crew energetically used up the expense account on running shoes, clothes, restaurants and motels. They were charming enough to tempt some of New Zealand's young women to stay for breakfast and gauche enough to boast about it afterwards.

After a Jacques-Tati like succession of missed encounters the two main teams were able to properly coordinate and destroy the *Rainbow Warrior*. As one South Pacific newspaper put it, 'they murdered it in its sleep'.

Two of the agents would have certainly escaped unnoticed but for one remarkable incident. A neighbourhood watch group, concerned about pilferage from their small boats, was patrolling the bay. They saw a Zodiac come ashore. They saw a man transfer some bags into a campervan. One of the bay watchers crept forward and took the numberplate of the van, suspecting he was in the presence of a petty thief rather than an international spy.

Two days later a French speaking couple calling themselves Alain and Sophie Turenge were detained when they returned the rented campervan. When it was determined they were carrying false passports the Turenges were held in custody.

In the following weeks, a succession of clues suggesting French involvement rose to the surface – these included a Zodiac raft and two small scuba bottles with Paris markings. It is interesting to recall how reluctant we all were to believe the French were behind this sabotage and murder. It was all a bit obvious, and after all, the French were our friends.

The *Ouvea* crew were questioned when the yacht stopped at Norfolk Island on its return trip to New Caledonia. The New Zealand police were very suspicious but had not at that time assembled enough evidence to make a confident arrest. The crew were allowed to leave, escaping by a hair's breadth. New Zealand police had given them the benefit of the doubt. Days later, when the police had assembled the evidence, it appears that the *Ouvea* was being scuttled and its crew transferred into a French submarine.

Meanwhile, the French Government abhorred the atrocity and strenuously denied any involvement. The French media peddled stories which identified the culprits as anything from South African mercenaries to British agents. The misinformation campaign might have worked but for the fact that locked up in an Auckland gaol were two French agents – Major Alain Mafart and Captain Dominique Prieur.

In the beginning, the French Government had disowned them. The agents refused to co-operate with the New Zealand police. The would not even admit to being French. At the time we thought they were probably mercenaries, in that no one, least of all a government, was accepting responsibility for them. When the agents first appeared in court they were careful to hide their faces, but an enterprising photographer with the New Zealand *Herald*, Ross Land, captured a picture which was spread across the world's press. British Intelligence recognized and identified the agents. Still the French Government said nothing. However, colleagues in the DGSE were unhappy about their friends being left to rot in far off New Zealand. The story began to leak. The French Government was being prodded towards accepting responsibility. That this affair would be a supreme embarrassment to President Mitterand was perhaps not so great a concern for an intelligence service whose power base had been eroded by the socialists.

In the meantime, some dedicated reporting by journalists in New Zealand produced a clearer picture of the movements of the French agents. This information, along with the leaked DGSE revelations, effected a change in the way the French media reported the affair. Sensing a French Watergate, they competed enthusiastically for new details of *L'affaire Greenpeace*.

The government had launched an official inquiry headed by a respected public servant Mr Bernard Tricot. When Tricot's whitewash appeared, it was rejected by a public well acquainted with cogent and contradictory evidence.

So, it wasn't until then, almost two months after the bombing, that the Mitterand government began its humiliating climb down. They admitted the agents in the Auckland gaol were theirs, but fell short of delivering to New Zealand Prime Minister, David Lange, the apology he sought. Eventually, the most recent champion of the French nuclear testing programme, Defence Minister Charles Hernu, was sacked.

The whole affair turned out to be a public relations misfire, one much greater than the one the sinking of the *Rainbow Warrior* was meant to avert.

Greenpeace had by now decided to send a larger protest vessel, the *Greenpeace* to Moruroa. Newspapers the world over condemned the French for committing what amounted to an act of war in the port of an ally – and all this to protect a nuclear testing programme which by now was unanimously condemned by South Pacific nations. In the face of such rising hostility, there was no contrition. President Mitterand took a Concorde to Moruroa to show the world, and his electorate, that France would remain the master of its own defence policy. French Opposition politicians were pointing to the gall of New Zealanders for daring to carry on their inquiries on French soil. And the tests continued.

A small underground detonation was watched by select cameras. Two filled champagne glasses showed the blast created but a ripple. Having disasterously lost the public relations battle over the *Rainbow Warrior* affair, the French were now able to make up some ground. Defence correspondents were not only invited to observe the tests but were given space on board the French Naval frigate, *Balny*, which was shadowing *Greenpeace*.

The journalists aboard *Balny* were courteously attended to. Journalists aboard *Greenpeace* had considerably more trouble filing their stories. A team from the French independent television service, 'Gamma', was unashamedly sabotaged when they attempted to transmit pictures. 'Gamma' had gone to considerable trouble to arrange flyovers of a small aircraft with videotape recording equipment on board. If the aircraft passed close enough to *Greenpeace*, pictures could be beamed up. The French cleverly thwarted the plans by placing a military aircraft in the area each time the "Gamma" plane took off. In that it was forbidden for a private aircraft to enter military airspace, the 'Gamma' plane was repeatedly forced to turn back. To add injury to insult, 'Gamma' later had its expensive television equipment seized and impounded.

On 10 October, *Greenpeace* retired when a generator failed. It had not entered the twelve-mile exclusion zone. The small yacht, *Vega* did make a run, was seized and its crew sent home. Both sides claimed a public relations victory.

The next chapter to be played out was to be the murder trial of Major Mafart and Captain Prieur. The first hearing was set down for 4 November. Their accomplices, who had sailed from New Zealand in *Ouvea*, would face no judge, being fortunate enough to have reached the sanctuary of France. A legion of press men and women crowded the Auckland court. They were astonished to hear the two agents plead guilty to lesser charges of wilful damage and manslaughter. Editors were telephoned and lengthy hotel bookings cancelled. There was undisguised disappointment that all the juicy details of this most bizarre affair, would for the moment, remain secret.

Alain Mafart and Dominique Prieur were sentenced to ten years imprisonment. At this time (December 1985) the New Zealand Government is showing a marked reluctance to bow to French pressure to release them. In turn the French Government is scoffing at New Zealand's claim of $A16 million compensation. The police investigation and trial of the agents cost a small fortune. The cost of Greenpeace is of course immeasurable, considering the loss of their flagship and one of its crew. However, France's Minister for External Relations, Mr Roland Dumas, has described the New Zealand Government's compensation claim as "ridiculous".

Viewed in exclusion, the *Rainbow Warrior* affair does seem bizarre. Viewed, however, in the context of French Polynesian history as revealed in this book, it is not so surprising. The vile treatment by France of the Tahitian autonomist group *Pouvanaa a Oopa* is not less shocking than the killing of Fernando Pereira. The decision to sabotage the *Rainbow Warrior* seems reasonably in keeping with a decision to set off an atmospheric test in 1966, when it was known that meteorological conditions would carry the fallout to populated areas. At the time, it was President de Gaulle's impatience which triggered the blast. 'Let them eat yellowcake', I can her him intone.

In 1985, many months after the death of the *Rainbow Warrior*, newspapers throughout New Zealand and Australia continue to publish protest letters. Australians and New Zealanders are beginning to learn what many Polynesians have long known. When they bomb and kill in a friendly port we could be forgiven for wondering whether being an enemy of France might not be safer than being a friend.

Chris Masters

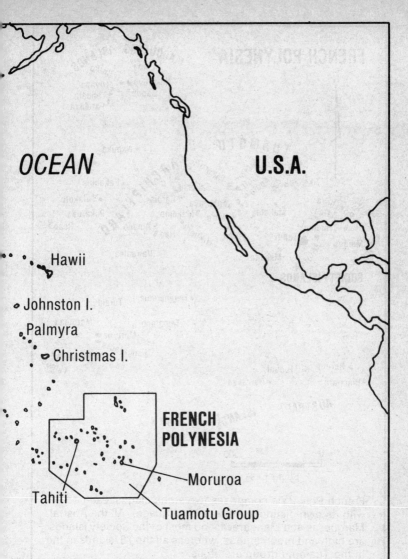

OCEAN   U.S.A.

Hawii

Johnston I.

Palmyra

Christmas I.

FRENCH POLYNESIA

Moruroa

Tahiti

Tuamotu Group

By 1985 islands in the Pacific Ocean had been used as a testing ground for 21 British, 106 American and 115 French atomic bombs.

The true name of the French nuclear base in the Tuamotu group is Moruroa — and not Mururoa as the French army mistakenly calls it. Construction of this base began in 1963.

FRENCH POLYNESIA

N

MARQUESAS ISLANDS
Eiao •
Nukuhiva • • Uahuka
Uapou • • Hivaoa
• Tahuata
• Fatuhiva

TUAMOTU

Rangiroa
Tikehau •
Manihi •
Takapoto •
Apataki •
• Takaroa
• Takume
Fakarava •
• Raroia
Makemo •
Kaukura •
Anaa
Hikueru •
Hao •
• Amanu
Vairaatea •

ARCHIPELAGO
• Napuka
• Pukapuka
• Fakahina
• Tatakoto
Pukarua •
Reao •

Maupiti •
Borabora •
Raiatea •
Huahine •
Maiao •
Mopelia •
Makatea •
Tahiti
Moorea
Meheita

SOCIETY ISLANDS

• Hereheretue
Tureia •
Tematangi •
Moruroa •
Fangatauta •
Marutea •
Mangareva •
Temoe •

Rurutu •
Tubuai •
Rimatara •
Raivavae •

AUSTRAL ISLANDS
Rapa •

0   500
Kilometres

French Polynesia comprises five archipelagos, each one
with its own distinct culture and language. All the Austral,
Marquesas and Mangareva, and most of the Society islands,
are high and mountainous, whereas all the 76 islands in the
in the Tuamotu group are atolls.

A comparison with Australia shows how widely scattered
the islands are: if Tahiti could be seen as Alice Springs, the
Marquesas islands would be located on the York Peninsula,
Mangareva in the Blue Mountains, and the Austral islands
in the vicinity of Port Augusta.

1 BEFORE THE FLOOD

The worst natural disaster that can befall the peoples inhabiting the scattered islands of the Pacific Ocean is not a hurricane but a *tsunami,* a succession of tidal waves produced by a submarine earthquake. Although a hurricane or cyclone can cause as much havoc, it is at least preceded by various warning signs such as a rapidly sinking barometer, gathering clouds, and an oppressive calm – permitting the islanders to seek refuge on higher ground or up in the trees. No such respite is granted by the enormous tsunami waves, suddenly appearing on the surface and racing across the ocean at aeroplane speed. The weather may be sunny and pleasant. Nobody on the islands lying in the path of the tsunami will be aware of the impending catastrophe. Men may be gathering food, cutting copra, or catching fish; the women cooking, plaiting baskets or mats, or tending their babies; the children playing on the village green or in the shallow lagoon; and the old people sitting quietly talking under the pandanus palms. Then all of a sudden they will all be engulfed in a roaring mass of water. As a rule no one is spared and no bodies are found.

The sudden flooding of the beautiful and peaceful islands of French Polynesia by twenty thousand foreign troops and merciless profiteers in the early 1960s, when General de Gaulle made his fateful decision to build nuclear testing bases there, is fully comparable, in both its swiftness and magnitude, to the destruction wrought by a tsunami. What made this brutal invasion such a uniquely tragic event was that it came at a time when the islanders had at long last almost recovered from the first fatal impact – produced two hundred years earlier by the equally unexpected appearance in their midst of foreign sailors, traders, and missionaries.

Of all the so-called primitive peoples, the Polynesians were probably the least well prepared to resist this first onslaught. Not only did they lack the physical means of defence (their sole weapons consisting of ineffectual wooden spears and stone slings) but they were also vulnerable because of their open, friendly, trustful dispositions, their customary hospitality and eagerness to please. The island where these Polynesian virtues could be found in the highest degree was Tahiti, as was clear from the enthusiastic descriptions of Lieutenant Samuel Wallis, who discovered the island in 1767. All succeeding visitors, of whom the most famous were Cook, Bougainville, and Bligh were likewise greatly appreciative of the ease with which they could obtain the basic necessities of life – fresh water, vegetables, pigs, and women.

For the same reason, the many whaling vessel captains who flocked to the new hunting grounds in the southern hemisphere from 1790 on called regularly at Tahiti. In exchange for their goods and services, the Tahitians received a few nails and tools, many firearms, even greater quantities of low-grade liquor and a wide assortment of hitherto unknown diseases. As a result, so many islanders were killed, either quickly by bullets or more slowly by alcoholism and disease, that thirty years after the discovery there remained only 15 000 or one-tenth of the original population. Among the departed ones were most of the native political and religious leaders, creating a sort of cultural vacuum.

At this stage, in 1797 to be exact, a group of Europeans of a very different type, arrived on the scene, who by sheer coincidence were well equipped to fill this void. They had been sent out by the non-conformist London Missionary Society (LMS) and consisted of four ordained ministers and fourteen pious men skilled in 'the mechanical arts'. Some of them were married and accompanied by their wives and children. They were as fanatical as they were enterprising and in less than twenty years had succeeded in converting, formally at least, all the inhabitants of Tahiti, Moorea, and the other Society Islands. Strangely enough the missionaries insisted that it was not enough to believe in the new god, read the Bible, and observe the ten commandments; in their view it was equally important for the neophytes to drink tea, eat with knife and fork, wear bonnets and coats, sleep in beds, sit on chairs, and live in stone houses – in other words, to live exactly like the English lower middle class, from which the missionaries had sprung. Consequently the natives needed money, and in order to obtain some they had to plant palm trees and make coconut oil. This meant still further changes in their lives.

The LMS missionaries tried to persuade their government to take over Tahiti and the neighbouring islands; but the British ministers of the Crown saw little reason for acquiring a collection of tiny palm islands and coral reefs and preferred to extend their conquests in Africa and Asia where there was to be found an abundance of gold, precious stones, ebony, spices, and other riches. The French government concurred that the Pacific islands were economically worthless. But was that the only measure to be applied? For instance Britain had taken possession of Australia solely for the purpose of using it as a safe dumping ground for a cumbersome surplus of convicts. For once, it seemed to many French politicians and ministers that their own government had something to learn from the British. Admiral Dupetit-Thouars, who had spent a few days in the Marquesas Islands in 1838 warmly recommended them as being ideally suited to that purpose. Not only were they located thousands of kilometres from the nearest continents, but were also sparsely inhabited by extremely ferocious cannibals, and thus particularly well adapted to absorb a surplus convict population. Grateful for this valuable suggestion, the French government sent out Dupetit-Thouars to take possession of the ten mountainous islands (or rather, high rocks) in the usual grand manner – with flag-hoisting, proclamations, and gun salvoes. Mildly and sometimes even greatly amused, the Marquesan chiefs attended. Of course, the only reason none of them protested was that they did not have the faintest idea of what it was all about. Buoyed up by this easy success, Admiral Dupetit-Thouars sailed on to Tahiti and annexed that island as well, in September 1842, though he had had no instructions to do so.

Quite understandably the French prime minister, Guizot, became furious upon learning of this act of insubordination. Unfortunately, the whole French press praised this 'gallant act of patriotism' and exulted over this 'glorious victory over perfidious Albion, this time unable to realise her rapacious plans'. (The editorialists were still bitter over the recent British takeover of New Zealand.) Dupetit-Thouars soon became a national hero and poor Guizot was forced to promote him instead of court-martialling him. The outraged LMS missionaries in Tahiti cried foul-play and managed to whip up such strong anti-French feelings in Great Britain that for a certain time there was some risk of the two nations going to war over these unknown islands that neither of them needed.

When it finally dawned on the Tahitians that the French were there to stay, they took up arms, such as there were. Most of them had only bush knives; the few owners of firearms had only antiquated muzzle-loaders. They wisely resorted to classical guerilla tactics, establishing camps in the rugged interior and carrying out swift raids again and again, preferably at night, on

13

the French garrisons, settlements, and coastal missionary stations. It took the well-armed and well-equipped French troops three long years to crush this determined resistance. The poor native queen, Pomare IV, who had been hiding out in the Leeward Islands all this while, reluctantly agreed to come back, and was reinstated as the nominal head of her realm, from then on a French protectorate. Actually the island was ruled by a French governor and the queen rarely understood or cared about the implications of the documents she was required simply to countersign.

One after another the French navy commanders who had the misfortune of being appointed governors quickly discovered that Tahiti was altogether as worthless as Guizot had maintained. Its only asset was a perennially warm, humid climate, producing several crops a year of any roots or vegetables. But this was offset by the extremely limited amount of cultivable land. The total area of Tahiti is not more than 1000 square kilometres, nine-tenths of it consisting of steep mountains culminating in a peak more than 2000 metres high. As for the possibilities of establishing copra, cotton, or coffee plantations on the available flat land along the coast, there existed another insurmountable obstacle: the Tahitians enjoyed an easy and pleasant life and had no desire to give it up in order to slave for foreign masters.

Nothing was basically changed by the eventual transformation of the protectorate into a colony called French Oceania in 1880, shortly after Queen Pomare's death, along with the subsequent annexation of a few more islands. As before, no Frenchmen in their right minds felt tempted to try their fortunes in these remote islands half way around the world. Actually, the only ones to make the four or five months' trip around the Cape of Good Hope and Australia were hapless army or navy conscripts stationed in Tahiti for the three years' duration of their service. Some of them married and settled down in the country. The more enterprising of these settlers, reluctantly yielding to fate, opened a tavern or a store, while the majority were quite happy to let their wives' relatives care for all their needs. Their children often married Polynesian men and women and, after a few generations, in most instances all that remained of their European cultural heritage was the family name. The same thing happened to the many English, American and Scandinavian sailors who jumped ship in French Oceania.

Therefore, today one may everywhere come across Martins,

Lagardes, Smiths, Browns, Andersons, and Johnsons – some with quite European features but most of them being of a thoroughly Polynesian type, living in completely native fashion and speaking only the native tongue. At the other end of the scale, there are many true Polynesians who have had a superior French education, love French culture, food and wines and speak only French. Those who have managed to strike a balance between the two cultures are called, and unembarrassedly call themselves, *demis,* literally 'half-castes'. Since the criterion is not racial but cultural, every foreign visitor or newcomer must find out for himself the correct label and category for each individual. The *demis* usually occupy posts in government offices, schools, and business firms serving a mixed clientèle where their double cultural affinity may be useful.

Both the remaining ethnic groups are easier to distinguish and define. They are the Frenchborn businessmen and the Chinese. That the former have never been numerous can easily be explained by the modest quantities of goods produced by the colony, which even at peak periods have rarely exceeded 25 500 tonnes of copra, 200 tonnes of vanilla, and 500 tonnes of mother-of-pearl shell a year. Most of the French merchants came out as representatives of some metropolitan* company and did not start their own firms until they had become thoroughly familiar with the local market. Even if we add on those who were primarily importers of wares from abroad, the total number of French businessmen was still only about 400 at the height of the colonial era in the 1930s.

By about that time, around ten times that number of Chinese immigrants had settled in Tahiti. Originally, they were all poor coolies who had fled from Kwantung via Hong Kong during the first quarter of the century, from the frequent famines and civil wars then ravaging China. After a few years of menial labour for the local businessmen and plantation owners, they would work their way up the social scale and establish themselves as storekeepers, restaurant and bar keepers, butchers, carpenters, and tailors. The cleverest and most ruthless of them made fortunes as wholesale dealers and ship owners.

However all political power remained in the hands of the governor and the French civil servants, who were rotated among

*In the local parlance, the term 'metropolitan' is synonymous with 'French-based', born in France, or simply 'French'.

the colonies every three years. They all lived in Papeete and received high salaries for the mental and physical 'hardships' they suffered in this remote and uncivilised part of the world. As a matter of fact, they lived in pleasant villas and with a monthly mail steamer they were hardly overburdened with work. When the governor and his closest collaborators occasionally left the capital to tour the other islands, they always travelled in grand style on a warship. On each island they were lavishly entertained with food, drink, dance, and song – in exchange for which the governor repeated the same patriotic speech in beautiful and flowery French, of which no one understood a word. If the governors and other officials had any closer personal contacts at all with the Polynesians, the latter were invariably young, sweet, though not always so innocent, girls.

If you were to presume that the French businessmen and the French colonial administrators had many bonds in common and saw much of each other, you could not be more wrong. Almost without exception their relationships were strained if not openly hostile. It is easy to see the reason for this. The businessmen were exasperated with all the stupid laws and decrees emanating from the government offices and constantly hampering their activities. Their Chinese colleagues shared this exasperation, but instead of loudly manifesting their disapproval, they got around their difficulties by appropriate gifts, discreetly distributed.

Popular representation was limited to the election every five years of a delegate to occupy a seat in the Colonial Council in Paris. All these delegates were French lawyers or professional politicians who never took the trouble to visit the colony whose spokesmen they were. Above all they were mouthpieces for the local French businessmen and planters. In principle, nothing prevented a Polynesian from standing as candidate, but nobody ever did because of the general belief, strongly supported by the French settlers, that in order to represent the territory in Paris it was indispensable or compulsory to be fluent in French and to have a law degree. Sad to say, this belief corresponded quite well with the factual situation. The Polynesians were not even considered qualified to be members of the Advisory Council, the only local body of a vaguely parliamentary character. It was no great loss for them, as the councillors were appointed by the governor and, if he did not like their advice, they were promptly fired and replaced by more docile persons.

There is no doubt, however, that this rigid caste system

concentrating all the French and Chinese in Papeete (with Uturoa on Raiatea as the only other centre) was to the advantage of the Polynesian people, leaving them in peace to be governed by their own leaders in keeping with customary rights and rules. The only significant break with the past was that the chiefs were no longer hereditary, but rather elected, officials or, more likely, native pastors of the Calvinist church. Of course in the Marquesas Islands, where 90 per cent of the islanders were Catholics, a French priest was sometimes the actual ruler.

Economically speaking, the Polynesians living outside Papeete or away from Tahiti had an even greater freedom and independence. The land still belonged collectively to the local families, each and every one of whom could grow adequate crops of taro, yams, sweet-potatoes, and bananas for its own needs. The sea teemed with fish and crustaceans; in a few hours a man, or even a young boy, could catch enough food for the whole family. Although the economy was thus of a simple subsistence type, there were plenty of opportunities to make money. Copra was the most common cash crop, but vanilla beans were also grown in the Society Islands. In the Tuamotus, a good diver could earn substantial sums by collecting high-priced mother-of-pearl shells in the lagoons.

The islanders spent most of their money on luxury items such as liquor, tobacco, fancy fabrics, mirrors, flour, rice, canned salmon and peaches, bicycles and cameras and could very well afford to do so. How unessential their cash income actually was could best be seen during the great depression of the 1930s. In America, Europe, Australia and New Zealand the depression brought suffering and tragedy. Not so in French Oceania, where the damping down of all trading activities forced the islanders to return to the simpler life and diet of their ancestors, making them healthier, stronger and happier.

2 FREE FRENCH FIGHT FOR ALL

The fall of France in 1940 created an unprecedented situation in Tahiti. The whole civil service, with hardly any exceptions, considered Pétain to be the rightful head of state and unanimously, with unflagging loyalty, obeyed all orders and instructions emanating from the Vichy government. For them, as for 99 per cent of the French people, de Gaulle was simply a traitor. Of course, in Australia and New Zealand the situation was just the opposite. From the day that Churchill recognised the Free French, de Gaulle became the hero and Pétain the villain in the tremendous war drama, the first act of which had barely begun to unfold. These Pacific countries, together with the United States, were the main buyers of French Oceania's copra, vanilla, and mother-of-pearl shells and were also the suppliers of practically all of the colony's imports of manufactured goods and foodstuffs. And the French and Chinese businessmen who controlled the import and export trade in Papeete did not take long to realise where their true interests lay. It was urgent for the colony to join in with the Free French Forces of General de Gaulle, which their trading partners, the governments of Australia and New Zealand, had officially recognised as their ally.

Of course, the Polynesians had never heard about de Gaulle. Pétain, on the other hand, was widely known as the great hero and saviour of France, and revered by quite a number of Tahitian veterans from the First World War. But when the leading French businessmen informed the population that only by siding with de Gaulle could they assure a continued supply of flour, corned beef, cloth, liquor, tobacco, and other necessities, there was a marked and rapid shift of public opinion in favour of the unknown general. A Free French Committee was formed, consisting of seventeen French businessmen and the most bemedalled Tahitian veteran of the First World War, Pouvanaa a Oopa. When the governor steadfastly refused to change allegiance, the Committee hastily organised a referendum on Tahiti and Moorea. This meant that only about half of the population in the colony took part. The organisers of the referendum maintained, with some justification, that due to the enormous distances and poor communications, it would have taken too long to consult the inhabitants of the remote archipelagos such as the Marquesas, the Gambiers, and the Austral Islands who, at any rate, were so ill-informed about world politics that they just might have made the wrong choice.

As it was very important to reach a quick decision, and there was no time to print up ballots, and envelopes were in short supply, the Committee simplified the procedure by distributing a number of exercise books, ruled up in two columns. Those who opted for de Gaulle were to write their names in the first column, and those for Pétain in the second one. On 2 September 1940, the day set for the referendum, the district chiefs invited the population to come and cast their 'votes'. No less than 5564 men, women, and even some children, followed the example and advice of the chiefs and signed their names in the first column. There were no more than eighteen who had the courage to declare publicly that they preferred Pétain. The Chinese were the only ones excluded from this popular referendum, a situation about which they were far from unhappy, for at that stage nobody could see how the war was to end.

De Gaulle's winning tally in French Oceania, 99.8 per cent, was even more overwhelming than that obtained by the evil enemy against whom the Free French and their allies were fighting, Herr Adolf Hitler, who had to be satisfied with 95–99 per cent Yes votes in his various, much more efficiently conducted, plebiscites. Confronted with these figures, the governor had the temerity to question the methods used. But after having been promised free repatriation to France via the United States for himself and all other civil servants, he eventually let the victors take over the administrative buildings. The eighteen courageous private individuals who had voted for Pétain were treated with much less magnanimity, for they were interned in the hot quarantine station on the two-hectare islet of Motu-uta at the entrance of Papeete harbour.

In some instances, however, the patriotic fervour stirred up by these events took much nobler forms, particularly among the simple Polynesian fishermen, planters, and copra makers in the remote districts and islands – who headed for Papeete by the hundreds and requested to be enrolled in the army and sent to Europe to help de Gaulle liberate the 'mother-country' that they had never seen. Within a week, enrolment had to be stopped for lack of uniforms and rifles. This relieved many of the French settlers and businessmen from the scruples they had sometimes felt for not having acted with the same speed and resolution as the Polynesians. When they reconsidered the situation, they clearly saw that this was the best solution for all concerned. For who was there left to govern the colony, make patriotic speeches, and run business, if they too left for the battle front in Europe? To prove that they were men of action nonetheless, they formed a local militia and locked up all suspect individuals. Even the members of the provisional government soon became suspect in their eyes and were likewise imprisoned. Inevitably, the jailers fell out amongst themselves and most of them ended up as inmates of the by then much overcrowded and very uncomfortable jail. Having all experienced these same inconveniences, the various groups of patriotic plotters from then on exiled each other in turn on the neighbouring island of Moorea. During all this strife and dissension, they all remained firm supporters of General de Gaulle. In fact, the aim of each fighting Frenchman in the colony was to prove that he was the purest and worthiest Gaullist.

When, in the summer of 1941, General de Gaulle at long last found time for such a minor problem as the comical vendetta that was going on in Tahiti, he solved it at once in a most efficient manner by sending out a Corsican air force colonel, Orselli, endowed with dictatorial powers. Being a military man, Orselli gladly left economic problems to the businessmen, who, in return, ceased their political intrigues.

The only person who seemed dissatisfied with this new order of things was the Polynesian war veteran, Pouvanaa a Oopa. By profession he was a carpenter and, while sawing and hammering, he commented freely on the events of the day to the growing crowd of friends and sympathisers who flocked to his small workshop in the centre of Papeete. Above all, he bitterly criticised the governor's hands-off economic policy, permitting a flourishing black market in basic commodities, thus placing them outside the reach of the Polynesians. No native had ever before behaved in such an insolent fashion. Some French settlers plausibly explained this apparent anomaly by saying that Pouvanaa was not a 'real' native, but the illegitimate son of a Danish sailor. True enough, he had blue eyes, hair almost blond, and a fair complexion. But he had been brought up in native fashion by his Polynesian mother on the unspoilt island of Huahine in the Leeward group, and was a true Polynesian at heart.

Colonel Orselli tried the only method of persuasion known to him: he put Pouvanaa in jail and left him there without any specific charges and for an unspecified length of time. It did not work at all. When Pouvanaa was freed in due time, he was even more adamant and impudent. So shortly afterwards he was locked up in the colony's asylum. Although it was only a hundred years old, it was a perfect replica of a medieval madhouse. This did not break Pouvanaa, either. So next, he was simply shipped back to his home island of Huahine, about 160 kilometres north-west of Tahiti. A gendarme was posted there, too, with the sole task of keeping watch over him.

The authorities considered the island a safe prison. The only communications with the outside world were maintained by schooners, on whose movements and passenger lists the gendarme kept very close tabs. At exactly the time that the gendarme was inspecting the weekly schooner, Pouvanaa put out to sea in a small lagoon canoe and paddled thirty kilometres across the open sea to a neighbouring island and quietly got aboard another schooner and sailed unnoticed back to Papeete.

By then the war was over. Orselli was replaced by a high-ranking civil bureaucrat, who disapproved of these strongarm methods – but solely on the grounds that they transformed 'a half-witted native' into a martyr and hero in the eyes of his fellow Polynesians.

3 THE RISE OF POUVANAA

While these patriotically inspired persecutions were taking place in the islands, the 300 Polynesian volunteers who had managed to enrol continued to fight with outstanding gallantry – first in North Africa, then in Italy, and finally in France and Germany. One-third of them were killed in action. The survivors had to wait a whole year before the first peacetime French government could find an old hulk having a fair chance of remaining afloat for the full six weeks needed to reach Tahiti.

Of course, they were given a hero's welcome. In one important respect, however, the new veterans behaved very differently from those who had fought in the 1914–18 war. Once the speeches, the parades, the music, and the banquets were over, they did not return quietly to their copra plantations and taro patches, but remained in town and wondered in a loud voice whether this was all the reward they were going to get for having risked their lives for the sake of liberty and democracy. Was it really asking too much of those who had stayed behind and prospered and enjoyed themselves to now make room for those who had suffered, bled, lost health and limb? Yet, this was exactly how Frenchmen in government and business offices were thinking.

Some of the war heroes remarked bitterly that this was not the only injustice. During the year they had spent in France they had also become aware of the fact that the whole society and system of government there was far more democratic than in the colonies. Yet no blame for this unfair treatment fell on General de Gaulle, for the very simple reason that, after January 1946, he was no longer at the helm, having voluntarily resigned in protest against the fact that the constitution and the parties would not allow him to rule in the same absolute manner as during the war.

One of the few persons in Tahiti who unreservedly sided with the war veterans was Pouvanaa, whose son Marcel was the most badly mauled and most frequently decorated soldier in the Tahitian battle unit. By then Pouvanaa was surrounded and assisted by a small number of bright young men, animated by the same fighting spirit, but far better educated. The most lively and ingenious of these was a 26-year-old typesetter, employed in the government printing office, with the preposterous name of Jean-

Baptiste Céran-Jérusalémy, totally un-Polynesian. Nobody in the colony knew for sure who his ancestors had been, nor where he had come from, and nobody really cared. According to local terminology, Céran (the usual shortened form of his name) was a *demi*. Therefore he possessed a talent completely lacking in Pouvanaa: he could read and interpret all those strange French laws, rules, and regulations that were always baffling and ensnaring the poor Polynesians. Last but not least, Céran was a first-rate organiser, and managed to form an action committee in which each member was assigned a distinct task.

In addition, at this critical time a high-ranking French civil servant did much to crystallise public opinion around Pouvanaa and Céran – albeit his assistance was quite unintentional. He was the secretary-general, acting roughly as vice-governor. Having served under Colonel Orselli during the war years, he had just been promoted to a similar position in a more important African colony. Quite unusually, he and his wife were returning to France via the United States. As his wife told the story, the purpose of this detour was to buy a new car, a fur coat, and some other goods that were then unobtainable in Europe. These outrageous plans were soon widely known in Tahiti. The secretary-general had also been head of the foreign exchange control. Thus the question that everyone wanted him to answer was where he had found the dollars he and his wife needed for all these purchases. Had he sent a demand to himself and approved it without consulting the board? Or had he bought his dollars illegally on the black market? Pouvanaa and his lieutenants went to see the governor, demanding an explanation. The governor was extremely evasive. But after Pouvanaa and Céran had organised a big protest rally, he suddenly gave in and announced that the secretary-general and his wife were returning to France by another route.

The situation had almost calmed down when, a few weeks later, a colonial inspector disembarked in Papeete. When he heard what had happened he became as furious as Pouvanaa, Céran, and the war veterans – but for a completely different reason. What angered Inspector Lassalle-Séré was the governor's timidity and passivity. If these impudent natives were not taught a severe lesson at once, complete anarchy would prevail. He did not have to wait long for an opportunity to demonstrate how to crush these agitators. At the end of July 1947 three new civil servants arrived on the government steamer from France to fill some low-rank posts in the administration, posts which had been coveted by the war veterans. As soon as this became known, Pouvanaa and Céran organised a new protest rally right on the wharf where the ship was to dock. Several thousand Polynesians, including most of the war veterans, attended and formed such a compact wall that no passenger could disembark from the ship.

Under strong pressure from Lassalle-Séré, the governor proclaimed martial law and sent out troops in the middle of the night to arrest Pouvanaa and six of his closest collaborators. Their alleged crime was 'conspiracy against the security of the State', with a minimum sentence of twenty years of hard labour. While the unhappy prosecutor set about looking for damaging evidence, the 'conspirators' languished in the cramped cells of the squalid old city jail where the daytime temperature rose to 35° Celsius. When the court convened at long last, Lassalle-Séré was no longer at hand, having been called away on a similar tour of inspection in another colony. The embarrassed judges mustered enough courage to acquit the accused men. By then, they had spent fully five months in jail and were all in extremely poor health.

The result of this clumsy attempt to get rid of the whole bunch of native 'agitators' for good was to greatly enhance their influence and prestige. When, two years later, Pouvanaa stood as candidate in the elections to renew the French National Assembly he won a landslide victory, with 10 000 votes as against 5000 for his main opponent, a respected and well-liked French Protestant missionary. Céran felt that the time had come to organise a full-fledged political party on European lines. He invited sympathisers from all of the island groups to attend a general convention in Tahiti at the beginning of 1950. The name chosen for the new party was *Rassemblement Démocratique des Populations Tahitiennes* (RDPT), though the word *Polynésiennes* might have better fitted the facts than *Tahitiennes*. The new party won eighteen of the twenty-five seats in the Territorial Assembly.

For the first time since the islands became French in 1842, the Polynesians had found in Pouvanaa a leader and a spokesman who was one of them, who understood them, and was understood by them, not only in the narrow sense that he spoke Tahitian but in the broader sense of sharing their very special way of thinking and doing things.

So, wherever Pouvanaa went, men, women and children flocked around him and asked for his advice and guidance on every imaginable matter or problem: a marital dispute, the excessive prices charged by the Chinese storekeeper, the correct interpretation of the Bible, the selection of a new pastor, the name to give to a newborn child, the best way to dry copra, and so on. Pouvanaa's formal education was limited to the few early years he had attended school on his home island. He had learned to read and write only in his own language. His limited French vocabulary just permitted him to carry on a simple conversation about well-known subjects, and barred him from a higher education. But like all Polynesians of his generation, he had studied the Bible every day and carefully meditated upon what he read. Therefore, when asked to act as arbiter or to find the solution to some problem, he had recourse to the teachings of the scriptures and invariably found, with a remarkable skill, the chapter and verse with the most appropriate answer. He loved Jesus' parables best of all and retold them in such masterly fashion that the Polynesian disciples sitting at his feet were instantly aware of how they should live and act.

In spite of his being only in his fifties, Pouvanaa appeared venerable and so imbued with the wisdom that usually comes only with age that everybody called him *metua,* father. This role of a latter-day prophet, almost a messiah, that Pouvanaa assumed, places him in the same special category as another contemporary politician, General de Gaulle. Both possessed an indefinable but extremely potent charisma, which explains why they were equally reluctant to formulate a party programme in writing. Actually, both Pouvanaa and de Gaulle often made completely self-contradictory statements without the slightest embarrassment, simply because they considered themselves inspired oracles in the classical sense, expressing divine truths. If someone asked Pouvanaa what his programme or aim was, he simply replied 'Polynesia for the Polynesians'. De Gaulle's ambitions for the French people were voiced in similar style.

At the time of the next elections to the National Assembly in 1951, Pouvanaa was re-elected with exactly 70 per cent of the votes cast, surpassing the count for any of the metropolitan deputies. However, this resounding victory did not change anything for the Polynesian people. The French government was trying hard to consolidate its colonial empire, which was already being threatened by various liberation movements. If need be, troops were dispatched, as for instance to Madagascar and Indo-China. True, some deputies from other French overseas territories also clamoured for reforms and more say for their own people in public affairs, but they did not number more than twenty, and the other 500 metropolitan deputies were definitely not interested in colonial problems, being too involved in their own far more important problems of getting as much money as possible for roads, hospitals, schools, and other public works for their own home constituencies.

As for the local parliament in French Oceania, the so-called Territorial Assembly, it was as little able as the National Assembly to change the colonial system, but for a different reason. According to rules drawn up in Paris, the Territorial Assembly was not empowered to discuss and vote on problems of a *political* nature. Not unexpectedly, all its requests for reforms were classed as political by the French administration, the sole judge in this case.

4 DE GAULLE'S FORGOTTEN SPEECH

Pouvanaa was the first to regret that de Gaulle's political career seemed to be over. Like everyone else in Polynesia – with the possible exception of the eighteen Pétainists, now free again – he sincerely believed that the liberator of France was the foremost French champion of the colonial peoples' freedom. The many speeches he had made to that effect left no room for the slightest doubt. Although it seemed unlikely that the general might be in a position to help them in their fight for freedom, the assemblymen invited him to visit French Polynesia. If nothing else came of it, they would at least have done their best to comfort an old friend who had come down in the world. De Gaulle answered that he was sincerely touched by their loyalty and that, having so little to do, he might just as well take the regular Sydney-bound French steamer, covering the distance between Marseilles and Papeete in about five weeks.

When he disembarked in Papeete on 30 August 1956, he was accompanied only by his wife and a secretary. No French newspaper or radio company had cared to send out a reporter by either ship or plane, simply because what de Gaulle did or said at this stage was no longer considered newsworthy. A recent poll had shown that only 2 per cent of the French people believed that he would be able to make a political comeback. In Tahiti, there were no newspapers and no foreign correspondents in 1956. Therefore it is not so surprising that no accounts of de Gaulle's visit were published in the French and international press.

Nevertheless, in retrospect, it is more than strange that de Gaulle and the editors of his numerous writings deliberately have omitted the texts of the speeches he made during his stay in French Oceania. The one most worthy of rescue from oblivion was made in the park in Papeete on the day of his arrival. The text was taken down and distributed by the local Gaullist party on the same day, and we possess one of the few copies in existence today.

In this deliberately forgotten speech, de Gaulle quite appropriately first reminded his audience of the dark days in the summer of 1940:

When France was wallowing in the depths, Tahiti did not lose faith in her. You were on the other side of the world from me, thrown up on the

27

English coast like a shipwrecked survivor, both of us harbouring the same thoughts and purposes at the same time. We both felt that France should not be subservient, humiliated, disgraced – and that it was worthwhile for us to fight for her liberation, victory, and greatness.

It was a tremendous consolation to me when I received the telegram at the beginning of September 1940 in which Messrs Ahnne, Lagarde, and Martin advised me that you had decided, by a vote of 5564 as against 18, to join the Free French. Thus was formed such a strong bond between you and me, between Tahiti and France, that nothing will ever break it.

This was old stuff, but it always appealed to the Tahitian masses. Next, the general turned his attention towards the future, describing the new trends that he could distinguish. Three were of particular relevance to French Oceania:

To begin with, there is a universal desire among peoples and ethnic groups to preserve their own culture and determine their own destiny. At the same time, they have a basic need of belonging to a larger economic, cultural, and political block, if they wish to escape material and spiritual poverty, avoid becoming prey to ignorance, and having their country transformed into a battleground for all sorts of ideologies fighting for world hegemony.

These were clever turns of phrase, at the same time satisfying Pouvanaa's followers, the war veterans, and the French settlers and businessmen. (Perhaps the Chinese, too, although they had stayed at home, as usual.) Therefore, everybody enthusiastically applauded the general, who continued:

Another trend in the postwar world is the constant growth of sea and air communications throughout the world, basic to all human contact, trade, exchanges, to all human activity.

Although de Gaulle from here on filled his speech with so many flowery metaphors and oblique allusions that it became almost unintelligible, his main message came through and was greatly appreciated. This growth of 'communications' and 'exchanges' meant more and more tourists. That was what everybody in Tahiti was expecting and some were fervently hoping for. But was it really such a happy prospect as the general suggested? Were there not serious risks that we were going to be exposed to the same ruthless exploitation which had taken place in the Hawaiian islands? The general had nothing to say about these very real dangers.

The third trend was – of course – 'the beginning of the era of nuclear energy, opening the way for either advancement and progress or the complete annihilation of mankind'. However, there was no reason for despair, the general told us, for 'being protected by vast, invulnerable expanses of surrounding ocean, tomorrow Tahiti may well become a refuge and a centre of rebirth for our whole civilisation'.

At the time when this speech was given, nobody in French Oceania was in the least troubled by the potential dangers of the misuse of atomic energy. True, the American government had exploded a certain number of atomic bombs in Micronesia and some innocent civilians, both islanders and Japanese fishermen, had suffered from radioactive fallout. But the Micronesian islands were located at the other end of the Pacific, with no communication whatsoever between them and the French islands. No newspapers were published in Tahiti and there was only one radio station, run by the government, whose few news bulletins dealt mainly with the price of copra, the arrivals and departures of ships, balls, local football matches, and receptions given by the governor. Consequently, the general's noble vision of Tahiti as a last refuge where our Western civilisation could hold out during a nuclear holocaust made no impact whatsoever on his Tahitian and French listeners standing in the shade of the *barringtonia* trees in central Papeete on that fine day, 30 August 1956.

5 A RIOTOUS TIME

The first effects of the decolonisation process that de Gaulle had described in his forgotten speech as a normal and unavoidable trend in the postwar world began to appear in Tahiti barely six months later. The general himself was still lost in the political wilderness, and the men who initiated this limited reform programme were two Socialist members of the new government: the minister of overseas territories, Gaston Deferre, and the minister of justice, François Mitterand. It was only after a long and bitter struggle against the Gaullist deputies, who resorted to every known parliamentary trick, that they finally succeeded in ramming through the bill. One year late, on 22 July 1957, the new law was promulgated in French Oceania, whose name was changed at the same time to French Polynesia.

The most important consequence was the creation of a new local executive body, called the Government Council, consisting of seven ministers elected by the local parliament or Territorial Assembly. Unfortunately, this excellent reform in the direction of establishing a responsible government was marred by a significant limitation: the Government Council was not presided over by an elected prime minister, but by an appointed career civil servant, who took all of his orders from Paris. The fact that he retained the old title of governor clearly indicates his dominant position. For instance, the governor alone decided which items should be put on the agenda. Even better, if the ministers did not give satisfaction, he could dismiss them.

The number of seats in the Territorial Assembly was simultaneously increased from twenty-five to thirty and it was given broader powers in economic and financial matters. But all political matters were still taboo and, if the Paris government thought that the elected representatives of the Polynesian people exceeded their powers, it could dissolve the whole Assembly by simple decree. While this reform was considered extremely audacious and liberal in France, it was felt, understandably enough, by Pouvanaa and his followers, to be a timid compromise. However, if it was, as alleged, simply the first step in a gradual and well-programmed decolonisation process, they were perfectly willing to give it a fair try.

The local French traders and planters were of exactly the opposite opinion, and protested violently against this disastrous decision to hand over all power to 'ignorant fanatics'. Although they did all in their power to warn the population against these false prophets, the RDPT candidates won a comfortable majority of seventeen of the thirty seats during the ensuing elections to the Territorial Assembly. The first name on the RDPT list was, of course, Pouvanaa; and, when the new Assembly elected the seven members of the new Government Council, Pouvanaa's name again figured prominently as vice-president and minister of the interior.

One of Pouvanaa's first acts was to suspend all further land sales and to order a careful examination of all existing land deeds. The frankly avowed purpose of these measures was to cancel fraudulent deals and stop speculation. At the same time, the RDPT members of the Territorial Assembly, who had elected Céran as its president, made an even more revolutionary move. They proposed a bill introducing a universal income tax. Hitherto all taxes had been indirect, mostly in the form of customs duties on imported goods. As the RDPT assemblymen pointed out, this was an unfair system – for the poor paid as much as the rich. (Or, using a slightly different formulation, the rich paid as little as the poor.) According to the proposed bill, taxation was to begin at an annual income of 100 000 Pacific francs (roughly $A1000), well above the income of the majority of the Polynesians. For higher income brackets the percentages proposed rose gradually from 5 per cent to a maximum of 20 per cent for an annual income of two million Pacific francs or over. Generous deductions were allowed for married couples with children.

The number of people who would have had to pay income tax according to these dispositions did not exceed 600, half of whom were Chinese who, as usual, said nothing. The remaining French traders and planters protested all the more vigorously. However, as they were defending only their own interests, their chances of blocking the new law were slight. What they needed was a clever spokesman, able to locate their problem within a broader and more suitable context. They decided to send for a smart Parisian 'fixer' named Rives-Henry, who later on became a Gaullist deputy and eventually was convicted for his participation in a gigantic financial swindle.

A few days after he had disembarked in Tahiti, in April 1958, Rives-Henry presented his own masterly analysis of the situation, which was as follows. There was no doubt that Pouvanaa and his followers had many base personal motives for trying to harm their political adversaries by proposing these oppressive taxes. But that was not all. In addition, they had another more important reason which they had so far managed to keep secret. They wanted to fill the treasury coffers with all this tax money so as to make the colony economically self-sufficient. As soon as they had succeeded in this, they planned to establish an independent Tahitian republic. In other words, it was the patriotic duty of all French settlers to refuse to pay taxes.

When Céran and the other RDPT assemblymen pursued their unpatriotic activities, their adversaries felt justified in using extra-parliamentary methods. The expression is very apt in this case, since they decided to gather outside the local parliament building early on the morning of 29 April. Their principal argument was a big bulldozer with which they hoped to impress the 'separatists', as they now called the RDPT politicians, strongly enough to make them give up their preposterous plans. If not, Rives-Henry and company openly threatened to raze the entire assembly building to the ground which, in the light of its state of decay, would have been an easy task. To finish off the assemblymen who managed to escape, there was a whole truckload of sticks and stones. Ten French gendarmes and thirty marines sent over at the last minute to keep order, stood passively by. After all, the order had not been disturbed – not yet. Luckily for the assemblymen, who were in the session hall upstairs, the whole Papeete police brigade, made up of Polynesians, hastened to the scene at an early hour and took up a position on the staircase leading up to the entrance.

Even more crucial was the determination with which these Polynesians met the first attack of the demonstrators: taking advantage of their superior strategic position and the law of gravity, they literally fell upon the assailants and cleared the staircase in a few minutes. Somewhat belatedly realising that these were the wrong tactics, Rives-Henry and the other anti-tax leaders called back their storm troops and walked over to the commander of the French *gendarmerie* detachment and told him, conveniently forgetting the presence of the bulldozer and the truckloads of stones, that their sole purpose was to discuss peacefully some important problems with the assemblymen. The commander felt compelled to persuade the Polynesian policemen to let the organisers of the demonstration through. When these latter reached the anteroom where Céran was waiting for them, however, they showed their true colours by making the following straightforward offer: 'If you give up your attempts to impose an income tax, we will at once tell the people to disperse. But if you insist, you will soon be in serious trouble.' That was enough for Céran, who told them to clear out, and the sooner the better.

All this while, 'the people' consisted of some hundred French settlers, a handful of Polynesians, and no Chinese at all. But their lack in numbers was well compensated for by their initiative. This time they attacked the assemblymen gathered at the windows with a shower of stones, breaking several glass panes. A couple of molotov cocktails followed, luckily producing no fires. Pouvanaa appeared in one of the opened windows and manfully tried to make himself heard; but the demonstrators possessed several loud-speakers mounted on vans, thus making it easy to drown out his voice. Thereupon Pouvanaa proceeded to throw back the stones that had fallen onto the floor of the session hall, and the other assemblymen followed his example. When they ran out of stones, they used ashtrays and boxes for missiles. While all these events were going on, the marines remained satisfied with looking on; but when the bulldozer began to move forward, they intervened at last and barred the way.

Seeing that the marines were considerably less friendly than the gendarmes, the demonstrators' brains trust quickly changed tactics and ordered the bulldozer to turn around and head at utmost speed for the governor's office, located in a huge garden in the centre of Papeete. The gates were chained together and padlocked; but the gendarmes and the marines had been left far behind during this complete volte-face and the leader could thus break undisturbed through the gates. In keeping with established tactics, the foot soldiers rushed through the gap and surrounded the governor's residence, loudly and alternately shouting 'Long live France' and 'Down with the income tax'. The governor, Camille Bailly, had taken up his position only a month earlier and was a typical bureaucrat, completely unprepared and unfit for the role he now had to assume. For a while he simply gazed with a perplexed expression on his face at the surging crowd from behind the balustrade of his veranda. When at long last he stepped forward to address the demonstrators, the gist of his rambling speech was a lame promise to do 'something' on the following day! The demonstrators deemed this a half-victory and pulled back.

Later in the evening, the demonstrators attacked Pouvanaa in his home. Before the police and the troops arrived, all the windows had been broken. The number of Polynesians who were on Pouvanaa's side and willing to defend him was of course ten or twenty times greater than that of the demonstrators; but they lived in the countryside or on the other islands, and the attacks against the Assembly building and Pouvanaa's home had been so swift and unexpected that but few of his followers heard about these events until they were over. Due to the siege of the Assembly building all morning, it was not until the afternoon that the hitherto imprisoned RDPT leaders were able to send out messengers in all directions, exhorting their faithful to converge on Papeete. The first trucks and buses loaded with hastily armed men began rolling into town during the night. The arms were of the simplest kind: wooden clubs, bludgeons, fish spears, with a sprinkling of hunting guns; whereas their numerically fewer adversaries had a far superior arsenal of modern firearms.

In this explosive situation, it was more urgent than ever for Governor Bailly to do 'something'. However, the only thing he could think up was to issue the following proclamation in the early morning hours: 'The governor expresses his disapproval of the tumultuous scenes that occurred yesterday during an un-authorised public demonstration. In the name of the French Republic which he represents here, he requests the population to show due respect for law and order.'

Unfortunately, at this point in time, 30 April 1958, all respect for law and order had long since ceased to exist in France. The savage fighting for a lost cause in Algeria threatened to spread like a cancer to metropolitan France, which was on the verge of civil war. It was only a question of time before de Gaulle would be called back to save the nation for a second time. While waiting for this to happen, the government, the ministries, and the adminis-tration were completely paralysed. Many high officials simply went into hiding. Seen from the Parisian perspective, the bloodless street demonstrations in Papeete seemed, anyhow, to be a ridiculously small and childish affair. Moreover, all cables emanating from Papeete made it abundantly clear that the patriotic forces were doing so well that it was unnecessary to send more French troops to the colony.

Therefore, everything now depended on Governor Bailly's next move. It consisted precisely of taking the step prescribed by the new constitution, which he had hitherto stubbornly refused to do – he convened the Government Council. The deliberation lasted about half an hour and when the governor reappeared on the veranda to announce the outcome, it was something of an anticlimax: considering the special circumstances, the Government Council had decided 'to refer the whole matter back to the Territorial Assembly requesting it to postpone the application of the new tax law'. Just because of its dilatory character, the decision served its purpose of defusing the explosive situation. In both camps, the orders were to return home, and they were strictly obeyed.

So everything would have been all right if Céran had not resented the outcome and managed to persuade his RDPT colleagues to boycott the meeting, suddenly convened that same afternoon in the Assembly, to act upon the request made by the Council. The governor, who exceptionally took part in the meeting, seized upon this tactical mistake by introducing a draft bill in which the key word *postpone* had been changed to *cancel*. Thereupon the assemblymen from the minority parties quickly passed it.

Although furious with Céran, Pouvanaa remained cheerful about the general turn of events. Exactly as foreseen, less than two weeks later, the Third French Republic foundered and de Gaulle was invested with powers that made him the sole master of France. With such a faithful friend and protector installed in the Elysée Palace, the future for the Polynesian people seemed bright indeed.

6 THE DEGAULLONISATION OF POLYNESIA

Pouvanaa had hoped that de Gaulle would come out to Tahiti and see personally to putting the house in order. He soon had to give up that idea. De Gaulle was too busy alternately making peace and war in Algeria to find time for a new trip to the antipodes. It really did not matter too much; before the end of the year the general was going to carry out his often repeated promises to give freedom and independence to all French colonies. In July the government radio station in Tahiti announced that a referendum was to be held throughout the French Empire on 28 September 1958.

Soon afterwards the text of a high-sounding proclamation was read and posted on all public buildings. The pretentious style clearly showed that de Gaulle himself had written every word of it. There was also the usual mixture of idealistic principles and hidden threats. It read:

AN APPEAL TO COMMON SENSE

We are in an age when it is necessary to belong to large economic and political federations, when a narrow nationalistic policy has become absurd. The worst thing about this form of nationalism is that even those who think that they benefit from it will sooner or later expose themselves to the deadly risk of being conquered or swallowed up by one of the big imperialistic powers. What France offers you, instead, is to become a member of a great community whose inhabitants will be equals and will retain their sovereignty and their freedom to run their own affairs.

It is up to you, the people, to choose, and you will express your choice freely.

If you say YES in this referendum, it means that you are willing to follow the same road as France, for better or for worse. Yet you are allowed to determine the form and degree of independence that you wish to enjoy within the framework of this new French Commonwealth.

If you say NO, it means that you prefer to fly under your own power, and France will not hold you back. She will wish you luck and let you lead your own life, without giving you any further moral or material help, since you will have come to think of yourself as grown-up and able to earn your own bread. That would mean secession.

Although you have this choice, I am sure of your answer and expect you to furnish me with the building blocks needed to put up this new edifice together.

General de Gaulle
President of the Council
of Ministers

Still thoroughly disgusted by the recent riots and the ambiguous role played by the governor, Pouvanaa wanted complete independence at once and therefore chose to say NO. Céran objected on tactical grounds. He feared that de Gaulle meant what he said and that all economic aid to the colonies that voted against him would immediately cease. Therefore it would certainly be wiser to follow the general's advice and achieve independence by a long but easy detour, rather than by the risky shortcut proposed by Pouvanaa. It was not the first time that Céran had disagreed with Pouvanaa; but on this occasion their disagreement took the form of a public quarrel. As a result many RDPT leaders either took sides or turned away from both of them.

With the enormous prestige he enjoyed, Pouvanaa was bound to win just the same, provided that he could reach and preach to his Polynesian voters. As usual, the chief difficulty lay in lack of communications. The territory of French Polynesia includes more than a hundred islands spread out over an area almost the size of Australia. There was no air service in 1958. Even if Pouvanaa limited himself to visiting the principal islands in each group, such a boat trip would require two or three months. The government was under legal obligation to put its schooner at his disposal. But by a strange coincidence, at exactly this time, when it was most needed, it had been taken into the navy yard for a complete overhaul, to take several months. Of course, the private French and Chinese ship owners flatly refused to take on board such an evil agitator whose sole aim was to destroy them all.

However, there remained one extremely simple and efficient solution to the problem, and that was to use the local radio station. Although Pouvanaa was leader of the majority party and vice-president and minister of the interior, the governor dug up some hitherto overlooked decrees which, according to his own interpretation, forbade all *local* politicians in the colonies to use the government radio during the forthcoming referendum. Only *metropolitan* party leaders enjoyed this privilege. For instance, de Gaulle easily qualified and his vibrant appeal to vote YES was accordingly broadcast several times a day in both French and

Tahitian for many weeks prior to the referendum, while all this time not a word was said about Pouvanaa's stand. Long since accustomed to following de Gaulle's lead, the inhabitants in the outer islands thus voted massively YES on 28 September, whereas the people of Tahiti and Moorea, having been able to attend meetings organised by Pouvanaa and loyal RDPT leaders, voted NO in their majority. This explains how the same voters who had re-elected Pouvanaa deputy a short while previously with a 70 per cent majority now cast 64.4 per cent of their ballots for his adversary during this seemingly democratic and free election.

Yet the defeat was far from final. After all, had not de Gaulle promised those colonial peoples who followed his paternal advice by voting YES that they themselves would be allowed to determine the form and degree of independence they wished to enjoy within the framework of the new French Commonwealth founded on the ideal of universal brotherhood? The RDPT was still the majority party. So it was now up to Pouvanaa and the other key leaders to elaborate this new contract for their continued association with France.

To their genuine surprise and indignation, not only did de Gaulle forget his high-sounding promises, but he took out his revenge on Pouvanaa for having opposed him. On 8 October, with a single stroke of the pen, he quite simply dismissed Pouvanaa and all the other RDPT ministers in the Government Council, although they were still supported by a firm majority in the local parliament or Assembly. Encouraged by this reprisal originating in the highest quarters of Paris, the storm troopers that had spearheaded the anti-tax demonstrations six months earlier took to the streets once again, even better armed than before. Fortunately for Pouvanaa, many of his followers, who had come in to town on the day of the referendum, were still around. To avoid any repetition of the previous events, they formed a solid ring of defence around Pouvanaa's home in Manuhoe, on the eastern outskirts of Papeete. Their task was made easier by the fact that it was a solid two-storeyed brick house in the middle of a courtyard surrounded by iron fencing.

It was only a matter of time before this confrontation of two hostile crowds would degenerate into a general bloody mêlée. A rapid police action was urgently needed and came early in the morning of 11 October, when all the available marines, gendarmes and policemen invaded the Manuhoe area. Of course, the normal and logical thing to do was to disarm and disperse all of the demonstrators. Instead the government forces surrounded Pouvanaa's house and summoned him to come out. Without the slightest hesitation or suspicion, Pouvanaa, wearing a white suit with his parliamentary insignia on the lapel, stepped out. Without explanation he was escorted by two armed soldiers to a police van and driven off. Thirteen of Pouvanaa's most faithful followers were likewise arrested and his home carefully searched. On the other hand, none of the many armed anti-Pouvanaa demonstrators was taken into custody or even questioned.

According to French law, a deputy or senator cannot be arrested, except when he is caught *en flagrant délit*, in the very act of committing a crime. This, indeed, was the accusation first made in the official news bulletin, issued shortly afterwards. But we and many other persons had seen with our own eyes that, at the time of his arrest, far from committing any crime, Pouvanaa was willingly and trustingly approaching the police, completely unarmed. Someone in government circles must have realised the mistake by then, for in the next news bulletin it was announced that several 'subversives' had tried to set fire to and burn down the town of Papeete. Their clumsiness and ineptitude were striking, as they had thrown four molotov cocktails into empty courtyards and gardens; three of these had immediately gone out, and the fourth produced such an insignificant fire that it could easily be extinguished. According to this official version, Pouvanaa 'was behind' this 'arson'. Even if this accusation could be proved, it certainly in no way constituted a *flagrant délit* as defined by law.

No further explanation of this criminal and legal enigma was furnished during the next twelve months, during which time Pouvanaa was kept prisoner in a small cubicle in the infantry barracks, while his alleged conspirators were locked up in the ordinary city jail. The reason why it took a whole year to prepare for the trial is to be found in the enormous difficulties the examining judges had in finding evidence against Pouvanaa.

Not surprisingly, therefore, when the trial at long last opened on 19 October 1959, the role of prosecutor was quickly taken over by Pouvanaa, who was incredibly alert and vigorous considering his long solitary confinement and the harassing interrogation methods used on him for a whole year. With his usual eloquence he denounced the shameful frame-up, and the political character and purpose of his imprisonment and trial. For, as everyone knew, his only crime had been to have told his supporters to vote

NO during the referendum. To sentence him for this, while talking loudly about the freedom and liberty being given to the colonial peoples was sheer hypocrisy.

The official prosecutor tried desperately to confine the proceedings to a demonstration of Pouvanaa's role in the attempt to burn down and destroy the town of Papeete. The exhibits comprised the following items found during the search of Pouvanaa's house on the fateful morning of 11 October 1958: half a dozen machetes, about twenty wooden clubs, and a few beer bottles that had contained petrol. Pouvanaa retorted that he and his followers had been compelled to arm themselves because the police had made no effort to protect them. He also wanted to know whether the gendarmes had made similar searches of other houses, for instance those of his adversaries, between the day of the referendum, 28 September, and the day of his arrest, 11 October. No, they had not, admitted the prosecutor. It was a great pity, concluded Pouvanaa, for if they had done so, they would have found large arsenals of much more modern weapons.

It gradually became more and more obvious that the outcome of the trial was to depend entirely on what the prosecutor's witnesses had to tell. The star witness was a *demi* who declared that he had actually heard Pouvanaa tell his followers to burn down the town. However, under strong cross-examination, he suddenly broke down and confessed that he had been paid by Pouvanaa's enemies to produce false testimony. In the end the only thing that the prosecutor could prove was that some of the Polynesians who had thrown the molotov cocktails had strong sympathies for Pouvanaa and the RDPT. Even so, there was not a shred of evidence that Pouvanaa was the instigator. As to the initial indictment for *flagrant délit* which had made the trial possible, it was completely forgotten, or at least passed over in silence by the court.

Pouvanaa and his fellow detainees had no reason to feel any serious apprehension as to the final verdict. Thus, their surprise and disgust were all the greater when it was announced on 21 October that Pouvanaa had been found guilty 'of having been an accessory to the attempted destruction of buildings, by having provoked, assisted, and furnished the means to that effect'. He was also found guilty of 'having been in the unauthorised possession of arms and munitions'. In consequence of this he was sentenced to eight years of solitary confinement, followed by fifteen years of banishment from French Polynesia, and finally and somewhat incongruously he was fined 36 000 Pacific francs

($A360). Of the other accused, twelve got prison sentences varying from eighteen months to six years, and the thirteenth got three years on probation. Pouvanaa alone lodged an appeal, but the only result was to have it confirmed in record time by a higher court.

On a dark night a few days later, Pouvanaa was put into a police van and driven out to an empty beach on the north coast of Tahiti, where a speedboat was waiting. It took him out to the regular French passenger ship that had left the wharf in Papeete harbour a few hours earlier. While the passengers slept soundly, Pouvanaa was taken on board and put into a cabin with a new safety lock. Not until his arrival in France five weeks later on was he told the chilling news that he was to be locked up in the dreaded Baumette prison in Marseilles, reserved for hardened criminals.

As soon as Pouvanaa's imprisonment became known in October 1958, the French National Assembly had vigorously protested against this complete disregard for the immunity that all deputies and senators enjoyed. But this was the dark period at the beginning of de Gaulle's rule when the new president held dictatorial powers as a consequence of the Algerian war. Therefore, exceptionally, the government could deprive a deputy of his constitutionally guaranteed immunity by the simple issuance of a decree.

Those who are not well acquainted with the Polynesian mentality may find it surprising that Pouvanaa's followers, some three-quarters of the population, did not rise up when their beloved leader was imprisoned and deported. One explanation for this passivity is the strong troop reinforcements that the Paris government sent out to Tahiti shortly after de Gaulle's takeover. Well equipped with modern machine guns as they were, these troops could and did easily stop all suspect vehicles approaching Papeete from the countryside on the two roads leading into town. Furthermore, a French navy boat was stationed in Papeete to control all sea traffic. To ensure instant action in case of new troubles, a former paratroop colonel, Sicaud, was dispatched to Tahiti to take over the slackening reins from the mild-mannered bureaucrat, Bailly. Last but not least, the RDPT leaders who had escaped imprisonment because they luckily had not been found in Pouvanaa's home on the fateful day of his abduction were scared and preferred to lie low and patiently wait for better times.

But that Pouvanaa still enjoyed the full confidence of the Polynesian people could easily be seen when new elections were held on 26 June 1960 to fill the seat in the French National Assembly left vacant by his disappearance from the political scene. The RDPT candidate was Pouvanaa's son Marcel, who had inherited none of his father's acumen and was dying from cancer. But he was his father's son and that was enough for him to win with a comfortable majority. Shortly afterwards, another election was held to fill the seat in the Territorial Assembly held by Pouvanaa. This time, his daughter-in-law, a genial woman with little schooling and knowing nothing about politics, became the symbol and focal point for those who believed in their *metua* and his innocence. They were so numerous that she, too, was elected with a sweeping majority.

7 NO FRENCH TESTS IN THE PACIFIC

Pouvanaa was sixty-four years old when sentenced to eight years of solitary confinement, to be followed by fifteen years of banishment from the islands. Even in the unlikely event that he might live to the age of eighty-seven, he would be a spent force. This meant that the only person in French Polynesia with a greater influence and prestige than de Gaulle had been removed forever. But why was this so imperative for the general? In 1958–59, the only plausible explanation for this brutal elimination would seem to have been de Gaulle's personal wrath, caused by Pouvanaa's refusal to play the decolonisation game according to his rules. This interpretation was based on the punishment meted out by de Gaulle to Sekou Touré of Guinea, who was the only other native leader to vote NO, and who then added insult to injury by winning the referendum. De Gaulle punished him with like severity by cutting off, on the same day, all economic aid and technical assistance.

However, in retrospect, there is not the slightest doubt that in French Polynesia de Gaulle acted in a much more cold-blooded and calculating manner when he 'neutralised' Pouvanaa, to use an oft heard official euphemism. By this time de Gaulle was fully aware that the Algerian war was lost, and it was urgent to find a place for undertaking nuclear testing other than the Sahara desert, a part of Algeria. The only other suitable French territory was the Tuamotu group in French Polynesia.

General Ailleret, who, on good grounds, loved to call himself and to be called 'the father of the French A-bomb', has well described the hard choice he had to make in 1957 in his book *L'aventure atomique français* (Grasset, Paris, 1968, p. 228):

On the map we made the rounds of the French territories suitable for the sort of tests we were planning. Like all Frenchmen, we had a rather sketchy grasp of geography and had thus imagined that there were many such territories. However, we quickly realised that we were left with very few choices. For example, the Kerguelen islands were too far away and the weather there too stormy, blowing with a force of twenty to thirty metres a second practically the whole year round. Clipperton was well isolated in the middle of the Pacific, but had to be left out because there was no room

43

there for building an airstrip. As a matter of fact, there remained only two possibilities: the Sahara desert or the Tuamotu group in the Pacific.

And the father of the bomb adds laconically that his reason for choosing the sandy Sahara desert was to some extent because it was so much nearer France than the watery Tuamotu desert, but above all because in the latter instance the most important prerequisite had not been fulfilled: there was no airfield in French Polynesia.

Therefore, the RDPT leaders' suspicions ought to have been aroused when de Gaulle, concurrently with Pouvanaa's imprisonment and trial, announced that a new airport for international jet traffic was to be built in Tahiti. But far from being suspicious, they, along with everyone else, were deeply satisfied by this decision. It was an old dream coming true at last, as the local Assembly had been petitioning Paris for ten years for funds to build such an airport, in the hope of attracting tourists and thus reinvigorating the flagging economy, based on uncertain exports of only three products: copra, vanilla and mother-of-pearl shells.

For the first time in Tahitian history, a construction programme was carried out with efficiency and relentless speed. Nor were there any financial problems. All this in spite of the magnitude of the task, for the airstrip was built by filling in the lagoon near Papeete with one million cubic metres of coral sand and stones fetched in from a valley ten kilometres away to the south. The fact that the constructor had previously built similar airstrips in Hong Kong and in Invercargill in New Zealand largely explains the smooth execution. The first load of stones was dumped into the lagoon in June 1959 and by May 1961 the first regular air carrier landed on the completed airstrip.

One of the first persons to benefit from the improved air service was the deputy, Marcel Oopa, Pouvanaa's son, whose health had deteriorated so much that he was flown to Paris to get more effective treatment in a cancer hospital. In July 1961, his father obtained a few days freedom and sat at his side when he died. Marcel Oopa was succeeded by his proxy, John Teariki, who had more or less the same social and cultural origins as Pouvanaa— thinking, speaking, and acting like a real Polynesian, and with a profound knowledge of the Scriptures. The main difference was Teariki's quite un-Polynesian business acumen and relative wealth, derived mainly from a shipping service between Tahiti and his home island of Moorea. Psychologically, he was considerably more ascetic and severe than Pouvanaa, who could be quite jovial.

Teariki had hardly taken his seat in the National Assembly when he heard a rumour that was so fantastic that he could not believe his ears. The gist of it was that, because of the impending military victory of the Algerian 'rebels', de Gaulle had already ordered the construction of a new nuclear testing site in French Polynesia. Teariki was still quite lost in the complicated parliamentary machinery of the National Assembly; but his colleague, Maurice Lenormand from New Caledonia found a way of confronting Louis Jacquinot, the minister of overseas territories with this rumour during the budget debate shortly afterwards. The honourable minister did not hesitate a second to declare solemnly that 'no nuclear tests will ever be made by France in the Pacific Ocean'. Both Teariki and the other RDPT leaders felt reassured.

As a matter of fact, when similar rumours began to circulate again in April 1962, the culprit to which all fingers pointed was not France but America. The ban on atmospheric testing agreed on by America and Russia that year was to take effect as of 1963, so both superpowers were in a hurry to complete their current test series, including several gigantic H bombs. So many accidents had already occurred in Micronesia that the U.S. government was reluctant to explode 20- and 30-megatonne hydrogen bombs there. Because of these qualms, it borrowed the uninhabited Christmas Island from the British government.

For the Polynesian assemblymen who had just convened in Papeete for a new parliamentary session, it made no difference whether the bombs to go off in their part of the ocean were American or French. What they found particularly distressing was the enormous size of these bombs, which were to be detonated only about a thousand nautical miles from the nearest islands in French Polynesia. Their apprehension was greatly increased by the unheralded arrival by the French TAI airline on 13 April 1962 of two specialists from the French Atomic Energy Commission (CEA) equipped with a wealth of instruments to measure radioactive fallout.

The Territorial Assembly immediately voted a strongly worded resolution, proposed by the senator for French Polynesia, Gerald Coppenrath, urging the French government:
(1) To ask the American government for more precise information about the Christmas Island nuclear testing schedule.

(2) To take a firm stand against all nuclear tests entailing the slightest health hazard for the populations in the neighbouring archipelagos, especially those belonging to French Polynesia.

(3) To require the American government to let French observers be present during these tests.

The only reply the assemblymen ever received to these demands came from the French CEA specialists who cordially invited them to a public lecture on radiation risks. Teariki and several other RDPT leaders turned up; all told, about a hundred persons attended. The first of the two experts to address the audience explained, somewhat unexpectedly, that he was a lawyer and therefore had nothing to say about the topic of the day. Since this was the only time he opened his mouth during the whole evening, it remained an open question whether he had made the long trip halfway round the world in order to prove that international law forbade the American government to poison the people of French Polynesia, or whether it was in order to show that it was legally impossible to stop other governments from following the evil example set by the Americans. (In retrospect, the latter seems the more likely alternative.) However the other man, whose name was Henri Jamet, claimed to be a 'specialist on atomic energy'. Whatever that means, he was certainly not a radiation biologist. The aim of his lecture, it soon appeared, was to dismiss all objections to the American tests on Christmas Island as scientifically untenable. Somebody in the audience reminded him of the well-known fact that the fish in the vicinity of the test sites in Micronesia were regularly radiated. What would happen when fish affected by radiation at Christmas Island were caught and eaten by Polynesian fishermen? Jamet had the perfect answer to that: Most of the fish died on the spot, and those that survived were so slow to reach the Marquesas and the Society Islands that they could by then be safely eaten. As for the danger of wind-borne radioactive fallout reaching our islands, a danger evoked by another person, Jamet was equally categorical: There was not the slightest risk that this might happen, as the Americans were going to explode their bombs only when the wind was blowing from French Polynesia towards Christmas Island. The whole audience protested that the wind might change, as had so often happened in Micronesia. No, that was not possible, declared the specialist, in this part of the ocean. All other objections were met by equally categorical and equally unconvincing denials.

Another French scientist, Louis Molet, an anthropologist by

profession and head of the local ORSTOM research institute, immediately sent a letter of protest to our only daily newspaper at that time, *Les Nouvelles*. Molet was particularly angered by an argument often repeated by Jamet: that the health hazards were insignificant, because of the low population density in the Pacific. After having enumerated the numerous accidents that had occurred in Micronesia, Molet concluded that the risks were the same in Polynesia. The fact that the *absolute* number of persons that would be contaminated was smaller in the sparsely populated Pacific islands than in the densely populated American and European continents did not make their exposure to the danger any less of a crime. His arguments were greatly strengthened by the simultaneous announcement on the first page of *Les Nouvelles* that a twenty-megatonne hydrogen bomb had just been exploded on Christmas Island.

Next morning Molet was requested to appear at once before the governor, who curtly told him to pack his bags and take the next plane back to Paris. The question that intrigued all the political leaders in Tahiti was why Molet had been punished in this severe manner for having criticised *American* nuclear tests. De Gaulle and his ministers had never hesitated to criticise America and the Americans, and anti-American feeling was widespread and unchecked in France. Could the explanation be that, in spite of all denials, the French government was shortly planning to follow the American example and use Polynesia as a testing ground for French bombs? These fears were echoed by the assemblymen, who now began to wonder openly why so many French warships had visited the Tuamotu islands since 1959. Was it really in order to carry out hydrographic surveys, as the government had claimed?

Less than a month later, the mimeographed Tahitian weekly *Les Débats* reproduced an article taken from a French metropolitan paper, under the title: 'The Unknown Dangers of the Christmas Island Tests'. Not only did the author explain these dangers in detail, but he advised his readers how to avoid them:

Do not be a vegetarian. Do not adopt a diet consisting basically of vegetables, fruit and milk. It has been established that the peoples of India, Portugal, Turkey, the Philippines and Japan, with vegetables as their main source of calcium, absorb a much greater amount of strontium 90 into their bodies than do other populations.

Do not eat too much fish either. Fish concentrate radioactive pollutants

47

from the rivers and oceans in their bones, as well as in other organs.

Drink as little rain water as possible. A nuclear blast produces several scores of radioactive elements of varying life-length. These dangerous particles are brought down by the rain drops. This is why rainwater gathered in cisterns often contains highly concentrated doses of radioactive matter.

If you live in a region where the soil has a low content of calcium, you will absorb infinitely more strontium 90 by eating the vegetables grown there than do the people living in a region where the soil is rich in calcium.

These were excellent admonitions – but impossible to follow in French Polynesia, where the islanders traditionally live on vegetables and fish. Furthermore, all drinking water is supplied by the clouds of the sky, and in the atolls rainwater is collected and preserved for weeks in concrete cisterns. Everywhere, the soil is devoid of calcium. If the article had been translated into Tahitian and widely distributed, the islanders, who knew nothing of atoms or radioactivity, might have become aware at that early stage of the possible dangers. As things then were, the article was read at most by some hundred French-speaking residents in Tahiti.

One of the most eager readers of local and metropolitan newspapers and magazines was a schoolteacher by the name of Jacques Drollet, belonging to a French family that had established itself in Tahiti many generations earlier. He was one of the eighteen RDPT assemblymen, and he intervened during the session of 21 June 1962 in order to read an equally interesting article he had discovered in a French weekly. Most of it was in the form of an interview with the left-wing deputy from the French overseas department of Martinique in the West Indies, Aimé Césaire, who related a conversation he had recently had with General de Gaulle. According to Césaire, de Gaulle had declared that the reason why he had given independence to the African colonies was that there had been no other choice, and that this was not a terrible loss for France, anyway. However, de Gaulle was firmly determined to maintain and even to reinforce the French hold on the islands of eastern Polynesia, since he needed them for many years to come as a nuclear testing ground.

With their usual honesty, or should we perhaps say naïveté, the assemblymen decided to write directly to the French government and ask how much faith could be placed in this article. The only dissident voice came from an astute French-born assemblyman

48

who was for a much more forceful course of action. He beseeched the colony's deputy and senator to go and lie down on the red carpet outside the president's office in the Elysée Palace and remain there until de Gaulle had sworn publicly that the whole article was an infamous lie. Unfortunately, the parliamentarians were too polite and too timorous to follow this excellent advice. It nevertheless stimulated the senator to take an audacious, non-parliamentarian step. He went to see de Gaulle's trusted trickster and executor of dirty jobs, Jacques Foccart, who revealingly enough had his office in the Elysée Palace, though he was officially only in charge of 'African affairs'. Foccart was excessively cordial and even went so far in his efforts to calm the senator's apprehensions as to write the following letter, which was read in the Polynesian Territorial Assembly on 28 June:

The Office of the President   Paris, 11th July, 1962
My dear Senator and esteemed Friend,

I hereby confirm my declarations concerning the information published in the weekly paper *Minute* on Friday the first of June.

This periodical's sources of information are to be taken with extreme caution. The statements attributed to General de Gaulle are pure fabrications and have no basis in fact. Mr. Césaire has not even been given an audience with the President of the Republic.

Very truly yours,
Jacques Foccart

The thirty Polynesian assemblymen rightly considered that it was their master's voice to which they had been listening and did not press the matter further, although they had never had the pleasure of an official reply to their written request.

Thus, everything would have gone along smoothly if (1) some unscrupulous French journalists had not continued to spread false rumours, and (2) Jacques Gervais, the owner, publisher and entire staff of the Tahitian weekly *Les Débats,* had not gone on reproducing articles taken from French magazines received by airmail which he deemed to be of local interest. One of these stories concerned the Mangareva, or Gambier Islands, east of the Tuamotu group and also a part of French Polynesia. De Gaulle planned, so the rumour now went, to build a missile base there. Less than a month later, in the issue for 20 August 1962, Gervais published a long front-page article with more detailed information, gleaned from the metropolitan press, about this project, under the title, 'Thirty thousand million in four years: Mangareva will first be a French and later on a European missile base'.

The key passage read:

The transformation of the Gambier group is to begin in 1963. Nearly 3000 French technicians are to be on the spot in 1964. It seems obvious that a rear base is to be located in Tahiti, but nobody knows whether the residential town for their families is to be built in the vicinity of Papeete or in some country district. . . It will cost France no less than 30 000 million Pacific francs to install these launching pads, gear shelters, and living quarters for the personnel.

The sorely tried governor became so upset over this irresponsible news reporting that he expelled Gervais without hearing or trial, as an old colonial decree from 1932 empowered him to do. Only a few weeks later a curious event made it seem more than likely that the real motive for this expeditious justice was that Gervais had told the truth, for all of a sudden the French minister of public works, Robert Buron, stepped out of a plane at the new airport. The assemblymen immediately invited him to come over and tell them what his mission was. Although it was plainly stated on the invitation that drinks and refreshments were to be served during this special session, the honourable minister sent back a message regretting that previous engagements did not leave him time to accept the kind invitation. Of course, this made the assemblymen, and everybody else in the territory, wonder what these other terribly important engagements might be. Perhaps some sort of construction in the Mangareva Islands? But if this were all, why surround the plans with so much secrecy?

The governor felt obliged to offer an explanation, which was far from convincing. Considering that there were to be new general elections in France on 18 November it was only natural for General de Gaulle and his ministers to refuse to say anything about long-range projects depending on the outcome of those elections. The Polynesian leaders retorted that it was usually just before an election that a government, uncertain of being re-elected, started all sorts of public works and saw to it that they received maximum publicity. Some RDPT politicians even went so far as to ascertain that de Gaulle had already decided to poison their island with his atomic bombs, and that it was time to denounce these criminal plans. That was exactly what Pouvanaa would have done, had he been a free man.

8   ELOQUENT SILENCE

It so happened that there were two other elections that same year, before the general elections. First the territory had to designate a senator. The incumbent, Gerald Coppenrath, a lawyer by profession, was a strong supporter of the existing colonial system. But compared to his predecessors, he was remarkably honest and intelligent and had done much to fight corruption and bureaucracy. Incidentally, there was a strong altruistic tradition in the Coppenrath family, which had come out from Germany one hundred years earlier. For instance, two of the senator's brothers were Catholic priests.

French senators are elected for a period of nine years, one-third of the senate body being renewed every three years, through indirect elections, open only to town (city and country) councillors. At that time in French Polynesia there were only about sixty of these electors, half of whom were town councillors in Papeete. Of course, the most influential of these latter was the mayor, Alfred Poroi. Like Coppenrath, he belonged to the *Union Tahitienne Démocratique,* the local branch of the Gaullist party. The party leaders all agreed that Coppenrath had done a good job and should be re-elected; but when the bulletins were counted, it appeared that Poroi had secretly persuaded his town councillors to vote for him, giving him enough votes to scrape through. This split the party into two warring factions.

Dissension was equally rampant in the Pouvanaa-ist ranks on the eve of the next elections for the renewal of the Territorial Assembly. The chief contenders were Teariki and Céran, both of whom claimed to be Pouvanaa's messiah. The break had become official earlier in the year when Céran, angered by Teariki's election to succeed Pouvanaa as president of the RDPT, had founded his own Tahitian Independence Party (*Pupu Tiama Maohi*). It was not only a matter of conflicting personalities, but also a choice between Teariki's tough stand and Céran's softer line of approach. The results of these elections, held on 14 October, proved Teariki right. The RDPT won fourteen seats, while the only *Pupu Tiama Maohi* candidate to win a seat was Céran himself. Several outsiders who claimed to have received Pouvanaa's blessings, although he was still being held incommunicado in France, managed to be elected in this deceitful manner. Once inside the doors of the Assembly building they joined forces with Teariki, giving the RDPT a majority of seventeen out of thirty seats. The new Gaullist party, *Union pour la Nouvelle République* (UNR), cleansed of Poroi and a few other 'traitors' won eight seats. Finally there was an independent named Pito who had been elected on an extremely original platform: the immediate abolition of the Territorial Assembly. His unforeseen success was undoubtedly due to the general exasperation with the ineffectiveness of that institution, what with the limited powers that Paris was willing to grant it.

In keeping with standard protocol, on 8 November 1962, the new parliamentary session was opened by the governor with a certain pomp. These purely ceremonial proceedings were traditionally presided over by the oldest Assembly member, who happened to be none other than Pito. Though actually against his principles, he very graciously consented to greet the governor on behalf of the whole Assembly, which he was still just as firmly as ever determined to do away with.

As usual, it was 26°C outside the Assembly building and 30°C inside. Nonetheless, parliamentary etiquette prescribed suit and tie. The hall was not air-conditioned. Therefore, on these occasions, the assemblymen were quite understandably in the habit of resting their heads in their hands and dozing off from time to time. But not now. They all sat bolt upright with wide-open eyes, when the governor put on his glasses and began to read from his typed manuscript. Like everyone else in the hall, they were all convinced that, at long last, the governor was going to announce what de Gaulle was up to.

The governor, an old career man, devoted the first ten minutes to a detailed analysis of the trade balance, or rather the lack of it. Both the quantity and the value of the colony's few exports had gone down. On the other hand more and dearer goods of all sorts had been imported. The only encouraging figures were those showing a certain increase in the number of tourists. In other words, we were harvesting the first fruits of General de Gaulle's foresighted and generous decision to build an airfield in Tahiti. At the same time the governor warned against an exaggerated optimism. The income from tourism represented only a small fraction of the total earnings, and it would take years and years to make it a major industry. At any rate the economy ought to be diversified and a special effort made to develop agriculture, animal husbandry, and fishing. The governor took a considerable time with a detailed description of the numerous measures he had decided upon. The senior assemblymen smiled discreetly, having heard the same promises a dozen times, and relaxed a bit.

Next came an appraisal of the state of the budget, which was even more catastrophic. The revenues remained at the same level, while the expenses increased by leaps and bounds, mainly because of the growth of public services. The governor evaluated the budget deficit at 100 million Pacific francs. If anyone feared that he was going to propose such a revolutionary measure as the creation of an income tax, any such fear was immediately dispelled. The logical and natural solution was rather to ask the beloved motherland to make up the deficit, the governor said. All the assemblymen, regardless of political allegiance, applauded vigorously.

Obviously inspired by this overt approval, the governor went on in a lyrical vein:

France will assume the obligations entailed by her historical role and the attachment shown by the noble Polynesian people, particularly dear to her. She will never abandon Polynesia and, believe me, is firmly determined to keep the tricoloured flag flying forever over these islands, which are French and will remain an integral part of the French Republic.

Long live Polynesia, French land in the Pacific.

Long live France.

Whereupon the governor collected his manuscript, shook hands with the senior president, Pito, and marched out of the Assembly Hall, his retinue following.

Surprise, perplexity and anger could be read on the perspiring faces of the assemblymen. Why suddenly make such a glowing declaration of love for Polynesia in the absence of even the slightest sign of encouragement? What counted for them was not all of this flowery rhetoric, but rather what the governor had *not* said. To make such a long speech without denying or confirming all those wild rumours about the establishment of military bases in Polynesia was an insulting slight to them.

Filled with a new fighting spirit, the assemblymen set to work and gave first priority to a request for the immediate release of Pouvanaa. All the African nationalist leaders who, like Pouvanaa, had been imprisoned because they had opposed the French colonial rule, had long since been liberated and allowed to return in triumph to their homelands. In their new roles as presidents of

53

independent states, most of them had even been received with due honours in Paris by de Gaulle himself; Pouvanaa was the only exception, still serving out his term for a crime he had never committed. The fact that he had recently been transferred from the Baumette prison to a convalescent home near Paris did not make the least difference, for he was not allowed visitors; neither could he correspond with his family and followers in Tahiti.

The governor replied at once in the following terms, which hardly contributed to appeasing the belligerent assemblymen:

Papeete, 9th November, 1962

Mr Speaker:

I acknowledge receipt of your letter number 788/1487 of the 8th November, 1962 advising me of the resolution adopted on the 7th November, 1962 by a majority of the assemblymen and requesting that Mr Pouvanaa a Oopa be permitted to return to French Polynesia.

I am compelled to call your attention to the fact that paragraph 45 of decree number 46–2379 of the 25th October, 1946 creating an elected Assembly in French Oceania and reconfirmed by later legislative texts, does not allow the Territorial Assembly to address remarks, requests, or resolutions concerning political problems directly to the Minister of Overseas Territories.

In the present case, the Territorial Assembly has exceeded its powers, as defined by the previously cited texts, which do not allow it to intervene in the administration of justice.

Respectfully yours,
A. Grimald

Confronted with this eternal recourse to specious legalistic argument, the RDPT leaders were determined to show the colonial authorities once more how little weight they carried compared to the political and sociological realities. When, two weeks later, the third election of the year took place, Teariki again stood as candidate for the deputy seat in the French National Assembly, his platform consisting solely of the same request: to release Pouvanaa without further delay. He was promptly re-elected with an even larger majority than during the previous election. However, this was to no avail as in France the Gaullist party won by a landslide. The new parliament included not less than 229 UNR deputies, and about fifty right-wing sympathisers, assuring the Gaullists of an absolute majority. Teariki's chances of making himself heard in the National Assembly were thus even slimmer than before.

9 DE GAULLE'S CHRISTMAS GIFT

There remained the little problem of the unbalanced budget for 1963. The deficit showing in the governor's draught version was roughly 100 million Pacific francs, or one million Australian dollars. There were several ways of solving this problem. Some assemblymen courageously suggested a corresponding cut in expenditure. They had even figured out exactly what kind of cuts could be made without imperilling the economy. There were more than 2000 civil servants in the colony, almost all of them stationed on the island of Tahiti with a population of merely 50 000 persons. That was far too many. So why not balance the budget by the simple expedient of dismissing half of these bureaucrats? Pito was even more radical. Without blinking he proposed in a firm voice that they show the way by realising his one-man-party programme: the immediate abolition of the whole Territorial Assembly. To everyone's surprise, as many as nine assemblymen voted for his proposal; but, of course, this was not enough to get it passed. Finally there was the usual RDPT proposal of instituting an income tax.

For his part, the governor showed an outright contempt for all these ideas. Why not adopt the classical solution, of proven effectiveness, and dispatch a begging delegation to Paris? By the way he expressed himself, it was abundantly clear that the French government would be only too happy to help. Another advantage of such an arrangement was that the delegates would be able to take up with the proper ministers such other matters of great concern to them as the release of Pouvanaa and the revision of the antiquated colonial statute. After a very short debate, the assemblymen decided to adopt this time-honoured solution. Each party sent one delegate; the senator Poroi and the deputy Teariki were also included in the group.

In the past, when similar delegations had travelled to Paris, they had always had to fight hard against the inertia of the metropolitan bureaucratic machinery. As a rule they had to wait for days and weeks before the ministers found time to receive them; and often they had to return time and time again to the ministries to remind the department heads of unfulfilled promises. But on this occasion everything was different. From the moment the Polynesian delegates stepped down from their plane at Le Bouget airport into the cold Parisian climate shortly before Christmas, all the French officials were immediately available, and trying to outdo Santa Claus. Confronted with this unaccustomed friendliness and generosity, the assemblymen quickly added a few more items to their Christmas list. They were immediately granted.

This aroused the suspicion of some of the delegates. Such a change of attitude could not be due solely to the Christmas spirit engulfing the French capital. It also seemed strange to them that their benefactors were so reluctant to discuss problems other than purely economic ones. The government officials had a handy explanation for this. All political questions were decided by the president of the Republic, whom they were going to see on 3 January 1963.

On the appointed day and hour, the Polynesian delegates arrived at the Elysée Palace where they were taken straight to the president-general's office to meet their former friend face to face for the first time since 1956. Without losing any time, their Territorial Assembly speaker, Jacques Tauraa, began to read the resolution requesting a revision of the whole colonial system of government. De Gaulle nodded, simply saying: 'In exchange, I promise you that France will stay in Polynesia'.

Before they had time to question him about the meaning of this sibylline statement, one of his collaborators began reciting the long list of aid projects being proposed or contemplated. De Gaulle listened with obvious approval and assured them in the end that he had personally instructed his ministers to see to it that all promises were faithfully kept. Without pausing for breath, he then added, as though it were the logical conclusion of all that had gone before: 'In the name of the French nation, I have also decided to build a nuclear base in the Gambier Islands. Not only will this test centre promote French military research, but it will also be highly beneficial from the point of view of the economy of the inhabitants of Polynesia.' There followed upon this a long eulogy of the patriotic Polynesian people who were among the first to acclaim him as leader of Free France and to join him in the battle for freedom and justice. Once more, he concluded with a superb anticlimax: 'I have not forgotten all that you have done, and this is one of the reasons why I have chosen to install this base in Polynesia'.

The new senator, Alfred Poroi, was so overwhelmed that he exclaimed: 'I am so grateful, General, that you have thought of us. It shows how much you in France love us.' The whole scene could hardly have been better directed if the script had been written by the great playwright de Gaulle himself. However, for the life of them, the other members of the delegation could not understand why poisoning their islands with radioactive fallout was such a marvellous token of gratitude and friendship. Although weak on French syntax and grammar, Jacques Tauraa managed to convey very clearly to the general the fact that he and everyone else in French Polynesia were firmly opposed to all forms of nuclear test – if that was what he had in store for them. Teariki added that the pastors of the local Protestant church considered the use of nuclear arms contrary to the teachings of Christ. Visibly annoyed by such stupid objections, de Gaulle nevertheless found a perfect reply: 'If so, Mr Deputy, I hope you will ask those pastors to implore the Almighty to prevent the Russians and the Americans from producing more bombs, in which case France will follow suit.' 'In order to avoid any further useless discussion, de Gaulle thereupon majestically waved them all out of his office.

At that point, Pompidou, Giscard d'Estaing and Foccart took over and were extremely voluble in detailing all the economic benefits the lucky Polynesians were to reap from this new military programme. On the other hand, they were considerably more restrained when it came to explaining the exact nature and characteristics of the scheduled testing centre. Upon his return to Tahiti, Frantz Vanizette, one of the delegates, made a statement to the local newspaper *Les Nouvelles*. It is quite revealing about the fiction that de Gaulle and his collaborators still managed to make sound convincing at this stage: 'As for the base to be built in the Gambier Islands, it will be used for testing missiles; in as far as nuclear tests are concerned, if such are to be made, they will take place in an uninhabited region of the Pacific, at such a distance from the nearest human settlements that there will not be the slightest danger'. As for the social and economic consequences, Vanizette let it be known that the French government had promised to form a committee composed of government officials, the armed forces, and the local elected representatives of the Polynesian people, to be entrusted with the task of supervising the installation, so as to avoid all harmful effects.

10 NOTHING TO WORRY ABOUT

Most of the assemblymen who had remained behind in Tahiti
while the Christmas delegation was being snowed under with gifts
in Paris, were openly hostile and told their colleagues that they
had not protested strongly enough. It was high time for the
Assembly to express officially its firm opposition to all nuclear
tests and all military bases. Vanizette then revealed that he had
been warned by several department heads that no money would
be forthcoming if the Polynesian Assembly 'began to stir up
troubles'. As so often happens, this revelation of attempted
blackmail produced exactly the opposite effect from that expected. The assemblymen unanimously adopted a resolution in
which they asked the French government to do nothing until
competent specialists had made careful on-the-spot studies of all
possible health hazards that might result from nuclear tests of the
kind contemplated.

The only reply they ever received to this reasonable request was
indirect and far from reassuring. It came in the form of a speech
that Governor Grimald made one month later, back from Paris in
his turn, after having received instructions from his bosses. He
began by admitting:
(1) that the planned missile base was to be built in French
Guayana in South America and not in the Gambier Islands;
(2) that nuclear bombs were to be tested on Moruroa, a small atoll
in the inhabited Tuamotu group.

Taking his cue from General de Gaulle, the governor next
dwelt with loving detail on the innumerable benefits that would
accrue to the population. The army was to build at least half a
dozen airstrips, open also for civilian traffic. The Papeete harbour
was to be enlarged and deepened. Of course, some wharves were
to be reserved for French warships. But there would be more than
enough space for new cargo ships bringing in marvellous goods of
all sorts for the local population. In the strictly military field, a
great number of barracks, offices, workshops and living quarters
were to be built. This would mean well-paid employment for
thousands of Polynesian workers. In other words, the bomb
meant peace and prosperity for all.

After a well-calculated pause, so as to catch the full attention of the audience, the governor added that he was well aware of the fact that certain persons were critical. However, he had taken into consideration all possible objections; therefore, he was happily in a position to give the following frank and honest answers:

(1) The amount of radioactive fallout will be negligible, thanks to the fact that Moruroa is located 1 500 kilometres from Tahiti and the tests will be made only when the winds are northerly and blowing towards the southern portion of the ocean where there are no islands.

(2) There is no risk at all that the islands will become military targets in case of an international conflict, as the enemy would only attack launching pads which in most instances are mobile anyway.

(3) The moral risks for the population are extremely small, since the majority of the military and technical personnel will consist of married men.

(4) As for the political situation, the newcomers will not be able to influence it, due to their small number compared with the local population of 85 000 persons.

(5) There will be no inflation thanks to the preventive measures that the government has elaborated and is about to apply.

(6) As for the tourist trade, the nuclear bases will have no impact whatsoever. Neither will Tahiti's beauty and charming way of life change in the slightest.

Only a few weeks later, the main executor of de Gaulle's nuclear policy, General Thiry, disembarked in Tahiti. Among the many gold-braided, uniformed men in his entourage was a civilian, Monsieur Philippe Giscard d'Estaing, president of one of the largest French construction companies, SODETEG. On 27 April General Thiry made the following statement about the remarkable security measures the French army planned to take in French Polynesia in order to protect the civilian population against radioactive contamination: 'It would be stupid to deny that there were any security problems at all. But it is equally true that they can be solved in such a way as to eliminate all risks. Considering the fact that radioactive fallout is short-lived and rapidly dissolves and disappears, all that has to be done is to enforce certain temporary prohibitions and injunctions.' As he explained it, with a big smile, certain islands were to be forbidden to human beings for longer or shorter periods of time, while similar interdictions against eating fish on specified islands were to be announced from time to time.

By then several persons in Tahiti had recognised General Thiry as the same officer who had visited Moruroa and the Gambiers more than a year earlier, in February 1962. He had at that time told *Les Nouvelles*: 'My aim is to organise rescue operations in this part of the Pacific and to examine the best sites for future airstrips. For instance, a project exists to build an airstrip in the Gambier group to serve as a convenient stopover for the air traffic between Tahiti and Chile via Easter Island.' *Les Nouvelles* had the gall to reproduce this statement now on its first page.

This further demonstration of how systematically and wittingly de Gaulle and his henchmen had deceived them for years was the last straw for the assemblymen. The angriest ones were those who hitherto had most trusted the general, that is the members of the local Gaullist party. During a stormy morning session on 16 May 1963, practically all the assemblymen expressed their disgust and their firm opposition to the establishment of nuclear bases in Polynesia. These are only a few representative samples of the opinions expressed on that occasion:

'Since there is really no danger at all, why does not the French government make these tests in the Marseilles harbour or in the centre of Paris? This seems to be an ideal solution for another reason, too: the great benefits that would accrue to the poor in France from such an enterprise.' (Felix Tefaatau, RDPT)

'If we ask a specialist who works for the nuclear test centre for advice, we know in advance what his reply will be. So why do we not ask the same questions of impartial scientists?' (Gérald Coppenrath, Gaullist)

'In the event of a new war, Polynesia will be a target. What steps has the government taken to protect the population?' (Tetuanui Ehu, Gaullist)

'Like all metropolitan Frenchmen, we say no to the bomb.' (Elie Salmon, Gaullist)

'The army will bring people in from the outer islands to Papeete, and these immigrants will become proletarians. But that is nothing compared to the difficulties that will arise upon the completion of the construction work when, if we are not to have general unemployment, it will become necessary to find new jobs for all the men who have been brought here. Meanwhile the rural areas will lose their farmers and planters and the production of copra, pearl shells, coffee, and vanilla will diminish. In other words, our whole economy will be in a shambles.' (Céran-Jérusalémy, Tahitian Independence Party)

'Another aim of these military installations is to provide refuge for thousands of Frenchmen in flight from former possessions in North

Africa. These people want to be our masters, and already with the next elections, they will be trying to take over. The former president of our Assembly is on their side, as he and his followers would like nothing better than to boot us out. This is why we people born in the islands must be on our guard against all these outsiders who settle here with the sole purpose of making money.' (Felix Tefaatau, RDPT)

The afternoon session was devoted to a debate about health hazards. Teariki had spent most of his time in Paris not in the National Assembly, but in bookshops and in scientific institutes studying nuclear safety problems. Therefore he was now able to present a detailed and highly critical report. To begin with he expressed his surprise that all specialists and officers asserted so categorically that the radioactive fallout from the bomb tests would be short-lived. What about strontium 90, for instance? Its half-life was twenty-eight years, a terribly long period for those exposed to this deadly poison. He went on to state:

This element has, moreover, the same chemical propensities as calcium, with the result that it can easily be absorbed into our bones. One-millionth of a gram of strontium 90 produces four million disintegrations per second and does enough harm to our marrow to cause leukemia. This explains why the official spokesmen have not mentioned strontium 90 at all. Yet this element will fall into the ocean where it will contaminate not only the fishes but also and above all the plankton, the basic food of all animal life in the sea. The plankton next contaminates the many small fishes which in their turn are swallowed by bigger fishes. At each step the strontium becomes more concentrated. All the while, the currents will carry the contaminated plankton to other ocean regions, without there being any possibility of our specialists determining its pattern of diffusion. Last but not least, we all know that many species of fish make long migrations the duration, direction, and seasonal variation of which we know nothing. Under these circumstances, what means are the specialists considering for our protection against these dangers? Probably none; otherwise they would not have made such absurd statements as to assert that the contaminated fish will lose every trace of radioactivity within a few days – before they are captured.

Teariki was equally sceptical about the trust the governor and the generals were putting in the meteorological service, quoting in particular their affirmation that 'the meteorologists are able to determine the strength and direction of the wind with such accuracy that the radioactive fallout produced by each blast will spread over only an uninhabited area of the ocean.' Teariki protested that meteorology was far from an exact science, as had unfortunately been demonstrated by the numerous accidents that had occurred during the nuclear tests in Micronesia.

For instance, on the 1st March, 1954, the Americans detonated a several megatonne H-bomb at Bikini. Radioactive fallout unexpectedly rained down over an area 500 kilometres long and 40 kilometres wide. Many Marshall islanders were contaminated although they were 160 kilometres from the bomb site and would certainly have fared much worse if their island had not happened to be located 35 kilometres off from the main axis of the radioactive cloud. Nevertheless they absorbed doses of magnitudes up to 175 roentgens. As it is extremely unlikely that these islanders had deliberately entered the proscribed danger zone for the fun of it, we must conclude that the reason for this disaster was that the wind changed direction at the last moment. In other words, nature does not always heed man's dictates.

The resolution he asked the Assembly to adopt was formulated in the following admirably concise and clear terms:

The RDPT majority therefore requests that the French government renounce its plan to undertake nuclear tests at Moruroa. If the government cannot give immediate satisfaction, we demand that the plans be submitted for the approval of the population in the form of a referendum. This is not primarily a political question but a matter of imperilling the health of the whole population. We assemblymen are all elected by the people to serve the people. That is why we should act accordingly and without exception vote for this resolution. Only in this manner can we show that we put the interests of the people higher than party politics.

Teariki's colleagues seemed all ready to vote for his resolution. But so many of them wanted to speak on the subject and did so that the closure of the debate and the final vote had to be postponed until the next session a few days later. During the interval, the governor asked Teariki to come over to his office, and right away launched into a long analysis of French defence problems. The point he was trying to make was how important and urgent it was for France to reinforce her defences. Only by doing so could another defeat like that of 1940 be avoided. Of course an effective defence was synonymous with a nuclear striking force. Consequently, common sense required Teariki's refraining from presenting such a preposterous demand as he had formulated in the pending bill. Completely unruffled, Teariki pointed out that the aim of his resolution was not at all to prevent France from re-arming, and at any rate the Territorial Assembly had no legal right to discuss metropolitan defence matters. His and his colleagues' aim was completely different. All they asked of the French government was not to make any nuclear tests in their islands. Realising that friendly persuasion would achieve nothing, the governor suddenly changed his tone and attitude and threatened to dismiss the Territorial Assembly if Teariki and company did not give in. The only thing Teariki could promise was to make this threat known to his colleagues.

The great advantage of the tactic initially chosen by the governor was, of course, that 'friendly persuasion' in his office, without witnesses, did not leave any embarrassing traces. This having failed, all the assemblymen would probably now vote for the resolution as a gesture of solidarity in defiance of the arbitrary dismissal that threatened them all. Therefore the governor used the traditionally less elegant axe method and quickly dispatched the following letter:

Papeete, 21st May, 1963

Mr Speaker:

On the 16th May, Mr John Teariki presented, on behalf of the RDPT group, a draught of a resolution concerning the installation of a nuclear testing centre in French Polynesia and it was decided that the debate was to continue on the 24th May.

I have the honour of informing you that this initiative and the request formulated in the pending bill constitute meddling in defence problems, which are the sole responsibility of the French government and the National Assembly. For this reason and because of the frankly political character of the pending bill, the Territorial Assembly has exceeded its powers.

At the same time, I can assure you that I am not trying to deny you the right of examining and discussing matters relating to the protection of the population's health; and I should like to repeat my assurances here in the name of the Republic that all necessary measures are being taken to guarantee that the population will not suffer in the slightest degree from the scheduled experiments.

On the other hand, it is my right and duty to warn you of the consequences to which you expose yourselves if you not only include in your agenda questions outside your competence, but also arrive at conclusions irreconcilable with the general policies of the Republic, and incompatible with the true interests of the territory as well.

Yours truly,
A. Grimald

The governor was perfectly right when he wrote that the assemblymen had very limited powers. Since he insisted so vehemently that they were not even permitted to debate problems of such tremendous importance as the mortal risks to which they were soon to be exposed, they could not help but think that their powers were *too* limited. However, instead of stoically accepting their fate as they had done in the past, the assemblymen concluded that it was high time they were given a greater say in the affairs of their own country.

Considering that by then the immense majority of the French, British and Dutch colonies were independent states, their demands were extremely modest and timid. But then we must remember that news about the decolonisation process, even in the Pacific islands, rarely reached Tahiti, due to the firm government control of all mass media. Fortunately, there were no legal obstacles preventing the elected representatives of the Polynesian people from following the same path towards greater freedom and even independence, if they so wished. For this right was clearly guaranteed by the French constitution, written by de Gaulle's closest collaborator, Michel Debré, and adopted by an overwhelming majority of the parliament in 1958. No less than fifteen African colonies had taken advantage of this constitutional right since that date.

As usual the only assemblyman to have carefully studied all of the pertinent legal texts was Céran. He had even gone one step further – on his own initiative he had drawn up all the documents needed for establishing an independent Tahitian Republic. His colleagues were taken aback and far from ready for such a drastic step. In an emotional speech Céran tried to win them over. But they all came up with the same objection. They could not make such a capital decision without having the full support of their respective parties. Fortunately, all local parties were shortly to hold their annual conventions, since the best period for convening the card-carrying party members was in July, when the inhabitants of the country districts and the outer islands came in to Tahiti to participate in the 14th of July celebrations.

Céran had foreseen these objections and presented a sort of questionnaire entitled 'Urgently needed reforms in French Polynesia' to his colleagues and asked them to bring it to the attention of their party convention constituents. His proposal was unanimously accepted.

11   THE PROBLEMS ARE LEGION

The last meeting of the Territorial Assembly before the 'Winter' break, which was to last until October, took place on 20 June 1963. Only a few minor matters were on the agenda. However, the whip of the RDPT group, Jacques Drollet, announced that he had an important declaration to make. These are the main speeches made during the ensuing debate:

Jacques Drollet, RDPT: When our delegation visited Paris in January and learned from General de Gaulle himself that nuclear testing was to take place in French Polynesia, some of his collaborators let it be known that the troops to be sent out here would include a component of foreign legionaries [soldiers of the French Foreign Legion]. We protested against these plans, and apparently our protests were heeded. A little later on in March I contacted several of the top men responsible for these nuclear bases and expressed once more our opposition to the use of foreign legionaries in our territory. In spite of all this, I have just heard that between two and three hundred men from the Legion's engineer corps will be sent out here to build these bases. I think that we should formally ask the governor to protest in Paris on our behalf against the use of legionaries in Polynesia.

Rudy Bambridge, Gaullist: Mr Jacques Drollet has made a proposal that I fully support and should even like to sign jointly with him. When I was in France last December and heard these rumours, I made the same objections to the same officials. In April I again discussed this serious threat to our population. We do not want any legionaries and must not believe a word of the talk we hear about their improved behaviour.

Jacques Drollet, RDPT: Let us all protest against the dispatch of the Foreign Legion personnel. A unanimous vote will carry some weight.

J. B. Céran, Tahitian Independence Party: I concur wholeheartedly with Mr Jacques Drollet. I have also heard about these legionaries and I have even hinted at this eventuality during a debate concerning the nuclear bases.

Gérald Coppenrath, Gaullist: I share Mr Drollet's views; as a matter of fact this threat has existed for several years. Recruitment has flagged. Therefore it has been suggested that the prospect of serving in a place with such a pleasant climate as Tahiti's would induce young men to sign up. This is why I have repeatedly explained in France, for many years now, that legionaries are not welcome here. I believed that the authorities had understood this. Unfortunately such does not seem to be the case.

Alexandre Le Gayic, Gaullist: I am fully in support of Mr Drollet's proposal.

Felix Tefaatau, RDPT: So am I, and I think that we ought not be too timid in expressing our disapproval. I should also like to recall what I said during a previous session about the risks of military rule. Today they are obvious. It is not hard to imagine what will be the consequence of having all these troops in our country. In the future they will shut our mouth with the help of their rifle butt. That's the main aim.

Jacques Drollet, RDPT: I should like to hear what the members of the Government Council think of this project of sending us a batch of foreign legionaries.

Jean Tumahai, Government Councillor: We have also learnt in an indirect manner that two battalions of legionaries are to arrive. We asked the governor whether it were true and he confirmed the rumour. He said that 40 per cent of the men in this engineering corps actually are legionaries.

Jacques Drollet, RDPT: Even if the percentage were .02 per cent, the number is too high. It is really farcical to pretend that only foreign legionaries are able to undertake these 'engineering' tasks. Are there not enough engineers and technicians in the French army? Why not use civilians? By the way, wouldn't it be possible to find or train the technicians needed here locally for this task?

At the end of the debate the four party whips jointly drew up the following motion:

Having been officially informed that two battalions of the engineering corps of the Foreign Legion are to be stationed in French Polynesia, we are greatly astonished that the authorities have not previously consulted us, and we express our complete disapproval. Even though the legionaries certainly do have soldierly qualities, the Territorial Assembly is painfully aware of the serious consequences for the peaceful inhabitants of these islands that will result from contact with individuals known for their brutality. Consequently the Assembly requests that if any army engineering corps has to be stationed here, it *must not* include any foreign legionaries.

The bill was unanimously adopted by the Assembly.

As could have been foreseen, the governor resorted once more to the colonial decree granting him almost dictatorial powers. The only difference was the particularly reproachful tone of his letter, probably due to the indirect slur cast by the assemblymen's protest on the Minister of Defence, Pierre Messmer, a former Foreign Legion officer. This is the full text of the governor's letter:

Mr Speaker:

On the 23rd June, your Assembly adopted a resolution expressing its opposition to the implantation of Foreign Legion troops in French Polynesia.

To begin with, I must again draw your attention to the fact that you have once more exceeded your powers, as defined by law. As I have previously informed you, the French government alone decides all questions relating to the army and the national defence.

Secondly, I must take exception to certain terms and formulations used by the speakers in the text of the bill.

It cannot be tolerated that some assemblymen, misled by cheap novels or by their own prejudices, freely use a libellous language when speaking of the Foreign Legion. The insults that have sullied this elite corps will be deeply resented by both the army and the veterans, and it is in their name that I protest vigorously against these slanderous remarks.

Therefore I request that you read this letter in the Territorial Assembly and I hope that the authors of the incriminating utterances referred to above will repudiate them and that, in the future, they will carefully consider and prepare the speeches they make about certain topics, so as to make sure that they are discussed in an impartial spirit.

Very truly yours,
A. Grimald

The assemblymen consented to the extent that they took up the whole question on their agenda a second time. They also proved how eager they were to act in an impartial spirit by changing the words 'individuals known for their brutality' to 'individuals hardened by war'. But as far as the basic problem was concerned they did not yield, but quickly reaffirmed their solid opposition to the use of Foreign Legion troops in Polynesia.

12 A TAHITIAN GARDENIA FOR FRANCE

The assemblymen might have spared themselves the trouble. While they were still debating the motion, the first Foreign Legion troops disembarked at Faaa Airport. They arrived by a regular UTA flight via Los Angeles, and in order to circumvent the American ban on the transit of foreign troops through the United States they were, (with the tacit approval of the government in Washington) attired in civilian clothes. Due to the great haste in supplying these, they fitted badly, making it easy to spot the foreign legionaries upon their arrival on this and many subsequent flights.

Shortly after the beginning of this sneak invasion, a UTA plane also disgorged an authentic French civilian on his way to the future bomb sites in the Tuamotus. He was none other than the minister for overseas territories, Louis Jacquinot, the same man who had sworn half a year earlier that France had no intention whatsoever of detonating nuclear bombs in the Pacific. The speaker of the Territorial Assembly invited him to come over and discuss 'some topical and urgent problems'. Jacquinot graciously promised to attend a meeting and make a speech; but as for the proposed discussion, he regretted that his schedule was so tight that he had to leave at once after his address. Although furious with this subterfuge, the assemblymen had to accept his terms, the only other alternative being a complete refusal on the part of the minister to appear. Furthermore, it was obvious that such a distinguished visitor must be greeted and introduced by the Speaker who, while doing so, was bound to touch upon topical and urgent problems of concern to the Assembly.

The greeting turned out to be noticeably devoid of warmth and within a minute after the opening phrase, the Speaker, Jacques Tauraa, was asking for 'frank answers' to two demands recently made by the Assembly. The first one concerned their unanimous wish to have the old colonial system of government replaced by a new statute granting them internal self-government. Secondly he asked point-blank: 'Your government has promised not to build any military testing bases in Polynesia without our consent. Can you guarantee that this promise will be kept?'

The honourable minister strode briskly up to the podium,

foreshadowing an equally brisk reply. Therefore it came as a complete anticlimax when he began to reel off, in a monotonous voice, a long string of figures, all intended to show how fabulously wealthy all the inhabitants were to become as a result of the construction of the very military bases that no one wanted. It was obvious that de Gaulle had decided to impose his will. Jacquinot's answer to the second question, which eventually came after another avalanche of statistics, was also a clear-cut refusal, although couched in even more muddled and evasive terms:

Thus even more closely united in mutual bonds of solidarity and common interests by the unforgettable memory of your historic rallying to the Free French forces, upon hearing the appeal of the great genius who has since restored France to her former greatness and glory, we shall continue together along the road of human progress towards honour, freedom, equality, and fraternity, which is the most significant feature of our French Commonwealth, and the true reason for its universal appeal.

It was a ludicrously poor imitation of de Gaulle's grandiose prose and the assemblymen were thus doubly disappointed and disgusted.

Still innocently believing that even de Gaulle must bow to the constitution, Teariki and the other RDPT leaders decided to take advantage of the clause that grants all French overseas territories the right to secede. The only difference of opinion among them was whether they ought to opt for immediate independence or rather, as a first step, be satisfied with internal self-government. In the past such differences had always been settled by Pouvanaa, and everyone was willing and eager to let him decide once more. But how? He was still being held in solitary confinement in France and denied the right to either write or receive letters. His family had not seen him for five years, so it seemed possible to evoke humanitarian motives for easing the prison rules. The party managed to scrape together enough money to send his nephew and daughter-in-law to Paris, and with the help of some metropolitan lawyers they were eventually allowed to see their *metua*. Pouvanaa had greatly suffered from lack of exercise and unpalatable food but otherwise seemed to be in a surprisingly combative mood. He listened attentively to what his visitors had to tell him – in Tahitian – and concluded that all that had happened in the islands during these five long years simply confirmed what he already knew: that de Gaulle and his collaborators were shameless liars without the slightest regard for the welfare of the Polynesian people. Therefore, the only way to escape the horrible fate held in store for them was to ask for independence at once. Upon receiving this message the RDPT leaders in Tahiti decided to call a special convention so as to have the historical decision formally approved. To that end they drew up telegrams addressed to all local branches of the party and duly delivered them to the post office. The aim of the convention was clearly stated in each telegram. Of course the secret police intercepted all of them and immediately informed their superiors in Paris. A few days later, on 6 November 1963, de Gaulle used the dictatorial powers he still held during the agitated aftermath of the Algerian war and by a simple stroke of the pen, without consulting parliament, dissolved the RDPT party, and for good measure Céran's small Tahitian Independence Party as well.

Naturally a dissolved party is not allowed to dispatch telegrams convening ex-members. In retrospect, this gave the post office legal justification for having obeyed the instructions of the secret police to refrain from sending them out. At the same time, the headquarters of the two banned parties were raided by the police, who confiscated a great many documents. Not being able to discover the slightest proof that Teariki, Céran, and company had committed any illegal acts, no further action was taken. But the principal aim had been attained: Pouvanaa's message never reached his followers and no special convention was held.

The explanation furnished by the governor for this anti-democratic procedure was highly original in both form and content. He organised a 'press conference' for the only newspaperman left in the colony, since the expulsion of the publisher of Les Débats. This newsman was perfectly happy to make a verbatim report in his paper, La Dépêche, of the flowery speech that the governor had made for his one-man audience. The key passage read as follows: 'General de Gaulle has thus chosen for the territory the goal that he knows to conform to the wishes of the majority of the population, that of letting the Tahitian gardenia continue to grow forever in the great French garden.'

Of course, what appeared in this small local newspaper had little importance as it was read only by some hundred Frenchmen. More annoying for the routed Tahitian leaders was a statement made shortly afterwards by Pierre Messmer, the French minister for defence, and reproduced in the New Zealand and Australian press. The occasion was an inspection of the future nuclear sites that he made in January 1964. On his return to Papeete he received a handful of foreign newspapermen sent out to cover the event. Among them was an Australian reporter nasty enough to ask a pertinent question about the local opposition to the tests. Messmer promptly replied:

In all democratic countries where freedom of expression exists, public opinion about important matters varies considerably. In Tahiti, the installation of nuclear bases is not always viewed in the same way, but these differences of opinion are certainly no greater than those occurring in Great Britain or in America when the construction of a nuclear power plant is proposed.

That was all.

The dissolved parties remained illegal; but, despite strenuous efforts, the police were still unable to discover any incriminating evidence that might be used to jail the RDPT leaders. In consequence, though they were no longer allowed to use the RDPT label, the assemblymen continued to sit and debate as before.

13 THE STRIKING FORCE
AT WORK

In mid-1964 Prime Minister Georges Pompidou came out to Tahiti to speed up the ravages of the CEP. The armed forces had by then already pushed out in every direction Moruroa and Fangataufa, for instance, the two atolls in the south-east corner of the Tuamotu group selected by General Thiry in 1962 as the most suitable test sites, were occupied by foreign legionaries – in spite of the vehement protests of the assemblymen that the land was territorial and could not be sold or leased without their express consent, which they absolutely refused to grant. Of course the local army commanders tartly replied that legal niceties were none of their concern; as good soldiers they simply obeyed orders from their superiors in Paris. The fact that the CEP took over the islands illegally with neither lease nor land deed probably explains one stupid error that has been perpetuated ever since: they misspelled the name of the atoll as 'Mururoa', whereas the true name, familiar to all local people, is and has always been Moruroa.

This island was favoured with an exceptionally wide pass and a lagoon deep enough to harbour huge ships in safety. Fangataufa, on the other hand, was a closed atoll communicating with the sea through only a few narrow channels in the solid ring of coral. Therefore detachments of legionaries were first dispatched to Moruroa. Thanks to the constantly warm climate, they could be bedded and boarded in hastily erected tents. As soon as they had built a wharf and an airstrip, regular troops began to swarm in. At the same time several former passenger ships from the now abandoned Algerian run, and bought by the French army especially for this purpose, were permanently moored at the wharf as floating hotels for a considerably more demanding category of military personnel.

The assembled forces then built two huge towers to be used as observation posts. According to the proud words of the army spokesman, not less than 46 000 tonnes of concrete and 16 000 tonnes of iron went into each one of these monumental constructions, deemed to be of such high priority that most of the materials were flown out from France. When completed, these death pyramids stood fifteen metres high and had walls six metres thick. Next, the foreign legionaries blasted a big hole in the coral ring on Fangataufa, and built another wharf and airstrip there.

Simultaneously, other military units had disembarked on Hao, another and bigger atoll 200 nautical miles north-west of Moruroa. It was inhabited by 800 Polynesians leading a peaceful existence, thanks to their island's isolation and barrenness. To their initial delight and amazement, they were suddenly surrounded by an enormous army camp where 2000 soldiers drove madly up and down straight 'streets' and 'roads', simply marked out on the flat, hard ground. Hao was to serve as a permanent rear base for assembling bombs, and a great number of storehouses and workshops were built along the lagoon shore. In order to avoid transshipping nuclear material through densely populated Tahiti with its many vocal critics of the whole scheme, the army command ordered still another airfield built on Hao, with a 3500 metre long runway permitting a shuttle service between the island and France, by using the French island of Martinique in the West Indies as a refuelling station.

The cost of building these bases, operating all these planes and warships, and maintaining all these troops at the antipodes had originally been estimated at 1000 million French francs. Within a year the actual expenses exceeded 2500 million. Less than a year later the official figure was 6000 million (about $A1000 million). Thereafter the high command wisely ceased supplying information about the financial side of the enterprise.

Having thus occupied three atolls in the Tuamotu group, the army might well have spared Tahiti a similar fate. But all the army personnel, from simple private to staff officer, found life on Hao, Moruroa and Fangataufa so terribly lonely and monotonous, and the climate so hot and unbearable that it was decided to have yet another rear base for rest and recreation – on Tahiti. The small capital with its numerous bars, restaurants, cinemas and shops was particularly attractive. As usual the first ones to secure a foothold in Papeete were the foreign legionaries who, in record time, built a number of corrugated iron barracks of unsurpassed ugliness. But competition was stiff from the navy high brass, who managed to spoil the natural beauty of several hundred hectares of palm groves by putting up small wooden cubicles to house the innumerable office personnel employed in their headquarters. However, they were all outdone by the Atomic Energy Commission (CEA), who took over one of the biggest beach properties just outside Papeete. Within a year accommodation had been provided, in and around Papeete, for not less than 7000 men – half of them staying for good, and half of them on a rotation basis.

Governor Grimald and General Thiry had solemnly promised that only married men were to be stationed in French Polynesia. Of course most turned out to be bachelors, and few of the married officers and technicians brought out their wives and families. They all received double salaries and were exempt from paying income tax. Consequently they could all easily afford cars, and the number of these increased by 3000 during the first year of the military occupation, creating monstrous traffic jams. Owning cars and having plenty of money, they could also find girls without any difficulty. Each new conquest meant that a local man lost his wife or sweetheart. This made the Polynesians so bitter and resentful that they began to attack blindly all uniformed men they encountered in town after dark. The soldiers, and most prominently among them the foreign legionaries, hit back when they had an opportunity, not much caring who their victims might be, as long as they looked like natives. Most of them used knives and this prompted the Tahitians to arm themselves with clubs and sticks. Each new fight was bloodier than the last, and now and then a Tahitian or a French soldier was knifed or beaten to death.

The army command issued a little guidebook to all newcomers containing advice of the following sort:

Do not walk alone in the streets. The danger of being attacked is particularly great after dark.

Walk on the left side of the street or road, for if you walk on the right side in the same direction as the traffic, you will be unable to notice the Tahitians on bikes or motorbikes who sneak up behind you and try to hit you on the head.

This did not help much, so the military brains trust went to work once more and came up with a most brilliant solution to the ever worsening safety due to the undeniable fact that the Tahitians could no longer stand the sight of a French uniform. The most logical deduction would have been: if all soldiers and sailors are taken off Tahiti, no more uniforms will be seen. Instead, the army staff concluded that it was enough to take the uniforms off the soldiers and sailors! In keeping with this seemingly logical reasoning, a general order was issued making it compulsory for all military personnel on leave to wear civilian clothing. Unfortunately the masterminds behind this scheme had overlooked one fact: that Europeans differ considerably from Polynesians both as to skin colour and racial type. Therefore it was simply impossible for the disguised French soldiers to blend imperceptibly into the crowd of natives milling about in the streets of Papeete. Even worse, authentic civilian tourists from Europe, the U.S., Australia and New Zealand were mistaken for soldiers. Their main reason for coming to Tahiti was the natives' wonderful reputation for friendliness and hospitality. So it was a hard blow indeed for them to be hit on the head when they tried to make closer contact with the Tahitians. Sometimes female tourists were taken for French army wives and savagely attacked and raped.

For several months the local press – now grown from one to two newspapers – published daily reports from the battlefront. But they made such a bad impression on the population that the military high command saw to it that publication of all such demoralising accounts cease. Only a few of these are reproduced here, showing that, right from the beginning, the French striking force was spearheaded by the elite Foreign Legion troops.

BRAWL AT THE PITATE CAFE

Who started the fight that took place yesterday between Tahitians and foreign legionaries? The former say that they were sitting at a table, quietly drinking red wine from a gallon bottle they had brought along with them when a Legion trooper derided them for being bad customers. In reply one of the Tahitians hit him with his fist. The trooper drew his knife, but stumbled at the very moment when he lunged forward. The Tahitians immediately fell upon him and gave him a good beating. Another legion trooper who tried to come to his fallen comrade's aid received the same treatment. At this stage of the battle, the Tahitians resorted to bottles and chair legs as striking weapons.

Trooper Valester Calamenos' version differs quite a bit. He claims that he and a friend of his stopped in at the Pitate Café only because a Tahitian sitting there at a table had very politely asked them for a match. But when he produced one, the Tahitian hit him in the face with such force that he fell over backwards. His mate drew his knife and tried to help him, but was attacked by a Tahitian armed with a chair leg. A general brawl ensued during which bottles, stones and chair legs rained over the legionaries, who therefore quickly fled the scene.

THE LEPINE DRAMA

One evening, Lépine, a young sailor from the French warship *Protet*, had a rendezvous with a Tahitian girl in a quiet corner of the harbour. He noticed two shadows, but before he had time to look up, he found himself on the ground with two men over him. His assailants hit him repeatedly in the face until he lost consciousness and then threw him into the harbour water. Next they turned upon the girl just as she was about to flee and raped her several times. However, thanks to the chilly water, the sailor recovered, escaped from drowning, and eventually managed to crawl back to the *Protet*. He was immediately hospitalised and for a long while seemed doomed, but is now beyond danger of losing his life. Within a few days, with considerable help from the girl, the police succeeded in apprehending the perpetrators of this outrage, 25-year-old Mara Enoha Vehia and 19-year-old Tiare Zakaria Tetaria. Both have made full confessions.

THE LEGION TROOPER'S REVENGE

A recently arrived German Legion trooper met one of those young Tahitian prostitutes who work their beat at Quinn's and the Lafayette, and decided that she was the ideal companion for him. He cemented their relationship by making the following vow: 'As long as you stay home, prepare my food, and remain faithful to me, every month I will turn over my whole salary to you'. The honeymoon lasted three months. But then came the 14th of July festivities. The *tamure* dance music was to be heard everywhere and acted as a magnet on the poor, secluded girl. After a while the trooper found her and seemed to forgive her. But during the tender reconciliation that followed, he suddenly reverted to his own savage self and bit off her most intimate female organ. She had to be hospitalised and is now and forever a mutilated, incomplete woman.

INNOCENT EUROPEANS ATTACKED

Two Tahitians, Tamatoa and Maitere, yesterday appeared before the court, accused of having attacked in cowardly fashion Flight Pilot Vossor and Cabin Steward Coussinet of the UTA Company, outside *Zizou's Bar*. Maitere readily confessed to having hit Vossor for no reason whatsoever, but said that he had never touched Coussinet. Tamatoa, who had previously committed numerous similar offences, flatly denied all charges, although several witnesses easily recognised him because he had been half nude and wore a flower lei on his head. Maitere seemed to regret to some extent what he had done, whereas Tamatoa treated all questions put to him with sullen silence. His defence lawyer explained that he hated all Europeans and that this hatred was the result of a recent deception. His *vahine* had left him for a handsome Legion trooper. Unable to find his rival, Maitere had taken out his vengeance on these two Europeans. It is worthwhile observing that, in addition to Maitere and Tamatoa, whose guilt has been proven, other Tahitians had availed themselves of the opportunity to kick and beat the two victims while they were lying on the ground.

14 THE STRANGE 'OUTLET' PROBLEM

To the people of Tahiti the root of the problem lay in there being too many men on the island. The military high brass explained the matter very differently. In their well-considered opinion, all these troubles stemmed from the fact, for which they could not be blamed, that there were too few women in Tahiti.

As early as February 1964 some former pimps in the Foreign Legion had tried to solve the problem by importing a batch of prostitutes and hiring them out. The assemblymen, however, were so outraged that the commerce was hastily abandoned. Jacques Drollet furnished another eloquent proof of his ingenuity. In a speech in the Assembly, he exhorted the army to organise the supply of badly needed female companions in a more honourable, if not thoroughly patriotic, manner. His main argument was as follows:

Who serve the officers, make their beds, sweep the floors, and so on? Exclusively male batmen. If you have an opportunity to visit the various military establishments, you will see that even the lowest echelon of officers have a chauffeur and a valet at their disposal. The waiters in the messes are likewise men. So it seems to me that the problem under discussion can be solved by importing women from France to take the places of all these men, freeing them for more useful work.

To everybody's dismay this extremely sensible suggestion was turned down by the military brass, who pointed out that there existed a classical solution of proven efficiency: the organisation of regular brothels. It seemed somewhat strange to us poor civilians in Tahiti that such a solution could be made in earnest in 1964, seeing that since 1946 it had been illegal to operate brothels in France. But we were immediately told that this law did not apply to the army, which was still entitled to organise brothels *during military campaigns*. And what with the continuous street fighting going on in the streets and bars of Papeete, who could deny that we were in the middle of a military campaign?

The Territorial Assembly still had no authority to discuss defence matters, and this important problem belonged entirely to that forbidden category, as the governor lost no time in pointing out. Nevertheless the assemblymen maintained that there were

79

several aspects of the problem that fell within their competence. To them it was, above all, a human and social problem and they expressed their disapproval, in the strongest possible terms, of the inhuman and antisocial solution proposed. The army immediately had recourse to some of its recently arrived specialists on 'psychological warfare' who had been transferred to French Polynesia from Algeria, after the final defeat. They wrote a series of unsigned articles and persuaded the local newspaper publishers to print them. The point repeatedly made in these articles was that the main concern of the army was to protect the civilian population, in view of the arrival of another five or six warships with crews totalling more than 7000 men soon to be stationed in Polynesia. The anonymous authors also explained that brothels had always been a feature of all higher civilisations. Finally, the brothels to be installed in Polynesia were to be run on the following humanitarian principles:

(1) They were not to be called brothels at all, but 'outlets' or 'relief stations' (*éxutoires*).

(2) Furthermore, they were to be housed on charming little ships, discreetly anchored in hidden creeks.

(3) The women to be employed on board were to be imported from abroad, probably from Hong Kong.

(4) Only French military and technical personnel working for the nuclear bases were to be allowed to visit them.

Teariki tried to answer these brothel specialists; but his open letter to the governor and the admiral was deemed to be so slanderous that it could not be published or read over the radio. Yet Teariki only propounded a few simple truths such as:

In the past, France let us partake of the most superb fruits of Western civilisation. French missionaries, teachers, doctors, and administrators have taught us their religion, their language, their culture, and brought us many other generous benefits. In other words, France has helped us to become a part of the modern world. But that world also contains dangers and evils from which it is France's duty to protect us. Unfortunately that is not what the present government is doing. Quite the opposite. It is exposing us to the most dangerous of all scientific experiments known to man, and to hideous vices. I insist that the guilty party is the *present government*, which will not last forever, and I am thus not accusing the French people. All I am asking is for France to remain faithful to her vocation and to respect the treaty binding us together. It is a matter of mutual esteem. That is why I am vigorously opposed to the introduction of the proposed vile form of prostitution, and it does not make the slightest difference whether the women to be thus degraded are foreign, French or Polynesian. Incidentally, there already exists a certain form of prostitution among us, although hidden behind flower leis, and there is every reason for us to help those who are trying to eradicate it, instead of promoting it on a larger scale. What we must do is to attack the evil at its roots and prevent it from spreading. The evil is caused by dispatching thousands of young bachelors for a long stay among us. At the root of the problem is the CEP nuclear testing centre. The present problem is only one of many that it has created and the only way to eliminate it and the many other even more serious problems is to get rid of this military outfit.

But to what avail was this protest since it was neither printed nor broadcast? The battle seemed irrevocably lost, when suddenly reinforcements arrived from an unexpected quarter. They were made up of students in the three Papeete colleges or high schools – one government school, one run by the Protestant church and one by the Catholic church. After having met and discussed the 'outlet' problem, the boys and girls adopted two separate resolutions, which they themselves deposited on the desks of the newspaper editors and the director of the radio station – who, after some initial resistance, gave in to their demands to make them known. In their open letter to the adults the boys wrote:

We think that those who are behind this project have been acting rashly without realising the fearful consequences. For what is it all about? What they are proposing is nothing less than a slave trade, which will certainly not be limited to importing foreign women. The pimps will also soon try to export Tahitian women to foreign brothels. Who can guarantee that they will not be kidnapped? We do not want to see our sisters and future wives sold on this slave market. We proclaim that the brothel system is totally unacceptable. It is clandestine, immoral, unfair and shocking – for it degrades woman to the level of an animal. It is a victory for deception and corruption.

The girls' manifesto provided a closer scrutiny of the legal aspect of the problem:

The army spokesmen defend their plans by saying that the brothels will be reserved for themselves. But this does not make them legal. A U.N. treaty dated 2nd December 1949 forbids all prostitution, and France signed this treaty somewhat belatedly on 25th November 1960. How then can the authorities permit the establishment of brothels in Tahiti, when they are

81

forbidden in France? Whoever the innocent victims are to be, we severely condemn this institution. . . Are the military leaders completely powerless? Are they unable to educate their men? Have they nothing to say? Our civilisation resembles the decadent Roman Empire just before its fall. All we ask for is a simple, quiet, and wholesome life and not a life filled with debauchery, filth and oppression. Yes, our future is at stake, as well as France's honour!

This strong attack from a new, unexpected quarter took the high brass completely by surprise. It can even be likened to a fifth column going suddenly into action, for many of these students were sons and daughters of high echelon officers. The effect was devastating. Within a few days, all plans to open military brothels in Tahiti were officially abandoned.

15 THE WHOLE COLONY CATCHES ELEPHANTIASIS

As though this brutal invasion of 7000 French troops, and as many sailors, were not enough, there began a simultaneous migration to Tahiti of thousands of Polynesians who had hitherto been living quietly in the outer islands. The blame for this new disastrous development must once more be laid squarely on the CEP and the army contractors, who were in dire need of cheap labour.

At that time the population of French Polynesia numbered about 85 000. Of these, 45 000 persons were living on Tahiti, mostly in Papeete or its immediate vicinity. At least 6000 townsmen were Chinese, less than 2000 Europeans, the remainder Polynesians. The latter worked for the first two groups in various capacities, such as dockers, fishermen, gardeners, road and house builders and low-ranking civil servants. Their salaries were modest, but then the cost of living was not very high either.

Thus the only unexploited labour force to be found was outside Papeete, in the rural areas of Tahiti and in the Tuamotu, the Gambier (Mangareva), the Marquesas, the Austral and the Leeward Islands. All Tahitian farmers and copra makers immediately left their home villages for Papeete when they heard that the CEP needed bricklayers, carpenters and masons to build barracks, offices and houses. At the same time navy ships were sent out in all directions to recruit workers for Moruroa, Fangataufa, and Hao. The salaries offered, of between 12 000 and 20 000 francs ($A120 and 200) a month, seemed fabulous, and on many small, remote islands the entire male population signed up for six months or a year and took passage on the warships right then and there. Within six months 5000 Polynesians had exchanged their tranquil existence as independent copra producers, farmers and fishermen for that of salaried construction workers.

Since they were all earning so much money, their families moved to Papeete where life was pleasanter and more fun. When the men did, at long last, complete their period of indenture, the right place to have a little well-earned fun was again Papeete. After their last franc was gone, the only course left open to them was to sign up for another period of six or twelve months. A few of them eventually discovered that a clause in small print on their contracts actually guaranteed them free passage back to their home islands. 'True enough, but there are no warships available right now' was the standard reply from the recruiting office.

So within a few years about 20 000 Polynesian men, women and children more or less voluntarily settled down in Papeete, during exactly the same period that French troops and technicians were infesting Tahiti. The only appropriate comparison to this artificial swelling of the town population is elephantiasis, the disease to which the Polynesians have been exposed since prehistoric times. As everybody knows, it is carried by the *anopheles* mosquito, which injects larvae into the human blood-stream. If this occurs frequently and the larvae are allowed to increase in number and size, they will eventually congest the lymph glands and cause abnormal swelling of the limbs and genital organs. Surgery is the only known treatment when this stage is reached.

The CEP rented all available houses and leased all the best land in and around Papeete for its officers and technicians but declined all responsibility for the social welfare of its Polynesian employees. The most it did was to lend some hundred homeless families army tents, which were set up on a treeless and dusty wharf. Little by little, the majority of these recent immigrants built small shacks of corrugated iron and fibreboard in the brushland in the valleys and on the hills behind Papeete. All land was privately owned and lease or rental to the owners was at least 2000 or 3000 francs ($A20–30) a month. The worst thing for this new category of Polynesian slum dwellers was the lack of water, as they were accustomed to bathing several times a day. Except during the rainy season when the slum areas were transformed into a quagmire, water had to be carried from far afield. The sanitary conditions are more easily imagined than described. The only person to take any interest in the problems of these poor immigrants was a French sociologist who, two years after the nuclear forces first struck French Polynesia, listed 3988 cubical one-room shacks inhabited by not less than 22 474 persons!

Of course there was no cultivable land in these slum areas. It was a long way to the lagoon and anyway none of the men had canoes, so they could not do any fishing. Therefore they were forced to buy all their food in the Chinese stores or at the market, where the prices rose steadily, and sometimes in leaps and bounds. The Tahitian producers of yams, taro, sweet potatoes and bananas had moved to town and become consumers; so these highly nutritious traditional food items became so costly that the slum dwellers had to depend almost entirely on bread, rice, macaroni, corned beef and similar foodstuff – deficient in iron, calcium, and vitamins. But even these were subject to the same steep price increases, although at the outset the governor had promised 'to take the necessary, quite simple measures to prevent all inflation'. Less than two years later, though, an official report admitted that 'during 1966 the prices showed an abnormal tendency to rise; for example fish now cost 35 per cent more, vegetables 84 per cent more, and fruit 57 per cent more.' One might like to know how the author of this official report had arrived at such precise figures since the scandalous truth is that the prices varied enormously from one store to another and that the authorities made not the slightest effort to check them. The only exceptions were the army stores, where all items were sold at cost price. Of course only army personnel and their wives were allowed to make their purchases in these stores.

The above-mentioned study of the slum areas contains a series of figures revealing the abysmal poverty of the people living there. Fifteen per cent of the men earned less than 7500 francs a month ($A75), 30 per cent less than 10 000 ($A100) and 50 per cent less than 15 000 ($A150), while only 5 per cent earned more than 25 000 ($A250). For purposes of comparison, it may be worthwhile mentioning that a decent meal in a cheap restaurant cost between 300 and 500 francs, a shirt 500 francs, and a pair of trousers 1000 francs. To make these figures meaningful, we must know the average number of people per household, which was seven, and the average income per household, which was 13 000 francs a month.

Even in the rare cases where the members of the household spent their whole income on food, fuel, clothes, and other essential items, their existence was precarious and their health impaired. In point of fact, in the great majority of households, money was rapidly squandered at the beginning of the month. How could it have been otherwise with the many temptations existing in Papeete? In every street there were bars, restaurants, dance-halls, cinemas, billiard halls, gambling dens, and cafés with juke boxes and one-armed bandits. For the simple Polynesians who had never seen or heard about these marvellous European inventions it was heaven. However, the greatest danger was the ease with which they could buy liquor, wine and beer in the numerous grocery shops all over town. In true Polynesian fashion, they never drank alone; but, whenever they had some money, they would invite all their friends and neighbours. Invariably the parties lasted until the last franc. Some storekeepers obligingly gave credit, with the result that the slum dwellers gradually sank deeply into debt.

Of course the ones to suffer most were the children. Education is compulsory in French Polynesia. But the school authorities never bothered to track down the new immigrants, which meant that the children attended school only when they wanted to, which was seldom or never. One may wonder why the parents did not supervise their children better. The reason is that they were completely bewildered and lost in their new surroundings and too fully occupied with their intense struggle to survive. The boys, following the example set by children in all civilised countries, formed street gangs and spent their time pilfering, stealing, robbing, fighting, drinking, and loitering. As for the girls, they soon found that the town was full of men eager to take them out, offer them drinks, dresses, and all sorts of gifts in exchange for the favours that they were accustomed to grant their boyfriends for nothing. Another more annoying consequence of their merry life was that they often had to seek costly medical treatment.

The few children who went to school and turned out to be bright and industrious did not fare much better, because they did not learn anything useful. So, when their formal schooling was over at the age of fourteen, they were unable to find a job. With hundreds of strong adult men still arriving every month from the outer islands, these teenagers simply did not have a chance.

Here is how a specialist sent out by the World Health Organisation, Dr Marcel Bonnaud, summed up the situation in 1967 after a thorough field study:

Out of the one hundred slum dwellers we interviewed, 80 per cent seemed lost and complained that nobody did anything for them, 10 per cent were completely apathetic, 5 per cent were aggressive, and the remaining 5 per cent found life in the slums exciting.

What happened in Tahiti between 1964 and 1967 can also be expressed in familiar socioeconomic parlance in this way: for the first time in French Polynesia there emerged a whole new class of proletarians. That no revolution has yet broken out is explained by the fact that the slum dwellers have never heard about Karl Marx's theories and are still completely ignorant of the fact that they are proletarians.

16 THREE LETTERS

Whereas declarations about the state of affairs in French Polynesia made by de Gaulle's ministers were given much space in the French press and read by the radio and TV announcers, Teariki and the other leaders of the dissolved Tahitian parties continued to protest, both inside and outside the Territorial Assembly, with just as much vehemence as ever against the military occupation and the nuclear tests. Although they regularly sent the full texts of their protests to the French mass media, not a line ever appeared in print and not a word was ever spoken in the radio and TV programmes. When, exceptionally, an editor or programme director took the trouble to acknowledge receipt of their bulletins, it was only to regret that nobody in France was interested any more in colonial problems.

Therefore Teariki resorted to stratagem. He wrote to several well-known French personalities asking for their support; a few of them actually replied. He next mimeographed several hundred copies of the more interesting answers and mailed them to French newspapers and radio stations. Only a few excerpts appeared here and there in the press; but nevertheless these worried the Minister for Overseas Territories, General Pierre Billotte, so much that he felt obliged to criticise Teariki publicly 'for airing fancied wrongs in view of promoting his own political career'. We will simply publish the following three letters here and let the reader judge for himself whether their publication can be considered an act of demagogy.

The first was written on 17 April 1964 by Doctor Albert Schweitzer and read:

Long before receiving your letter, I was worried about the fate of the Polynesian people. I have been fighting against all atomic weapons and nuclear tests since 1955. It is sad to learn that they have been forced on the inhabitants of your islands. Yet I knew that the French Parliament would not come to your assistance. The deputies do not have the courage to resist and they do not dare to oppose the military brass who are determined to undertake nuclear tests in your country. Those who claim that these tests are harmless are liars. Like many other persons, I am ashamed of the Parliament's attitude in this serious matter. The Parliament and the

87

general public are sacrificing you. I feel sorry for you and shall continue to do so. I have had a great pity for you ever since I first learned that the army had decided to use your Islands for testing their Atomic bombs. Who could have imagined that France would be willing to deliver its own citizens to the military in this manner?

The second letter was from the famous biologist Jean Rostand of the French Academy who wrote on 22 August 1964:

You have asked me what I think of the possible effects on the genes of exposure to radioactive fallout from an atomic bomb explosion. All I can do is to repeat, with the same conviction and force, what I have already said in many articles and during many lectures, to wit: that there does not exist a 'threshold' below which radiation is so feeble that it is no longer harmful. Every increase of the radioactive dose, however slight it may be, enhances the probability of a mutation. Or in other words, more changes will take place in our genetic heritage and these variations are always, or practically always unfavourable.

The author of the third letter was the future Nobel prize winner, Théodore Monod, and he wrote thus on 23 October 1965:

I should like to thank you for your courageous speech in the National Assembly during the debate on the military budget. I was equally moved by your earlier speeches in November and December 1963, which also fell on deaf ears.

You are perfectly right in simultaneously denouncing the official lie that there is no radioactive pollution from the tests, and the social and moral disasters they have led to in your country in the form of alcoholism, prostitution, etc.

I have just written to the president of the French Protestant Federation reminding him of the Christian duty we all have to take a stand, and of how urgent it is for the Church to speak up about these problems.

Incidentally, if these nuclear tests are as harmless as the government alleges, why does it not carry them out in Corsica, Landes, or Seine-et-Oise? Can the reason be that the government finds it easier to deceive the islanders than the metropolitan voters?

I am at a loss as to how to help you and your countrymen, so gravely threatened by these madmen, but believe me, Mr Deputy, I feel very strongly for you and send you my most sincere greetings.

17 DE GAULLE'S COUP DE GRACE

After Pouvanaa had managed to convey to his followers in Tahiti the message that they should try to achieve independence as soon as possible, the doors of his prison remained closed for the next two years. He was neither allowed to receive visitors nor to send out any mail. By burying him alive, the government evidently hoped that his people would gradually forget him.

In October 1965, the stiff, grim-faced, and eternally floundering Governor Aimé Grimald was replaced by an elegant and good-looking technocrat named Jean Sicurani, who might easily have been mistaken for an international oil company executive. His chief qualification for the job was that he had acted as secretary to the minister for defence, Pierre Messmer, during the fateful years when the army occupied Polynesia. The governor's first act was to invite the ex-RDPT politicians, Jacques Tauraa and Jacques Drollet, respectively speaker and majority leader of the Territorial Assembly, to come over to his office for a little chat. To their surprise the governor quickly brought up the painful subject of Pouvanaa's fate. As he explained it, the government had made a complete about-face and was now willing to set him free. Perhaps right after the presidential election that was to take place on 5 December – provided that de Gaulle was re-elected.

It may seem very strange – and so it appeared at first to his guests – that the governor was so eager to fish for the Polynesian votes (about 35 000 altogether) when de Gaulle could certainly count on two-thirds of the 28 million votes cast in metropolitan France. Unfortunately, the Polynesians could not influence the outcome of the presidential election; nevertheless, the way they voted was of some concern, especially to the governor. After all it was the first big election since the beginning of the glorious nuclear era and a massive vote in Polynesia for the anti-bomb Socialist presidential candidate, François Mitterand, would certainly make a very unfavourable impression on public opinion in France and abroad. Consequently a victory for de Gaulle in Polynesia would be greatly appreciated in the Elysée Palace and facilitate the governor's future career.

After careful consideration of the pros and cons of the proposed deal, practically all of the ex-RDPT party leaders were for it and some of them could hardly suppress their malicious joy over the stupid way that Sicurani was walking into his own trap. Did he not realise that the first thing Pouvanaa would do upon his return would be to declare independence and kick out the whole military outfit? Therefore the proper tactic to follow was not to press their political demands too strongly during the election campaign, so as to avoid arousing the governor's suspicions.

The only one to speak up against this self-proclaimed Machiavellian policy was Teariki who, as usual, preferred principles to stratagems. For him not only was it dishonourable to compromise with the enemy, but also extremely dangerous. In his opinion, all previous experience had shown that the French governors and ministers could not be trusted. To believe it possible to cheat the cheaters was sheer folly. So instead Teariki wanted the party to carry on a vigorous campaign for François Mitterand, who had taken a firm stand against the nuclear tests and promised to free Pouvanaa, if elected. The other party leaders were indignant and in their turn accused Teariki of opportunism. How did he dare propose in earnest that they vote for a Socialist? They were all sincere Christians and would have nothing to do with horrible atheists like Mitterand and his cronies in the French Socialist and Communist parties, against whom their priests and pastors had so often warned them. Teariki, who belonged to the synod of the Protestant church, stuck to his choice and begged them at least not to canvass for the candidate responsible for all their woes.

It was certainly no coincidence that the French government had decided in 1964 to build a TV station in Tahiti; it was completed just in time for these presidential elections. While waiting for the official opening of the campaign, the new TV station showed a long series of documentary films glorifying the great war hero and saviour of the Republic, General de Gaulle. There was no noticeable break between this series and the following campaign films. Due to some never fully explained 'technical mishap', the reel containing Mitterand's forty-five-minute speech against de Gaulle's military follies and colonial policy never did reach Papeete.

This was as nothing, however, compared to the difficulties

Teariki experienced when he wanted to address the population over the radio. His letter of protest, mailed to the governor on 6 December 1965, is extremely revealing:

General de Gaulle has been unable to obtain the required majority during the first ballot and there will thus be a second ballot on the 19th December. Therefore, Mr Governor, I feel compelled to denounce some illegal actions of concern to me.

Although not allowed to do so by electoral law, both the mayor of Pirae, Gaston Flosse, and the mayor of Papeete, Alfred Poroi, have been given time on Radio Tahiti in order to praise one of the candidates, General de Gaulle. However, when I requested permission to make a similar radio speech in favour of François Mitterand, whose officially appointed representative I am, I was told that this was not possible. I refused to accept this verdict and maintained my request. As a result, on the afternoon of the 3rd December, I was allowed to record two speeches, one in Tahitian and one in French. They were to be broadcast the same evening. To my own and everybody else's surprise, this was not done.

The following day, the 4th December, Monsieur Delabrousse phoned me on your behalf, that you had not authorised the scheduled broadcasts on the pretext that I advanced 'political theses that were unacceptable'. Yet I had very carefully refrained from personal attacks and the use of violent language. To crown it all, on the same evening, during the Tahitian language programme, the facilities of Radio Tahiti were put at the disposal of the Assembly speaker, Jacques Tauraa, the *Te Ora* party president, Tony Bambridge jr., the mayor of Papeete, Alfred Poroi, the president of the local Gaullist party, Rudy Bambridge, and the chief of Tautira, Raiarii, for the express purpose of praising de Gaulle and his actions, retelling the old tale of our adhesion to the Free French movement, ending up with an exhortation to the audience to vote for the general on the morrow.

It is a scandal that the Guallists can break the electoral law in this manner and go unpunished, the same law that is wrongly invoked to prevent me from using the radio, and this with your own approval and that of the other civil servants. It is a strange way indeed of guaranteeing equal rights for the candidates.

In conclusion, in order to reinstate impartial treatment of the candidates by fairly and adequately informing the voters, I request that, as François Mitterand's official representative, I be given equal time on the radio to that granted General de Gaulle and his spokesmen. Therefore, please advise me when the studio personnel will be able to record the speeches which I insist on being entitled to make.

The governor was so shaken by this impudent language that he forgot about ordering the director of Radio Tahiti to make the recordings. So Teariki wrote again on 10 December, repeating his request in even more urgent terms. The governor pulled himself together and managed to reply some four days later, but only to say that he had just discovered that he had no authority to intervene in this matter. Requests of this sort were handled by a special committee formed according to instructions 10445/TOM/AP/BEL issued on 18 October 1965 by the minister for overseas territories. In a new letter to the governor, Teariki indignantly pointed out that his reason for protesting was precisely because these instructions had not been respected by the director of the radio station. At the same time he asked the governor pertinently why he had *personally* stopped broadcast of the pro-Mitterand speeches recorded on 3 December, instead of referring the whole matter to this committee. Could the reason be that the committee was non-existent, due to the governor's strange neglect of acting in accordance with prescribed legal procedures?

The governor eventually admitted his mistake at the same time that he regretted that it was too late to do anything about it. Thus it happened that Teariki was never allowed to explain over the radio to the people of French Polynesia why it was in their interest to vote for Mitterand and not for de Gaulle.

On 19 December, the day of the second ballot, therefore, the following disparate categories of voters deposited ballots with de Gaulle's name:

Most of Pouvanna's Polynesian followers.

All Europeans who were against Pouvanaa.

Those who were for the nuclear bases.

Many who were against them.

All anti-Communists.

Plus some who were genuinely for de Gaulle.

On the other hand, only the following groups voted for Mitterand:

Some Polynesians who were for Pouvanaa.

Some persons who were against the nuclear bases.

Not surprisingly this resulted in a victory for de Gaulle, but his winning margin was the smallest ever recorded in Polynesia, only 59.72 per cent. Nevertheless the governor could be quite happy with this outcome, since in metropolitan France de Gaulle's score was a meagre 54.50 per cent. Let it be added that, against all logic and justice, the ballots cast by the military personnel temporarily serving on the nuclear test sites were not tallied up in their home constituencies but in French Polynesia.

The 'machiavellian' ex-RDPT leaders who, for tactical reasons, had concluded a deal with the governor and campaigned for de Gaulle, were jubilant and did their best to forgive and comfort Teariki. Everything would be all right now that their *metua* was coming home. The governor had confirmed that Pouvanaa would soon be pardoned, and told them that, if they so wished, they might bear him these good tidings themselves. All of them – except Teariki – hurriedly set off for Paris, eager not to miss the opportunity of appearing as Pouvanaa's saviour in the eyes of the local electorate. To their great consternation their *metua* received the marvellous news very coldly. He had nothing to ask pardon for, he said. The only thing he wanted was a new trial so that his innocence might be established. The governor was less affected by this uncooperative attitude. After all, nobody had asked Pouvanaa for his consent when he was jailed, so why do it now? In the event that he persisted in ignoring what was best for him, it was no more difficult to throw him out of jail than it had been to throw him in. At any rate the new minister for overseas territories, another general by the name of Billotte, was to explain the government's intention, during his forthcoming visit to Tahiti.

Billotte arrived as announced on 24 February 1966 and immediately organised a spectacular press conference attended by all local journalists, whose number had now increased from one to two. The message was short and to the point. Without further ado, de Gaulle had pardoned Pouvanaa. The ex-RDPT party bosses at once dispatched a telegram to de Gaulle in the prescribed and obsequious style that had not been fashionable in France since the time of the Emperor Napoleon. It read:

The assemblymen of the ex-RDPT and UT-UNR parties are deeply touched by the pardon you have granted Mr Pouvanaa a Oopa and wish to express, in the name of the whole population, their gratitude for this generous gesture, here interpreted as a mark of the warm sympathy the mother country harbours for French Polynesia.

Instead of blindly signing the telegram, Teariki asked to be shown the relevant government decree and sat down to study it. There was no doubt but that Pouvanaa had been pardoned at the last possible time after having served seven years and five months of his eight-year sentence. But Teariki also discovered the following paragraph in the decree about which Billotte had said nothing:

The above-specified Pouvanaa Tetuaapua Oopa is forbidden, for a period of fifteen years, counting from the 25th February, 1966, from living in or visiting French Polynesia and the other French territories, including the New Hebrides, governed by the High-Commissioner of the Western Pacific.

What a despicable comedy! Pouvanaa had originally been sentenced to eight years in solitary confinement and to exile from his home country for fifteen years, *counting from the day of his arrest on 11 October 1958*. Not only had this latter part of the sentence not been stricken out but the two generals, de Gaulle and Billotte, had moreover conspired to change the wording so that his exile was now to be counted *from the day of his 'liberation', 25 February 1966!* As he was more than seventy years old, this meant that, in spite of having been 'pardoned', he would have to remain in exile far away from his country until the end of his life.

At long last, some of the clever 'machiavellian' party bosses began to realise what dupes they had been all along. Others were more furious with Teariki than with the governor, de Gaulle and Billotte. It was because he had not played the game that the French authorities had not kept their promise, either, they insisted. The majority of them concocted a new telegram, slightly less reverent in tone than the previous one, in which they asked for a retrial of Pouvanaa. They were sincerely surprised and pained that de Gaulle did not even take the trouble of answering them.

Teariki waited patiently until 2 July 1966, when the defunct RDPT party, now rebaptised *Pupu here aia* (Patriotic party), held its annual convention or congress. Right from the beginning, it proved to be explosive. The first blast was delivered by the military high command who chose this exact moment to detonate a nuclear charge on board a barge anchored in the Moruroa lagoon. The pastor who opened the party convention with a prayer, in true Polynesian manner, implored the Almighty 'to stop these satanical bombs that have begun to spread their poison in our sky'. Blast number two was purely verbal and delivered by Teariki. Like an Old Testament prophet he thundered mightily against the fourteen assemblymen, including the speaker of the house, for having made such a stupid and dishonourable deal with the enemy.

The party delegates, coming from all of the islands of French

Polynesia, did not hesitate a second. They decided unanimously by a show of hands to exclude all fourteen traitors and to elect Teariki president of the reborn, cleansed party. The bulletin issued at the end of the convention preserved the Biblical flavour, for the key passage read: 'Thus ends this sad story. It is to be regretted that men who in the past honestly did their best to fight for the people became so corrupted that they willingly served our oppressors'.

After this crushing victory Teariki had become the undisputed leader of the biggest political party in the territory. It was particularly important to have this popular support considering that, within a few months, he was to stand face to face with the person responsible for all the calamities to which the Polynesian people had been exposed since 1963 – General de Gaulle himself.

18 MR PRESIDENT!

It had been officially announced shortly before this party convention that de Gaulle planned to visit French Polynesia in September 1966. On his way he stopped over for a few days in both French Somalia and Cambodia to make moving speeches in favour of peace and freedom for all oppressed peoples. The people of French Somalia demonstrated their complete agreement by revolting against the colonial rule and police terror exercised by de Gaulle's government. When the street fighting eventually ended there were four dead and seventy wounded. The reception was considerably more cordial in independent Cambodia where de Gaulle, speaking in the main stadium in Pnom Penh filled with 250 000 people, severely criticised 'those big powers whose armies invaded other countries where they have no business being'. He even told the cheering audience which particular nation he had in mind, decrying the American crimes in Vietnam and exhorting the United States government to pull its troops out at once.

Teariki had innocently taken it for granted that de Gaulle was going to examine, discuss, and propose solutions for all the social, economic, and political problems plaguing the Polynesian people ever since the nuclear forces had taken over their islands. But when he was eventually shown the schedule for this visit, he discovered to his dismay that the President-General was first to spend three days in Tahiti making speeches and attending parades, dinners, and dance shows – and then watch an atomic blast at Moruroa. No meetings or discussions at all had been scheduled with the elected representatives of the Polynesian people. The only reply he received to his protests was that the programme had been prepared in Paris and that no last-minute changes could be made. Although these were not the exact words used, the governor made it abundantly clear to Teariki that de Gaulle was too preoccupied with great international problems to waste any time on petty local problems. It was almost an insult to suggest that he be bothered with them.

The only scheduled opportunity for a meeting between Teariki and de Gaulle was during the protocol reception for important persons to take place in the intimacy of the new government council room the day after de Gaulle's arrival. To show the tremendous change that had occurred in his status since his previous private visit in 1956, de Gaulle arrived this time aboard a big plane accompanied by a staff of fifty persons. It had also been deemed necessary to post out hundreds of gendarmes at short intervals along the road leading from the airport to the country house where General and Madame de Gaulle were to stay. The precaution was completely unnecessary, for few people turned out and none of them were bomb throwers. Well-rested and fit, the President-General arrived the next morning, 7 September, at the council building. Luckily for Teariki, protocol placed him almost at the head of the waiting line; it also assured him of a private audience, about which he felt less happy. As soon as he was whisked into the presence of his adversary, he pulled out a manuscript and began to read the following address:

Mr President!

Ten years ago you honoured us with a visit. You were then a simple citizen, but at the same time, in the eyes of many of your fellow countrymen the greatest living Frenchman. For us Polynesians, who were once among the first to heed your appeal to continue the fight for freedom, you were not only the heroic leader of Free France but also, and above all, the liberator who proclaimed for the first time at Brazzaville the right of the inhabitants of the French colonies to equality, freedom, and self-government. This is why, even as early as 1956, we already received you with the honours due to a president and, even more important, with the cordiality that one reserves for one's best friend.

Today you are back among us as president of the republic for the purpose of witnessing the detonation of the most powerful atomic bomb France has produced to date. This is why your present visit differs from your earlier one, both in its formal aspect and in respect to the feelings we harbour for you.

You are being received with all the honours due to your rank. Like your cabinet ministers before you, you will be listening to many speakers assuring you in most solemn terms how attached we are by eternal bonds to you and to France. These rhetorical exercises are probably of some value for your propaganda apparatus, but I am sure that it is easy for you to make out the true character of all these more or less official, forced, and guided declarations. You are too shrewd and experienced, Mr President, to be deceived. At the same time I regret that all your information emanates from your secret police, and I am very happy that protocol has made it possible for me to draw your attention to the main issues opposing our two nations.

A widespread uneasiness exists in Polynesia and is worsening from day to day. It is due to the Fifth Republic's policy since you took over the helm, a policy consisting right from the beginning of a long series of attacks against our liberties, threats and acts of force aimed at reinforcing the colonial system and the military occupation of our islands. Or in other words, as has now become evident, your policy has had only one aim, that of being able to freely dispose of our country as a testing ground for your nuclear weapons. Since then our destiny, our health, our social, economic, and political institutions have been geared to your military needs.

To less well-informed persons than you, my conclusions might seem unfair or downright unpleasant. But you know, Mr President, that I speak the truth. You know as well that the much lauded prosperity is wholly artificial and short-lasting, and accompanied by an appalling inflation. During the last year for instance, the fish prices at the Papeete municipal market have increased by 85 per cent, those of vegetables by 84 per cent, and those of fruit by 57 per cent while the legally guaranteed minimum wage rose, between 1960 and 1966, only from 27.45 Pacific francs [27 cents] to 37.50 Pacific francs [37 cents] an hour. This shows that all social categories do not benefit from the marvellous prosperity ascribed to the CEP.

In fact the situation is even more disastrous than that. Not only has your government done nothing to avoid these economic disorders, but it has wittingly exploited them in order to reinforce the military occupation of Polynesia. You have thus adroitly made use of our constant budgetary deficits as pretexts for letting metropolitan ministries take over more and more of the local administration, a policy that will eventually remove any possibility of our running our own affairs. But beware! If you continue in this policy, the risks are great that you will lose the slight trust that we Polynesians still have in you, becoming instead a target for our wrath.

After alluding to the recent wrath of another colonial people in French Somalia, Teariki went right to the heart of another serious matter:

Pouvanaa's case is purely political. Governor Sicurani considered it so when he held out a promise to free our deputy in exchange for a massive vote for you during the last presidential elections. That you look at it this way yourself, Mr President, is proven by the fact that on the same day you released Pouvanaa, a few months before having served his full term, you instructed your minister for overseas territories to issue a decree banishing him from all French possessions in the Pacific, because you feared the political power of this old man whom all Polynesians venerate. But we are not so easily deceived and you can be sure, Mr President, that this aggravation of Pouvanaa's penalty will aggravate all political problems in the islands. This is even more certain after the bloody events in Somalia have shown how arbitrary and opportunistic your actions are. For example, while Pouvanaa was condemned to exile, in Somalia the leader of the *Union Démocratique Afar*, Mohammed Ahmed Issa, was released two days after having been apprehended in the act of fighting in the streets of Djibouti armed with a gun. Is Pouvanaa's crime that he had not spilled any blood? Is it really too much, Mr President, to ask that you show him the same clemency you have just shown Mohammed Ahmed Issa?

Let us then examine the other problem obscuring our relationship; your decision to install nuclear bases in French Polynesia. You made this decision without consulting us Polynesians, although our health and that of our children will suffer from the tests. This is a serious breach against the French constitution and the charter of the United Nations. Your propaganda department disregards the most elementary truths by alleging that these atomic and thermonuclear blasts are completely harmless to our health. I do not have enough time, here and now, to refute all of these propaganda lies. Suffice it to say that the reports of the UN Scientific Committee on the Effects of Atomic Radiation for 1958, 1962, and 1964 have firmly established that each radioactive dose, however small, is harmful to those exposed to it, as well as for their descendants – that it is consequently recommended to avoid increasing natural radio-activity – that there exists no efficient method of protection against the harmful effects from widespread radioactive fallout from the explosion of atomic and nuclear bombs. Which is why all these reports reaffirm the necessity of stopping all nuclear tests.

While reminding you of these basic scientific facts established by this highly qualified international body, however, I harbour no illusions whatsoever that you will share my fears and abandon your plans to set off the atomic explosion you have come to witness. No government has ever stopped nuclear testing until having acquired all the atomic weapons it wanted. No government has ever been honest enough nor had the cynical frankness to admit that its nuclear testing entails health hazards. No government has ever hesitated to expose other peoples – particularly if they are small and defenceless – to these dangers. The Americans exploded their most powerful bombs among the inhabitants of the Marshall Islands. The English used Christmas Island, surrounded by atolls peopled by Polynesians. The Russians preferred to make their tests among the peoples of Siberia. The Chinese government chose a region inhabited by Tibetans and Mongols. The French first exploded their bombs in Africa and are now ready to do so in our islands.

Yet I must tell you, Mr President, on behalf of the whole population, that in as far as France is concerned, it is sad and bitter for us to see that Pasteur's country, the country that has done the most to defend human rights, has followed this shameful road and joined what Jean Rostand calls 'the atomic gangsters'.

This is all the more to be regretted in the light of the magnificent speech you have just delivered in Pnom Penh, fully comparable to those you made during the war in London and Brazzaville. In this speech you took the side of an unfortunate people, victim of a war outside its control and crushed by the bombs and grenades of its 'liberators'. You strongly condemned American intervention and exhorted the United States government to follow its traditional vocation of defender of liberty. In conclusion you said that only by giving up its attempt to impose its will on the people of Vietnam can America win back its greatness and the esteem of the rest of the world.

Like the 250 000 Cambodians who listened to your speech, I enormously appreciate your courage in stating such evident truths. But I also ask myself whether the purpose of your visit here is so very different from the United States' involvement in Vietnam and whether the Americans could not criticise you for acting in the same way here. It seems to me that I have an even greater right than they do to use such language, and this is the prayer I formulate:

Mr President, please apply here in French Polynesia the same noble principles that you enumerated in Pnom Penh for the benefit of the Americans and re-embark your troops, your bombs, and your aeroplanes at once.

If you do so, you will never be accused of having caused cancer and leukemia here in our islands.

If you do so, our descendants will not blame you for the birth of monstrously deformed children.

If you do so, the friendship of neighbouring peoples will not be tarnished by any atomic clouds.

If you do so, France will become a model for the whole world. For this would mean that, for the first time in history, a great nation will have renounced freely, without having been motivated by fear of blackmail or gain, the use of nuclear power for mass murder, thereby proclaiming its faith in reason and inciting other nations to follow suit.

If you do so, we Polynesians shall be proud and happy to be French citizens and we shall again become your best and most faithful friends.

It is hard to see how de Gaulle could have avoided being touched by the sincerity and the anguish that Teariki expressed so eloquently. Actually he listened without moving a muscle or saying a word. It was also in complete silence that he took the text of the speech when Teariki offered it, and put it in his pocket. Whereupon he shook Teariki's hand as though nothing had happened, turned around, and strode briskly out of the room into a large hall where the other notables were waiting.

The official bulletin relating this historical meeting behind locked doors was more than succinct, relating it in these lines:

The head of state also received the deputy of French Polynesia, John F. Teariki, in the new council building, amounting to a sort of inauguration. The latter touched upon three topics with which he is much preoccupied: the statute, the liberation of Pouvanaa, and the CEP.

That was all.

Teariki had had a premonition that the official press was not going to make much greater efforts than this to make his speech known. So, as a safety measure, he had prepared several hundred mimeographed copies of it in advance, which he distributed among the many journalists who had come out from France to observe the event. None of them reproduced a line of it. As for the three local papers, only one of them published anything at all, and then only the official bulletin quoted above, with no further comments. The local and French radio and TV stations, although devoting many hours every day for a whole week to de Gaulle's visit, completely ignored the whole incident.

De Gaulle himself made not less than five speeches in Tahiti, but did not say anything about the three grave problems evoked by Teariki. He also carefully avoided alluding in any way to his splendid visions of a decade earlier of French Polynesia as the last peaceful place of refuge in a world threatened by nuclear holocaust. Instead he repeated over and over again the same old rhetorical stereotypes about how rightly proud the Polynesians must be of being allowed to participate in the great national defence efforts, etc.

On 9 September, de Gaulle flew out to the Tuamotu group for the event that was, literally, to highlight his trip, an atomic blast at the Moruroa test centre. Already four years earlier, after numerous tests in the Sahara desert, the French military technicians had succeeded in producing a considerable number of small seventy-kilotonne plutonium bombs that henceforth equipped the so-called striking force of thirty-six Mirage aeroplanes. The chances of these slow planes ever reaching their targets in

Russia, however, were absolutely nil. This explains why the French atomic scientists and technicians kept up their research and testing. What de Gaulle wanted to do now was to see for himself exactly how much progress they had made, since the military bases in the Sahara desert had been closed by the new, independent Algerian government. It had been decided that he was to watch the big bang from the deck of the cruiser *De Grasse*. Therefore, immediately upon his arrival at Moruroa, he boarded that ship, which then put out to sea.

When he appeared on deck early the next morning, 10 September, the sky was cloudy and a strong wind was blowing – from the wrong direction. Not only at sea level, where in fact easterly winds are the rule throughout the year, but also at much higher altitudes. If the bomb were to be detonated right away, in keeping with the schedule made in Paris, too much radioactivity would fall out over the inhabited islands to the west; the Tuamotus, the Societies, the Cooks, the Samoas, and the Fijian islands, etc. De Gaulle's face darkened at the bad news and gradually became so stony that the admiral in charge of the operation hesitated several hours before announcing that the test had to be postponed. The worst blow was nevertheless still to come. When the cruiser approached the island again, the general discovered that the object dangling in the air from a helium-filled balloon over Moruroa was not a sleek operational bomb at all, but an iron box of the size of a big family refrigerator.

After another night spent in the cabin he had taken over from the admiral, at sunrise on 11 September, de Gaulle marched up on deck with a determined look on his face. The wind was still blowing strongly in the wrong direction at all altitudes. In no uncertain terms he let it be known that many urgent problems were piling up in Paris and that he could not cruise around in this way forever. The poor admiral was in a terrible quandary. If the bomb did not explode soon, the general would. Having weighed these two risks against each other, he decided that the latter disaster would be the worst. So before the day was over, the plutonium box was detonated.

The yield of the explosion was only 120 kilotonnes. But, as predicted, the radioactive fallout reached all the islands west of Moruroa in a matter of hours or days. For instance in Apia, the distant capital of Western Samoa, 2000 nautical miles downwind, the radioactive content of the rainwater catchment tanks four days later was estimated by the National Radiation Laboratory of New

Zealand (report F 47, pp. 14–15) to be 135 000 picocuries per litre. Almost equally alarming measurements were made in the Cook Islands and in Fiji. The exact amount of radioactive fallout received by the inhabitants of French Polynesia, living in the shade of the atomic mushroom, has never been announced by the CEP high command.

19 PROBLEMS OF ELECTION AND SELECTION

Shortly after de Gaulle's visit, a huge section of the local electorate was given an excellent opportunity to take sides in Teariki's and his followers' bitter struggle against the general's colonial rule and policy of military grandeur. The event in question was the extra municipal election to be held in October 1966. Practically all Europeans and Chinese and most of the *demis* lived, or at least voted, in this constituency. Therefore, despite its equally important Polynesian population, Papeete had always been a Gaullist stronghold. Its perennially re-elected mayor since 1942 (!) was a fervent admirer of de Gaulle; he was the prosperous *demi* businessman, Alfred Poroi, who, as previously related, had made such skilful use of intrigue in 1962 that he was elected senator for French Polynesia, too. It may also be worth recalling that Poroi alone of all the delegates received by de Gaulle in the Elysée Palace on the fateful day of 3 January 1963 had been overjoyed by de Gaulle's decision to install nuclear bases in Polynesia. His enthusiasm reflected that of all his business colleagues in Papeete, who mainly regarded the thousands of soldiers, sailors, and foreign legionaries invading the town as so many new customers. The other newcomers, the Polynesian immigrants from the outer islands were, as we have seen, overlooked in the general stampede to get rich quickly. They felt very little sympathy for Poroi and his consorts, who therefore barely scraped through during the regular election in 1965.

Quite exceptionally the results were contested. The defeated *Pupu here aia* candidates representing above all the Polynesian electorate asked the French State Council to cancel the election on the grounds that not less than 2574 voters had been illegally barred by Poroi and company from taking part in the election. The State Council ruled that the fraud was amply proven and ordered new elections to be held on 2 and 9 October 1966. De Gaulle's visit to Tahiti on 6, 7 and 8 September could hardly have occurred at a better time as far as Poroi was concerned, and the general had no scruples about giving a helping hand to his old admirer and supporter. In a long speech held in the Town Hall courtyard, with a beaming Poroi standing at his side, de Gaulle generously promised – without having consulted anybody – not less than 7000 million Pacific francs ($A70 million) for a mountain road that nobody needed, but from which the Polynesian immigrants (and voters) were going to benefit in the form of new job opportunities. As usual the governor, the whole administration, and the military staff did their best to help Poroi during these new elections. An important part was played by the army specialists on 'psychological warfare', whose existence had been revealed during the lost battle for military brothels.

Poroi's adversaries were Teariki, Céran, Vanizette and a *demi* newcomer to the political game, Tetua Pambrun, who formed a coalition. Their slogan was well chosen: *Clean up Papeete, sweep out Poroi*. They succeeded magnificently. All twenty-seven seats in the municipal council fell to them. The new council promptly elected Tetua Pambrun mayor. In their post mortem of the elections the winners said:

Poroi was the government's and the governor's candidate. They supported him openly or secretly in every conceivable manner. Everybody in de Gaulle's entourage showed their preference for 'Dear Poroi'. We cannot express how surprised we are over this support for a candidate who had just been condemned of fraud by the State Council. This once more proves how eager the government always is to interfere in local politics. Only this time it backfired, or as Poroi himself said after the election: 'It is the CEP's fault that we lost'. What he meant was that the military 'psychological warfare' experts had too visibly been distributing their stupid propaganda.

Barely six months later, in March 1967, it was ballot time again, and once more the Gaullist forces took a severe beating. At stake this time was the deputy seat of Teariki himself in the French National Assembly, which was being renewed at the expiration of the full five-year term. Teariki stood again and made the nuclear tests the central issue by condemning them more vigorously than ever. The local Gaullists tried a clever move. They chose as their candidate a man who had almost the same social and religious background as Teariki. His real name was Elie Salmon, but he was known to everyone as Nedo. Like Teariki, he was an influential leader of the Protestant church and a great orator in Tahitian. By profession he was a school teacher which meant that he was well educated and spoke excellent French, besides. His proxy was the only female medical doctor in Tahiti, Andréa de Balmann, who belonged to a local *demi* family.

Among the many other candidates, the only one who seemed to have a fair chance of scoring well against Teariki and Nedo was a newcomer to politics, Francis Sanford. In spite of his English name, inherited from his American great-great-grandfather, he was a typical French-Tahitian *demi*. He too had begun his career as a school teacher and happened to be stationed on Borabora in February 1942 when an American task force took over the island and transformed it into a navy supply base for the duration of the war. Thanks to this fact and to his fluency in English, Sanford became the ideal liaison officer between the American forces and the local government in Tahiti. After another twelve years of teaching, he was appointed government interpreter and eventually head of the governor's staff. Then suddenly, in 1965, he gave up his well-paid position to form a new party, *Te ea api* – The New Way. It won its first victory a few months later in the suburban slum town of Faaa whose mayor Sanford became.

What worried Teariki and Nedo most was Sanford's universal appeal, for he would surely attract as many votes from the French, *demi* and Chinese as from the Polynesian electorate. Like everybody else during the war Sanford had been a Gaullist, or rather a militant in the local ranks of the pro-allied movement, whose figurehead de Gaulle became in the absence of any other contender. However since the war Sanford had concentrated on his work, first in the administration and then as mayor of Faaa and had never formulated in public any opinions about de Gaulle's nuclear and colonial policies.

Governor Sicurani's first action in favour of the Gaullist candidate, Nedo, was to install special polling booths on the nuclear bases in the Tuamotu islands for the convenience of the French troops and technicians stationed there, although no legal text existed permitting him to do so. The navy commanders followed suit by offering Nedo and his election staff free transport on warships to distant islands lacking regular boat or air service.

As the constitution stipulated, there were to be two rounds of balloting, the first taking place on 5 March. The result was a resounding defeat for Nedo with no more than 4526 votes against 8222 for Teariki and 6820 for Francis Sanford. Unruffled, Governor Sicurani declared that, after all, the main purpose was to defeat the anti-bomb, anti-French candidate, Teariki. So nothing had really been lost. On the contrary, the situation was quite hopeful. If Nedo pulled out of the contest and asked his followers to vote for Francis Sanford, this would give the latter

4526 votes in addition to his own 6820, or 11 346 altogether. As a result he was going to beat Teariki with a margin of 3000 votes!

For once the Gaullist party bosses disagreed with the governor. It was wholly unrealistic, they said, to expect such an automatic and complete transfer of votes. Moreover they claimed to know Francis Sanford better than the governor and assured the latter that he was as bitterly opposed to the nuclear tests as Teariki. The only sensible thing to do, therefore, was to let Nedo stand again. Even in the quite likely event of defeat, he would gain useful experience for better results in future battles. Basically it was a matter of principles.

This insistence on adherence to principles was strongly disapproved of by the national headquarters of the Gaullist party in Paris. At ten o'clock the following morning, Nedo received this telegram:

State matter
Elie Salmon
Papeete

The Action committee for the Fifth Republic congratulates you on excellent results obtained in first election round and wish to thank you for having fought so well for our cause. It is now absolutely necessary to achieve complete victory by giving full support to Sanford who is in the best position of all the candidates who are for General de Gaulle. We therefore request that you stand down and canvass during the second round for Sanford who thus becomes the Fifth Republic candidate. Friendly greetings.

Georges Pompidou
Valery Giscard d'Estaing
Jacques Baumel

The time limit for the formal declaration that each candidate must make as to whether he wanted to stand again or withdraw expired the same day at midnight. Therefore the local Gaullist leaders hurriedly met again in order to consider this telegraphic request. Their reaction was entirely negative. They decided to maintain Nedo's candidacy, even in the event that the Committee for the Fifth Republic was no longer willing to endorse him. The unpleasant task of informing the French administration of their decision was entrusted to the new, young party secretary, Gaston Flosse, a local-born businessman who had entered the political arena by winning the municipal elections in the suburban district of Pirae in 1965, at the same time that Sanford had won in Faaa.

However to Flosse's immense surprise, the government secretary flatly refused to record his verbal declaration that Nedo was maintaining his candidacy. To do so, he declared, a handwritten letter was required, signed by both the candidate and his proxy, Doctor de Balmann. It was past eight o'clock. Nedo's home was far from Papeete on the west coast. Flosse jumped in his car and pressed down the gas pedal. At half past ten he was back with the precious document duly signed by Nedo and Doctor de Balmann, who lived in Papeete. The government secretary read it very slowly and carefully, and seemed disappointed at being unable to discover any mistakes. Nevertheless he refused to deliver a receipt, as the electoral law required. The governor was to furnish all explanations and would be there in fifteen minutes.

Flosse had the bright idea of phoning Nedo, whose wife answered that her husband had been picked up by a member of the governor's staff, who had reached their home in a car quite a while ago. Flosse was luckier when he phoned the proxy. She was home and promised to come over right away. She arrived at the same time as the governor and Nedo, who were engaged in an animated discussion. They stopped half-way up the staircase leading to the government secretary's office on the first floor. The time was now 11.25 p.m. and Flosse shouted to Nedo to hurry. The governor angrily told him not to interrupt them, but thanks to this intervention Nedo gathered up enough courage to break away, dash forward, and slip through the door being held open for him by Flosse.

The government secretary stared for several minutes at the door. When it remained closed, he eventually took this as a hint that the governor had given up the chase and handed over a receipt. It was then 11.37 p.m. The next minute the telephone rang. It was the ministry for overseas territories in Paris and the government secretary ran out to fetch the governor, who, to everybody's surprise, was still waiting on the staircase. The governor listened respectfully and then explained that it was now more necessary than ever for Nedo to withdraw. According to the latest forecasts, there seemed to be a real risk of the national elections ending up in a draw. So the final outcome might be decided by the voters of French Polynesia and Nedo could perform a great service to the whole French nation by standing down in favour of Francis Sanford.

Nedo tartly replied that it was too late and left the office, together with his proxy and Flosse. This answer was patent nonsense to the Gaullist bosses in Paris. How could it be too late when it was only a quarter to midnight? The one to insist most strongly that the game should not be given up so easily was de Gaulle's dirty-trick man, Jacques Foccart, who called from Paris at this exact moment. On Foccart's order the government secretary rushed down the staircase and out into the street where Nedo was sitting in his car, ready to go when the traffic light changed. He repeated in an even firmer voice that it was too late; and when the light turned green, he drove off with a roar.

It would have been wiser for him to take the call, for without any regard to the fact that it is night in Tahiti when it is day in Paris, his home telephone began to ring as soon as he got into bed. Now, at the other end of the line, was the minister for overseas territories, General Billotte. The reply was the same, making the general terribly unhappy. Nedo had barely fallen asleep when the phone rang again. It was the exuberant Foccart, who simply wanted to be assured that Nedo had changed his mind. He soon realised that the only change was that Nedo was in a murderous mood, and he quickly hung up. At four o'clock in the morning Nedo was once more awakened by jingling telephone bells. He could hardly believe his ears. It was Prime Minister Georges Pompidou himself to whom he owed the honour. As if unaware of all previous conversations he affably repeated the whole sad story of the close race in France and the significant contribution to the Gaullist cause Nedo could make by standing down.

Nedo began to become worn down by the high pressure tactics. Nevertheless he gathered up enough strength to protest that it definitely *was* too late to stand down. The deadline had gone by. There was nothing he could do any longer. He could not have been more mistaken, he was told the following morning by the governor, who of course knew all of the night's news. Even after the expiration of this *legal* delay, a candidate could, *de facto*, abandon the race simply by omitting to distribute his bulletins and campaign material. The case was foreseen in paragraph R 100 of the electoral laws. Nedo objected that this might be done in France where communications were good; but how was this to be done in the hundred widely scattered islands of Polynesia where the bulletins and the propaganda leaflets for *both* the first *and* the second round had been distributed simultaneously weeks ago? No problem, replied the governor; I shall see to it that radio telegrams be dispatched instructing all local election officials to destroy your bulletins, posters, and leaflets. Nedo realised that it no longer made any difference whether or not he consented. He had already been withdrawn.

Thanks to this unexpected and unasked for help from the very active Action Committee for the Fifth Republic, Francis Sanford won the second round with an exceedingly thin majority of 13 633 votes as against 13 289 for Teariki.

If some readers find it hard to believe that all these grotesque events actually took place behind the scenes, we shall be only too happy to reveal our sources. The whole account, with an impressive number of sworn affidavits by all the principals, including Flosse, may be found in the brief that Teariki submitted to the French State Council in support of his request that the election be quashed and a new election held. When the verdict of the State Council (the nearest thing in France to a Supreme Court) was finally handed down, it went against Teariki. The only irregular act proved was the installation on the nuclear testing sites of special polling booths for the metropolitan troops and technicians. But this was not considered to be a grave enough infraction to warrant new elections.

20 PROFESSOR PERRIN'S PRODIGIOUS PROMISES

Up until 1966 when the first nuclear explosion occurred at Moruroa, the various spokesmen for the French government and the CEP assured us that it would be enough to make such tests every two years. But, as de Gaulle had been able to see with his own eyes from the deck of the *De Grasse*, the progress made by his nuclear physicists and military technicians since the transfer of the bases from the Sahara desert to the Tuamotu atolls was pitiful. The worst thing was the utter failure of the new Pierrelatte plant in France to produce the uranium 235 required to make an H-bomb, which after all was the sole aim and justification for the ambitious and costly French nuclear programme. Therefore de Gaulle gave his scientists and engineers a severe scolding, another 1000 million francs, and strict orders to step up the speed of production. Among other things, this meant that henceforth tests would have to be made every year at Moruroa and Fangataufa.

When announcing this decision in September 1966 shortly after de Gaulle's visit, Jean Lorrain, the admiral in charge of the whole programme, provided the following explanations:

We expect to begin our new series of tests in June 1967 at which time the winds begin to become more favourable. Several blasts have been scheduled but they will be less powerful than those made this year and all bombs will be suspended from balloons. The goal will be to prepare the ground for thermonuclear explosions in 1968. Our greatest problem during the next season will be how to decontaminate the site from one blast until the next. As a matter of fact Moruroa will not be inhabitable before November this year, and Fangataufa not before January 1967. The best solution would be to cover these two atolls with concrete, since it is easier to clean a concrete slab than the coral ground.

Well before the explosion of the first bomb at Moruroa on 2 July 1966, Teariki had written to the head of the French Atomic Energy Commission (CEA), Professor Francis Perrin, asking him for more precise information about the radioactive dangers threatening the population and what safety measures he was planning to take. Teariki was particularly worried about the health hazards entailed by contamination of tuna, bonito and other kinds of migratory fishes. What would happen if contaminated fish swam from Moruroa over to other inhabited islands and were captured and eaten there? Perrin replied by return mail, but like the typical absent-minded professor forgot to add the extra postage needed for airmail. As a result his letter did not reach its destination until two months later, by surface mail, on 19 July. Two nuclear devices had already been detonated. Here are the less than reassuring explanations furnished by Perrin in his belated reply:

Let us first consider the possible consequences of radioactive fallout occurring on uninhabited islands. This fallout will cause the ocean to become highly contaminated, but this contamination will rapidly diminish, as most of the radioactive elements have short lives. In addition we have such radioactive elements as strontium 90 and caesium 137 with long lives. Therefore their contamination of the environment and eventually of the fishes does constitute a problem, and considering the importance of sea products in the Polynesian diet, we must pay special attention to it. To begin with it will be necessary to prohibit the islanders from visiting uninhabited islands exposed to radioactive fallout, just as long as we are not certain that the contamination has decreased to a low enough level.

However these prohibitions in the area exposed to radioactive fallout do not solve all the problems. For there is also a risk that migratory fish such as tuna, after having spent a few days in contaminated waters, may move on to other distant regions and be captured and eaten. In this case, however, we must remember that it is only during the first days after a nuclear explosion that the fish will be contaminated to such a point as to constitute a health hazard for the inhabitants, as the radioactive elements are rapidly scattered over the ocean and diluted in huge masses of water. Another prerequisite to attaining a dangerously high level of contamination would be for the islanders to eat contaminated fish repeatedly over a long period; when eaten occasionally such fish do not cause any harm. For all these reasons we have deemed it necessary not only to foresee the exact place where the radioactive fallout will occur but also to study the environment and particularly the marine biology, and last but not least to verify the actual consequences of the nuclear explosions.

The means at our disposal allow us to observe how the radioactive fallout is formed and spreads, to determine which species, if any, are contaminated, and finally when necessary, to prohibit the eating of these fishes. Every time such a prohibition is made, the islanders will be duly recompensed for their losses. All migratory fishes, particularly tuna, sold in the principal market place in Papeete will be checked by radiobiologists, so as to remove any possible fears that the population may still harbour.

As soon as Perrin's letter became known, members of the new municipal council of Papeete, during their almost daily visits to the market place, began to look out for radiobiologists in the process of sampling and testing the huge quantities of fish sold there, about 200 tonnes a month. None was ever to be seen. On 17 November, after the fifth bomb of the 1966 series had been detonated, the disappointed town councillors adopted the following resolution:

We hereby request the mayor to ask the admiral and military unit responsible for the protection of the civilian population from radiation about the exact nature of the measures they have taken since they were first charged with this task, and more specifically, in what manner do they supervise the food sold in Papeete, both in the market place and in private stores. Moreover we should like to have the facts and figures obtained so far, i.e. the radioactive fallout measured in the air, the sea, the soil, the rainwater, the drinking water, and the food in Papeete and its vicinity – before, during, and after the tests made this year. It is urgent for us to receive an immediate reply, and we also expect, in the future, to be kept regularly informed about all studies made of the radioactivity and the subsequent safety measures decided upon.

Several weeks passed. Even months. The municipal council repeated its request. Still no reply arrived. In May 1967 the French fleet came back, which was a sure sign that a new series of nuclear tests was in the offing. The councillors adopted a more strongly worded resolution in which they expressed their surprise over this six month long silence, 'amounting to an admission by the authorities of their guilt or incapacity to do anything to protect the population'.

Three months and three nuclear explosions later, having still had no word from the governor or the admiral, the councillors adopted a third protest against 'the open contempt shown by the civilian and military authorities for the elected representatives of the Polynesian people'. For good measure they sent copies of their resolution to the local newspapers. It was the right course to follow. Four days later the governor replied. Here is what he had to say, after having thought the matter over for a whole year:

Although it is quite natural for you to feel some anxiety, I am obliged to remind you that the municipal council is not empowered to adopt

113

resolutions relating to matters outside its competence, as defined by articles 25 and 44 of the decree of the 8th March, 1879. Consequently the municipal council *cannot make public* any protest or petition, and the recent distribution to the press of a note dated the 1st September, 1967, is thus an illegal act.

Whereupon the governor advised the councillors to read the local newspapers, listen to the radio broadcasts, and watch the TV programmes, if they really wanted to learn about all 'the special safety measures taken during the nuclear tests'. Of course the councillors had very closely followed what the mass media had to say about the tests and the reason why they had protested and kept on protesting was precisely that all these official bulletins repeated ad nauseam the same vague assurances that unspecified 'security measures' were being taken, without ever giving a single fact or figure about the only subject that mattered: the actual amount and dispersal of the radioactive fallout.

Nevertheless the councillors felt a bit sorry for the governor. For there was no longer any doubt as to the real reason for its having taken him a whole year to compose a reply to them: he had been obliged to go through eighty-eight thick volumes of the *Journal Officiel*, from the present time back to 1879 before coming across a decree that could be used to muzzle them.

In conclusion it should perhaps be noted that this decree had been issued in France for metropolitan municipalities one year before Polynesia became a French colony and eleven years before Papeete became a town, and in all likelihood had no legal value whatsoever. But as the governor well knew it would cost the council a fortune in legal fees to prove him wrong, discouraging them from ever making the attempt.

21 LONG LIVE SELF-GOVERNING POLYNESIA

The one person most bitterly opposed to the governor's autocratic rule backed up by obsolete colonial decrees was the new deputy, Francis Sanford, whom the Gaullist high command had made such strenuous efforts to have elected in March 1967. During his first parliamentary session, on 13 June 1967, he addressed the following formal request to Prime Minister Pompidou:

Mr Sanford draws the attention of the Prime Minister to the fact that during the last general elections, 80 per cent of the electorate in French Polynesia voted for candidates who had campaigned for internal self-government. The French constitution guarantees all peoples in the French overseas territories the right to determine for themselves the form of government they want and Mr Sanford thinks that the time has come to organise such a referendum in Polynesia. Consequently he would like to see the Prime Minister propose a law for the purpose of undertaking a peaceful and orderly consultation of the people of Polynesia immediately after the renewal of the local Territorial Assembly on the 10th September, 1967. The question to be asked is whether or not the Polynesian people wants internal self-government.

In keeping with parliamentary rules, Pompidou had as long as he wished to furnish a written reply. The 'normal' delay was anything from three to six months. While waiting for Pompidou's answer, no one less than General de Gaulle himself made it emphatically clear what he thought of requests of this sort. The occasion was his famous visit to Canada, culminating in his salute to free Quebec. A few days later, Sanford's party, *Te ea api*, distributed broadside leaflets in Tahiti with the following text:

EVERY PEOPLE'S RIGHT TO GOVERN ITSELF
General de Gaulle has been to Quebec and made the following speech:
'The drive here has reminded me of the liberation of France. It is a sign of our times that every nation is becoming self-governing and I feel that this is what is happening here tonight.
'What we are witnessing here is the same event occurring in so many parts of the world: the coming of age of a people, ready to take its own destiny in hand and become fully self-governing. Not only have you

survived but you are strongly determined to use every modern means at your disposal to liberate and develop your country.

'Long live Free Quebec!'
In the same spirit, *Te ea api* proclaims:
'Long live self-governing Polynesia.'

In the few other French colonies that had not opted for immediate independence in the 1958 referendum, much more political progress had since been made than in Polynesia. For instance the Comoros Islands, located in the strait between Madagascar and Mozambique, had attained internal self-government in 1961, leaving only defence and foreign affairs in French hands. Far-reaching reforms had likewise been granted in Somalia after the bloody street demonstrations during de Gaulle's visit in 1966. These were excellent precedents and Prime Minister Pompidou really admitted this when his written reply to Francis Sanford was at long last delivered on 26 August. Pompidou's only reservation concerned the proposed method of consulting the Polynesian people. In his opinion it was unnecessary and superfluous to organise a separate referendum. As the elections to renew the Territorial Assembly were to be held soon, on 10 September, and all candidates had strong views about the form of government they wanted, why not simply let the new Assembly decide? Teariki and Sanford saw no reason to oppose such a procedure, particularly as they were certain of victory. They were right on this point. Their parties, *Pupu here aia* and *Te ea api*, both favouring self-government (*autonomie interne*), won seventeen seats out of thirty and another four independent assemblymen fighting for the same goal formed a loose alliance with them. Among the losers were Céran and all the old RDPT leaders excommunicated by Teariki, who had tried their luck as independent candidates.

During the first meeting of the new Assembly Teariki and Sanford jointly presented a resolution for immediate self-government. To avoid all intentional or unintentional misinterpretations, they specified just what such a reform meant. Their demands were quite modest. The most important concerned the executive post. They wanted to replace the governor, appointed by and acting on the orders of the French government, by an elected president or prime minister appointed by and responsible to the Territorial Assembly. In other words what they were asking for was simply the sort of democratic parliamentary system existing in France. Much nearer to hand, it was the system of government introduced into the Cook Islands in 1965, and following the example of Albert Henry, they were perfectly willing to let the 'mother-country' continue to handle defence matters, foreign affairs, and monetary policies. The Territorial Assembly promptly adopted Teariki's and Sanford's proposal and it was transmitted to Paris for immediate implementation.

The two Autonomist party leaders were again of one mind when another urgent problem came up for discussion, the nuclear tests. They both severely criticised the French authorities for their refusal to inform the Papeete town council about the exact nature of the much heralded 'safety measures'. They also wanted to know why these important tasks had not been entrusted to the French National Radiation Laboratory, the special agency created for just this purpose – but to a nondescript army outfit, taking orders from the same CEP-CEA bosses guilty of polluting the islands with their nuclear devices. It was as preposterous as though the accused were to be at the same time his own judge. No wonder, then, that in this case the bomb people exonerated themselves. The debate ended with the adoption of this resolution:

The Territorial Assembly is anxious to find out the exact nature and amount of radioactive contamination to which the environment has been exposed by earlier A-bomb tests and to which it is to be exposed by future H-bomb tests in the Tuamotu islands. We therefore ask the government of the French Republic to invite three foreign specialists on such problems from, respectively, Japan, New Zealand, and the USA as well as the three French scientists Monod, Kastler, and Rostand to visit French Polynesia in order to study the radioactive pollution of the environment on the spot.

22 DECOLONISATION IN THEORY AND PRACTICE

Thanks to unsolicited Gaullist help, Francis Sanford had narrowly defeated John Teariki during the general elections in March 1967, henceforth becoming deputy for French Polynesia. In France the Gaullist party lost so much ground that it had to seek a coalition with Giscard d'Estaing's supposedly liberal party, the *Républicains Indépendants* – Independent Republicans – in order to remain in power. But even so the various opposition parties occupied exactly the same number of seats – 243. Therefore the last deputy to be elected, Francis Sanford, held the balance of power in his hands. He was immediately approached by the Independent Republicans, who promised him their support in exchange for his decisive vote. Having nothing to lose and everything to win, he accepted the deal.

The first test of the willingness of the coalition government to change its colonial policy came six months later on 7 December 1967, when it presented a bill in the National Assembly giving the small French overseas territory of the Comoros Islands in the Indian Ocean complete self-government, transferring practically all powers to the local assembly and an elected prime minister. This provided a perfect opportunity for Francis Sanford and the deputy from New Caledonia, Roch Pidjot, to propose that the same liberal reforms be extended to all French overseas territories. The minister concerned, General Billotte, replied suavely 'that the government is very aware of the strong and genuine aspirations of all the overseas territories towards self-government and is ready to take appropriate action'. So, he continued, it was extremely regrettable that article 91, paragraph 3 of the Assembly rules prevented him from including any such amendment in the bill proposed by the government. However this objection could easily be overridden. All it took was for the Assembly to introduce a new bill right away, formulated in keeping with Sanford's and Roch Pidjot's wishes. Unfortunately, for some strange reason, all the other forty-two deputies representing the Independent Republicans were absent. Even more suspect was General Billotte's rather happy and relieved smile when it was announced that Sanford's and Pidjot's bill had been defeated due to this unexplained desertion of his coalition partners. It was meagre solace for the two Pacific deputies that, a few minutes later, the Assembly unanimously agreed to giving the Comoros Islands complete self-government.

Furious over this treachery, Sanford left Giscard's party to become a truly independent Assembly member. The French press which had previously refused to give space to the Polynesian leaders' many protests against the nuclear crimes committed by the French government in Polynesia, suddenly discovered Sanford's existence and published long articles about 'the native from a remote South Sea island who had upset the governmental majority'. Needless to say, these articles were full of picturesque details about this noble savage's Parisian adventures, but completely failed to inform their readers about the real issues.

Nevertheless the government was so annoyed that it hit back at Sanford where it hurt most. On 17 February 1968, Prime Minister Pompidou replied in the following terms to the Polynesian Territorial Assembly's request of November 1967 for internal self-government:

This request has been formulated by a group of assemblymen who are not entitled to speak on behalf of the territory as a whole, since they represent only a fraction of the local electorate; consequently there is no justification for changing the statute enthusiastically adopted in 1958, a statute from which, moreover, the Polynesian people have drawn great benefit ever since.

Sanford and Teariki promptly pointed out that this was a strange criticism indeed, coming from a prime minister running France with the support of 243 deputies against 244, whereas the Polynesian Autonomist parties held 17 seats out of 30 in the Territorial Assembly. As for the notorious 1958 referendum, the outcome of which was not binding for an eternity, it were better to talk about it as little as possible since the methods used had been blatantly fraudulent. If Pompidou's last statement implied that his government had bought the right to treat the Polynesians as it liked, this constituted a serious insult, deeply felt by all the islanders.

The majority of the Polynesian assemblymen were so outraged that they decided, on 21 March 1968, to send a delegation to Paris to press their constitutionally recognised rights to run their own affairs. Of course, at the same time they planned to repeat their perennial demand for Pouvanaa's immediate release. Actually this second aim was the more urgent. Pouvanaa had had a serious stroke on 16 February, and his strength was rapidly ebbing. He was still vegetating in a small flat in an ugly tenement house in the Parisian suburb of Vanves, assigned to him by Pompidou's government two years earlier in consequence of his continued banishment from the French Pacific islands. The delegation was made up of the new speaker, Jean Millaud, its vice-speaker, John Teariki, assemblyman Henri Bouvier, and the deputy, Francis Sanford. Having in the past often criticised the abusive practice of sending huge delegations to Paris on the slightest pretext, they all agreed to pay their own expenses.

As soon as Minister for Overseas Territories General Billotte learned about these plans, he instructed the governor to tell the delegates that they would not be received by him, nor by any member of the government. The reason advanced for this flat refusal was their decision to pay for the trip themselves, making it legally impossible to consider them *official* delegates. The pretext chosen could not have been worse. For in the meantime two members of the local minority parties, Rudolf Bambridge and Frantz Vanizette, had announced that they, too, were going to Paris, likewise paying all travel expenses themselves. The purpose of their mission was of course to persuade the government *not* to listen to the demands of the Autonomist delegation. As a result Billotte and the governor quickly forgot their own strictly legal objections, and the Autonomists took the regular UTA plane for Paris, together with their sworn enemies, on 29 March 1968. Among the passengers embarking at Nouméa was a delegation of New Caledonian Autonomist assemblymen who were to act jointly with their Polynesian colleagues.

It was Saturday when the plane disgorged this motley crowd at Le Bourget airport in Paris. But as soon as the ministries opened on Monday – which incidentally was All Fool's Day – the Autonomists asked for an audience with Billotte. Two days later they received a short letter signed by his secretary, Pierre Angéli, expressing 'sincere regrets that the Minister has such a heavy workload that it will not be possible for him to receive the Polynesian and New Caledonian delegates within the near future'. It was furthermore suggested that, instead, they discuss their problems with Angéli! The delegates immediately rejected this meaningless offer of using a department secretary as messenger boy. The same day the Parisian newspapers informed them about the exact nature of Billotte's 'heavy workload'. He had been discussing Polynesian problems with the self-appointed minority delegates, Bambridge and Vanizette. According to these press reports, 'the government has no intention whatsoever of granting the request for internal self-government (*autonomie interne*), made by some Polynesian assemblymen'. The two delegations sent out a press bulletin (partially reproduced by two or three newspapers) pointing out that they represented the *majority parties* in their respective Territorial Assemblies, and asking why the minister received only envoys representing the *minority parties*.

Obviously finding his earlier pretext a little bit too thin, Billotte instructed his secretary this time to inform them that the single true reason why he had not received them was that they wanted to discuss a 'question of a political nature'! The delegations retorted:
(1) that they had been elected on a political platform just like all Gaullist deputies and ministers in France and that it was absurd to forbid politicians from dealing with politics;
(2) that at any rate, the purpose of their present visit had nothing to do with politics; all that they wanted to discuss was the long overdue reform of the colonial statute stifling Polynesia, and Pouvanaa's release, made ever more imperative by his rapidly deteriorating health. (The New Caledonian delegation asked, besides this, to be given complete control over its own mineral resources, which had hitherto been exploited by private firms, subject only to authorisation granted by the government in Paris.)

Having reached this dead end, Billotte tried another approach. He told one of the majority leaders in the National Assembly, Jacques Duhamel, that he was willing to meet Sanford and Roch Pidjot 'privately'. As intended, Duhamel informed his Polynesian and New Caledonian colleagues about this strange offer. They replied at once that they did not mind where and how the meeting took place. What mattered to them was to obtain a firm assurance that the government was at long last going to meet their demands. A few days later a blushing Duhamel had to confess that Prime Minister Pompidou had overruled Billotte and vetoed the scheduled 'private' meeting. What saddened the Polynesian delegates most, of course, was that they had to return to Tahiti without Pouvanaa. They were all convinced that it was the last time they would see him alive.

Upon their return they contrasted their own experiences with the French government's officially proclaimed decolonisation policy. It had been summarised in a particularly succinct manner by de Gaulle himself, and the Autonomist parties now printed and distributed this speech in which the general said, among other things:

The spirit of our times implies changes not only in our own country but also overseas. It is unnecessary to enumerate all the reasons obliging us to bring the colonial era to an end. By undertaking reforms, by educating an élite, by encouraging all liberation movements, we have shown that we recognise all colonial people's right to self-government. Besides, to refuse them this right would have violated our ideals and resulted in a long, useless struggle, mobilising world opinion against us. To no avail, for eventually we should have lost the battle. It is understandable that certain individuals dream themselves back to the time of the colonial empire, as others regret the disappearance of oil lamps, sailing ships, and horse drawn carriages. But what are such nostalgic thoughts worth? Only realities count in politics.

During this month of May, 1968, while the Polynesian Autonomist leaders were decrying this striking discrepancy between practice and theory in de Gaulle's treatment of their country and people, the French students and workers were revolting against his reactionary policies at home. It thus became the perfect opportunity for the Autonomists to begin building barricades in the streets of Papeete. In reality, the Polynesians paid very little attention to what was going on in Paris. To the extent that they watched the TV news, they strongly disapproved of the stone-throwing students and wanton destruction of cars, shop windows, and public property. As a matter of fact, the only persons in Tahiti to become somewhat agitated were the local Gaullists who tried to organise a sort of 'Patriotic Front', to maintain their local supremacy in case the general's rule came to an end in France. They did not calm down until the governor sent for military reinforcements and declared that he was not going to tolerate any disorders – however patriotically inspired.

As we all know, the excesses committed by the students in Paris created such a strong resentment among all classes of French society (particularly in the provinces) that de Gaulle managed to remain in power. The backlash lasted long enough to assure the Gaullist and other conservative parties a crushing victory during the ensuing general elections held on 23 and 30 June; they won not less than 358 of the 487 seats in the National Assembly. Due to the rashness with which de Gaulle had acted, it proved impossible to organise a simultaneous election in French Polynesia, which therefore took place one week later on. The local Gaullists confidently expected the incumbent deputy, Francis Sanford, to be swept away by a similar wave of popular indignation and did their best (or worst) to depict him as a red revolutionary. The candidate to vote for was Nedo Salmon who, as a true Gaullist, was already on the winning side, and once elected would be in an excellent position to obtain funds and all sorts of favours for Polynesia.

The identity of views existing among all Autonomist party leaders was confirmed when Teariki consented to be Sanford's proxy. In addition to Sanford and Nedo there was a third candidate, the young trade union leader, Charles Taufa, who was for a vaguely pro-French policy, meaning above all more French money for public works, from which his sympathisers were to be the chief beneficiaries. As usual the civil and military authorities did their utmost to help the Gaullist candidates and all the French technicians, officers, soldiers, and sailors temporarily stationed in the islands were once more allowed to cast their ballots at the local polls and thus provide a counterbalance to the Polynesian electorate. In spite of all these handicaps, in the first and only round, Sanford/Teariki obtained 14 701 votes, or more than twice as many as Nedo whose score was 7135. As for Taufa, he did better than expected with 3349 votes. In New Caledonia the Autonomist deputy, Roch Pidjot, was re-elected by a wide margin.

23 GONE WITH THE WIND

Completely unaffected by all this political turmoil, the CEP-CEA high command continued to lay the groundwork for the most impressive and poisonous nuclear testing programme to date. With military precision the admiral in charge of the whole operation proudly announced in May 1968 that no fewer than 5936 men in uniform and 2265 civilian technicians were already at their posts on Moruroa, Fangataufa, Hao and Tahiti. Furthermore, one aeroplane carrier and three cruisers were steaming at full speed towards Tahiti, with another 7018 men on board.

Simultaneously the French government let it be known that the Pierrelatte processing plant had at last succeeded in producing enough uranium 235 for the manufacture of, if not exactly an H-bomb, at least a crude thermonuclear device. On 4 July 1968 *Le Monde* wrote:

This first French thermonuclear blast will result in extensive damage to the test site, i.e. the atoll of Fangataufa, chosen for these H-bomb experiments . . . This atoll will not stand more than two thermonuclear explosions, and if they are not successful it may become necessary to find a new site. We must also keep in mind that in spite of all possible security measures that have been taken, a thermonuclear explosion will cause extensive radioactive pollution. So much so that we must ask whether, in the case of a successful blast, it will prove justifiable to undertake the scheduled second explosion.

All these figures and forecasts made the Polynesian leaders, if possible, more gloomy and angry.

With their customary lack of judgement and common sense, the military high brass chose to detonate the first bomb for the season on 7 July, the same day that the Polynesians went to the polls and re-elected Sanford as their deputy. According to the short official news bulletin, it was 'only' an ordinary A-bomb. The following day, Henri Bouvier, the shrewdest of all the Autonomist leaders, made a strange discovery, which he recounted in these terms in the Territorial Assembly:

On Monday the 8th July, when the election committee, of which I am a member, met in the Courthouse to proclaim the official results, we discovered that there were no figures at all from two islands, Maiao and Tureia. In the first case the explanation was quite simple: the radio transmitter on the island was out of order and the stormy sea prevented any boats from calling there. As for Tureia, the other members of the election committee seemed to be of the opinion that it was useless to expect any results from that island, but refused to tell me why and how they had arrived at that conclusion. I am therefore afraid that the whole population has suddenly disappeared.

At Bouvier's suggestion, the assemblymen decided to ask the governor and the military high command:
(1) Whether the population of Tureia had voted in the general election on 7 July 1968.
(2) If not, what the reason might be.
(3) In the event that the islanders were still on Tureia, what had happened to them and what fate lay in store for them.

This was not the first time the Territorial Assembly had expressed its concern for the welfare of the fifty or so inhabitants of this small atoll, situated but seventy-eight nautical miles to the north of Moruroa. As early as 1963, as soon as it became known that Moruroa was to be the principal nuclear testing site, several Autonomist assemblymen had voiced strong fears about the health hazards to which the people of Tureia were to be exposed. As previously related, the governor gave firm assurances that 'the tests will be made only when the winds are northerly and blowing towards the southern portion of the ocean where there are no islands. 'Consequently,' he said, 'there was no need at all to evacuate Tureia.'

Faced by an angry storm of protests that there were never any northerly winds during the southern winter in the region where Moruroa and Tureia were situated, the CEP then admitted that the governor had made a slight mistake and furnished its own, equally preposterous explanation. According to the admiral in charge, tests were to be made exclusively when the winds in the stratosphere were westerly, blowing every particle of the radioactive cloud out over the empty ocean between Polynesia and South America. The Autonomist leaders, many of who were sailors and captains who had spent all their lives studying sky and wind, objected that in the first place the ocean east of Moruroa was not altogether empty but contained at least a dozen inhabited islands. Secondly they pointed out that *at sea level* the winds were constantly easterly, and thus likely to carry radioactive fallout in the wrong direction, towards the mass of inhabited islands of the Tuamotu and Society groups. In an impassioned speech in the Assembly that same year, Teariki had shown that adequate meteorological data for making reliable forecasts were non-existent in French Polynesia. The first and only meteorological station had been set up in Papeete as late as 1932, and its budget had been so piteously inadequate that the skeleton staff had only been able to observe and record rainfall, wind direction, and temperature at sea level. Worse yet, the whole station had burnt down in 1948 and all records had been destroyed. So how could the bomb testers now have the temerity to pretend that they were able to foresee when the winds were going to blow in the 'right' direction? Teariki's own forecast was that the admiral would soon have to take back every word he had uttered and mount a last minute emergency operation to evacuate Tureia, and about six other inhabited islands.

Two years went by without any noticeable changes in official policy concerning the protection of islanders living on atolls in the immediate vicinity of the test sites. On 15 May 1966, the CEP announced that the first blast was soon to take place and sent out a warning to all ships and aircraft to keep out of a danger zone 'extending in a 400 kilometre radius around Moruroa with a wedge-shaped, 740 kilometre prolongation in an easterly direction'. Teariki immediately protested that no fewer than seven inhabited atolls were located inside this danger zone. The CEP high command was terribly sorry. A mistake had been made. The correct radius of the danger zone was 222 and not 400 kilometres. This did very little to calm the apprehensions of Teariki and the other assemblymen. To begin with, they wanted to know how the military bosses could make such fearful mistakes. It testified to a carelessness that shook everybody's faith in the CEP's whole safety policy. However that might be, Tureia was still inside the danger zone, even as defined by this 'corrected' figure. Were the fifty Tureians to be evacuated or not? And what about the people on the eight other islands situated just outside the limits of this reduced danger zone? What guarantees could the military give that the wind would not shift a few degrees, exposing them to heavy radioactive fallout? The assemblymen were particularly worried about the fate of the 700 Polynesians living on the high island of Mangareva.

The strange disappearance of the whole population of Tureia just before the elections in July 1968 was equal to a belated admission that Teariki had been right from the beginning in this instance, and that some health hazards existed after all. For there was no doubt that the fifty men, women, and children on Tureia had been spirited away and hidden for the duration of the tests, on orders from the CEP high command. When after a week the Assembly had still not received any reply to its enquiries about the fate of the Tureians, it tried to stop any further tests by adopting the following bold resolution, presented by Francis Sanford:

On the 11th January, 1968, our Assembly asked the government in Paris to invite three foreign scientists from respectively Japan, New Zealand, and the United States – the three French scientists Jean Rostand, Théodore Monod, and Alfred Kastler – plus a group of technicians from the French National Radiation Laboratory (SCPRI) to come to our islands for the express purpose of studying the radioactive pollution of the environment caused by the CEP's atomic activities. The French government never replied to this request. Therefore as soon as I learned that a new series of tests including thermonuclear devices was to occur this year I forwarded, on the 30th May, 1968, a written request to the minister for French overseas territories, urging him to bring a cease to all further nuclear testing in our islands. This having not been done, I propose that we take the matter into our own hands. Fortunately there exists a legal possibility for us to do so. I am referring to decree 57–912 of the 22nd July, 1957 where it is clearly stipulated in article 40 that the Territorial Assembly can make laws concerning:

'Agriculture, forest, and coastal waters, as well as the protection of soil and vegetation.

'Hygiene and public health, with the exception of preventive treatment against tuberculosis, leprosy, and elephantiasis.

'Town planning, housing, and the suppression of dangerous, incommodious, and unhealthy buildings or establishments.

'Monuments and historical sites.'

Nobody can deny that the testing of A and H bombs is harmful to the soil, vegetation, and waters, and constitutes a health hazard for the population. Nor is there the slightest doubt that the buildings erected by the CEP on the sites must be defined as 'dangerous and incommodious'. Consequently the Territorial Assembly hereby forbids all further nuclear testing in French Polynesia.

Of the twenty-two assemblymen present, fourteen voted for and six against the resolution, while two abstained, considering the whole procedure worthless, convinced as they were that the governor would, as usual, declare the new law null and void.

24 HAPPY TUREIANS, HAPPY GALLEY

But what had become of the fifty-odd inhabitants of Tureia? Some enterprising reporters with good connections in the army soon came up with an answer to this mystery, intriguing everybody in Tahiti. According to their sources, the Tureians had all been shipped to Tahiti and hidden away in an army camp. Various spokesmen for the CEP emphatically denied this rumour for a whole week, until so many embarrassing facts had become known that the only escape left was to do a complete volte-face and declare that this was of course exactly what had happened, while innocently asking what was wrong with that?

As a smiling press officer now laid out the text, the secret removal of the whole population of Tureia had nothing whatsoever to do with the nuclear tests. It just so happened that these fine people had petitioned the French navy on their own initiative two days before the first nuclear blast for a free trip to Tahiti. The reason for their sudden desire to make such a trip? Nothing was easier to explain. In true patriotic spirit they wanted to participate in the 14th of July celebrations. Yes, it was a bit unfortunate that they had missed the elections, but it was their own decision. The whole tribe was now living in a recreation camp in Mataiea on the south coast of Tahiti as guests of the CEP. Each family had its own house with all modern conveniences. They were all given free meals in the first-class army restaurant. How did they spend their time? As well-to-do tourists. During the daytime they water-skied, swam, or sailed. But some preferred to play billiards or bowls. In the evening they watched movies. But had they not come to Tahiti to participate in the 14th of July celebrations? Of course they had. They were transported every day in buses all the way, about fifty kilometres, from Mataiea to Papeete. The admiral and the governor generously gave them free tickets to all the best shows in town.

The Autonomist leaders had the bad manners to openly state that the French navy and army had kidnapped the poor islanders because of their island's nearness to Moruroa. To show how completely wrong these accusations were, a few Tureians were shown on a special TV programme. They warmly thanked the admiral and the governor for their kindness, adding that the two men who had refused to leave the island would be green with envy when they eventually learned what they had missed. The TV reporter who interviewed them (with the help of an interpreter) did not hesitate for a second to ask them a question that was uppermost in most viewers' minds: Were they not afraid of the bomb tests at Moruroa? The Tureians laughed. They had already seen or heard eight blasts, and contrary to what they had originally feared, nobody had fallen down dead. How long did they plan to remain in Tahiti? Well, they did not know exactly. Probably several months. Which meant that they would not see any of the beautiful thermonuclear explosions. But it was not a matter of great regret. They were all very happy with their Tahitian holiday.

This sudden willingness of the programme director to discuss nuclear problems on TV gave the assemblymen an idea. Why not organise a TV and radio debate with the principal local politicians, the CEP and CEA bosses and some French specialists on radioactive pollution and environmental problems? Even the Gaullist assemblymen voted for this resolution. In spite of having been unanimously adopted, it met the same fate as all previous bright ideas emanating from the Assembly; it was quickly buried in the governor's special drawer for lost causes.

Half jokingly Sanford made another proposal, bound to join the previous one. He had just discovered a clause in the statute making it possible to regulate by special legislation the importing and utilisation of all radioactive matter. The text adopted by the Assembly at his instigation read:

Article 1: It is illegal to import, transport, sell, stock, and spread in the air, the sea, the rivers, and on the ground all radioactive matter except when the purpose is strictly medical.

Article 2: The trade and use of TV sets and watches and alarm clocks with luminous figures is exempted and will later be regulated by a separate law.

Article 3: Henceforth all radioactive matter found in the territory will be confiscated and returned to the country of origin, at the expense of the importer.

Article 4: All transgressions of the present law will be punished by the maximal sentence prescribed by governmental order No. 238/M I/A A of the 19th March, 1958. In addition all dispositions of the criminal and penal laws existing in the territory may be applied.

It was a most timely intervention but of course totally ineffectual, for the next day, 24 August 1968, a 2.5 megatonne thermonuclear device exploded in the Pacific sky above Fangataufa. The minister for scientific research, Robert Galley, who had come from Paris to witness the test, exulted during a press conference over this tremendous scientific achievement, adding that 'the radioactive cloud rose rapidly and drifted eastwards between the Actaeon and Reao atolls following exactly the bisector of the triangular escape zone'. This sounded fine to all Parisian correspondents, ignorant of the topography of the Tuamotu group. But local people, who knew that Tureia was situated only 40 kilometres off this bisector, were much less impressed. On his return to Paris, Galley summarised the significance of this thermonuclear blast for *Le Monde* (see the 10 September issue) in the following terms: 'The more successful our tests are the fewer we shall make. The reason for this is obvious. We do not want to increase the contamination of the stratosphere excessively unless we are certain to reap some benefits from an additional blast.' This way of reasoning did nothing to calm the hypersensitive assemblymen, for it implied that if the French government were convinced that further technical progress would result from continued tests, it was prepared to go on polluting the southern hemisphere forever.

In keeping with this officially admitted principle, the CEP-CEA detonated a second thermonuclear charge two weeks later on Moruroa as Fangataufa was still too 'hot' to approach. The French technicians had thus, at long last, been able to repeat the 1957 performance of their British colleagues. The only thing that remained for them to do now was to produce a nuclear bomb. For what they had just detonated on Fangataufa and Moruroa was nothing of the sort, and the euphemism used, *ébauche d'engin expérimental* (a rough cast of an experimental device), very imperfectly hid the sad truth that the 'engin' was a big, formless charge. During the next crucial stage of production, this crude device had to be transformed into an operational bomb small enough to be mounted as a warhead on a missile, and hardened enough to pierce the enemy's radar screen. According to the estimates made by the French military technicians themselves, it would take at least four more years to realise this difficult task. The cost was of course astronomical, and at this precise juncture the economic situation in France was disastrous due to the month-long work stoppage during the May revolution. Some savings had to be made and the Minister for Defence, Pierre Messmer, did not hesitate to cut down on non-essentials, announcing that the personnel was to be cut by one-third during the 1969 tests and no navy ships were to be sent out to Polynesia to patrol the danger zone. In return, the budget appropriations for the production of more and better nuclear weapons could be maintained during the coming year at the originally designated level: 6500 million French francs, or roughly $A1100 million.

25 A HUMANITARIAN MEASURE

The year 1968 was memorable, too, because of three anniversaries full of profound regret for all Polynesians. To begin with, exactly twenty years had gone by since they had made their first public demand for internal self-government. Furthermore, ten years had elapsed since Pouvanaa had been imprisoned on trumped-up charges. Finally the military occupation and pollution of Polynesia was five years old.

The Autonomist leaders commemorated this triple anniversary by trying in turn to solve these perennial problems. As we have seen their first attempt was unsuccessful, since their delegation had never been received by the responsible ministers in Paris. Next they had also tried in vain to stop the havoc wrought by the nuclear striking force by legal means. Undaunted by these reverses, during the last quarter of the year they decided to do their utmost to have Pouvanaa liberated. The composition of the new government, appointed by de Gaulle after the landslide victory in the summer of 1968, encouraged them to hope for a slightly more liberal treatment. Their most determined and hateful adversaries, Prime Minister Pompidou and Minister for Overseas Territories Billotte, had been replaced by the suave career diplomat, Couve de Murville, and an obscure deputy named Inchauspé from the Basque provinces near the Spanish border.

By profession Inchauspé was a wool dealer, which was not particularly useful for his ministerial activities in the French overseas territories, where the only existing sheep were black and two-legged. As a matter of fact, he had never been overseas. But in Polynesia, the new minister's complete ignorance was rather favourably commented upon as it might herald a more unbiased approach to their problems. This positive attitude was strengthened when Inchauspé came out to Tahiti shortly after his appointment and proved to be a genial, round-faced man, full of talk and good-humour: the perfect antithesis to his stern, stiff, and ceremonious predecessor, General Billotte. Neither did he keep the Polynesian leaders at respectful distance with the help of an out-dated protocol, as all other Gaullist ministers had done. On the contrary, he invited Teariki, Sanford, and all the other shunned Autonomist leaders to 'a frank discussion of all Polynesian problems'. When greeting them he strongly stressed the fact that he was a Basque and thus a born Autonomist himself. After having listened patiently to their complaints, he even went so far as to admit that 'in April when you were in Paris, the door was closed in your face; but I want to open this door again'.

Francis Sanford took him at his word. On 4 November during the budget session of the National Assembly, he had one of the rare occasions offered him to make an address and he devoted the whole seven minutes at his disposal to plead for Pouvanaa's release, a reform of the colonial system, and a complete stop to the nuclear tests. He described the continued imprisonment of Pouvanaa, now seventy-two years old and partially paralysed, as 'an act unworthy of a great liberal nation like France', and exhorted the French government to give the people of Polynesia at long last the self-rule the leaders of the majority parties were clamouring for. In conclusion he said: 'The nuclear tests have been forced upon us by the military, and we are worried and in constant fear every day of discovering new cases of leukemia and cancer. I know what I am talking about for I am speaking from personal experience. Why has the government never organised a referendum? Why has it condemned us, without a hearing, to becoming guinea pigs to be sacrificed on the altar of the French nuclear striking forces?' The personal experience Sanford was referring to was the recent death from leukemia of his 14-year-old son.

His Basque friend Inchauspé was considerably more vague when replying than during their frank discussions in Papeete, and asserted that 'the CEP is very popular among the islanders and has rendered the inhabitants of the atolls numerous services. I am therefore quite surprised to hear such complaints. But I hope to be able to continue our discussions and to dissipate all misunderstandings.' As for Pouvanaa, the minister stated even more cryptically that he had 'personally investigated the case in Papeete. The government is evaluating the facts in a positive spirit, but in order to find a solution a more dispassionate climate is required.'

Sanford suspected that the mastermind behind this new, more flexible policy was de Gaulle's trusted trickster, Jacques Foccart, still sitting in his office in the Elysée Palace, untouched by all the recent changes within the government. Using the latter's own favourite weapon, a bluff combined with a thinly veiled threat,

Sanford sent Foccart a strongly worded letter the next day, warning him that Pouvanaa had only a few days left and that the news that their *metua* had died in exile was going to have an explosive effect on the Polynesian people. He ended with an ultimatum: Pouvanaa had to be returned alive to Tahiti before 1 December.

This was the right approach. Only four days later, the official news agency, AFP, sent out the following bulletin: 'Looking forward to the Armistice Day celebration, commemorating the 11th November, 1918, General de Gaulle has signed a decree pardoning Mr Pouvanaa a Oopa and abrogating his banishment. The decision can be viewed as a humanitarian measure, particularly appropriate as the beneficiary is a veteran from the 1914–18 war.' This sounded fine in France – provided that anybody was interested in what happened to the Polynesians, which was hardly the case at all. In Polynesia, on the other hand, this attempt to label a political manoeuvre as a 'humanitarian measure' was taken for what it was: pure hypocrisy.

What had finally made the French government release Pouvanaa was above all the negative report of the doctors sent to examine him. They all concurred with Sanford's diagnosis that Pouvanaa was dying. Consequently he was put on a Tahiti-bound aeroplane before the end of the month. As to be expected, the thousands of Polynesians who had flocked to the Faaa airport to greet him in the early morning hours of 30 November 1968 saw a tired old man emerging from the plane, unable to walk down the staircase without the firm support of Francis Sanford and Teariki, who then half carried him across the tarmac to the open, flower-bedecked car. Pouvanaa seemed barely to notice the crowds lining the road and lifted his hand only a few times in thanks for the countless flowers thrown to him. At his destination, the Papeete Town Hall, he sat almost motionless through a cruelly long programme of music, songs and speeches. The most telling proof of how little strength he had left, however, was his own short speech. Nothing could have been more remote from his customary fiery rhetoric than the few stuttering words he uttered, mainly to thank God for his deliverance. He also let it be known that it was more necessary than ever to work together for the common good. His only demand concerned the trumped up charges on which he had been sentenced. He wanted a retrial.

Pouvanaa's simple home was located near the Town Hall. So most of his faithful followers accompanied him there on foot.

Nothing had changed much since the fateful day, 11 October 1958, when he had been taken away. The furniture in the big living room on the ground floor was very sparse, since most members of his family still preferred to sit, sleep, and eat on pandanus mats on the floor. As in all Polynesian homes, however, the middle of the room was occupied by a small, round table covered with a white, knitted cloth upon which lay a Bible in the Tahitian language. Next to it stood the only comfortable chair, in which Pouvanaa sunk down. He bowed his head and closed his eyes. It was obvious to all of the reverently silent onlookers that he had reached the limit of what he could endure.

26 SPRINGTIME, SEASON OF HOPE

Shortly after Pouvanaa's return, the Paris government came to another decision highly appreciated by the people of French Polynesia. It cancelled all nuclear tests planned for 1969. To be sure the decision was dictated solely by a shortage of funds; France was still on the brink of bankruptcy. But who knew, might not this enforced pause give de Gaulle and his ministers enough time to reconsider and eventually give up their whole crazy attempt to outdo the two big superpowers, America and Russia, in the nuclear arms race?

At any rate, for the time being there was only one important demand left on the agenda of the Autonomist leaders, immediate self-government. To their great surprise, at just that time the mass media began to devote more and more space to talk about a new reform, proposed by none less than General de Gaulle himself, and aiming at the decentralisation and democratisation of the whole French administration. The key provision was the transfer of as much power as possible from the technocrats in the various government departments in Paris over to the provincial councils. For once Sanford and Teariki agreed wholeheartedly with de Gaulle, happily pointing out that this was simply another way of phrasing the Autonomists' old request for internal self-government. Their enthusiasm knew no bounds when de Gaulle announced that this reform was to be submitted to the people in the form of a referendum, to be held in early spring, this being 'the season of hope'.

It was not until 4 February 1969, however, that the Territorial Assembly received the first official communication concerning these wonderful plans. Strangely enough it consisted of this short and cryptic letter and nothing more:

Mr Speaker,

        In view of the regional reform I should greatly appreciate receiving from you, not later than the 14th February, a reply to the following question:

        In your opinion, which form of participation by social and

economic groups in local community life does best reflect the spirit of the
regional reform?

> Sincerely yours,
> On behalf of the governor, absent on a mission
> The Secretary-General
> R. Langlois

As everybody knew, Governor Sicurani had been recalled to
Paris to be promoted as a reward for the fine job he had done
during his four-year stint in Polynesia. (Shortly afterwards he was
appointed secretary to the new Prime Minister, Chaban-Delmas.)
The subterfuge that he was 'on a mission' was being used because
no successor had yet been appointed, the difficulty here being the
superabundance of colonial governors out of work and pestering
the minister for this choice post. The assemblymen did not care
who signed the letter but strongly objected to the imperious
injunction to furnish forthwith their opinions about a reform bill
the text of which they had never seen. It did not help them in the
least that the secretary-general sent them a propaganda leaflet the
next day, containing exhortations by de Gaulle and his ministers
to vote for this unspecified reform.

Being extremely reform minded the Territorial Assembly
nevertheless assigned two of its sharpest dialecticians, Henri
Bouvier and Daniel Millaud, the task of producing a report within
the prescribed period. They succeeded in doing so and prefaced it
with a few pertinent questions:

First of all we should like to know who is responsible for the formulation of
the question we are supposed to answer. Is it the secretary-general himself
or is he acting on orders from somebody else?

Moreover it would be useful to have some of the terms contained in this
letter more clearly defined. For instance, what social and economic groups
are being referred to?

Finally, we cannot understand why the author of this letter wants us to
reply 'in the spirit of the regional reform'. Suppose we dislike the spirit in
which this reform is undertaken. As the question is formulated, however,
anything we say will be interpreted as acquiescence on our part.

In the absence of any other guidelines or documents, Bouvier and
Millaud had carefully studied the booklet containing excerpts
from various ministerial speeches. Unfortunately they were
forced to report that they had been unable to discover a single

statement as to how this reform was to be carried out in the French overseas departments and territories. On the other hand there seemed to be no doubt but that de Gaulle wanted to create in metropolitan France large 'regions' made up of two, three, and occasionally more departments, and that considerable powers of decision in social and economic matters were to be given to an elected council in each region. The two assemblymen therefore concluded that to act in the spirit of this reform in the Pacific region implied the creation of such a council, grouping together elected representatives from all the French possessions there, to wit: Polynesia, New Caledonia, and Wallis and Futuna.

But if this were the case why had the secretary-general not said so, instead of talking vaguely about the participation of un-specified social and economic groups *in the local community life*. Bouvier and Millaud had made some investigations of their own and were in a position to be able to inform their fellow assemblymen that these 'social' and 'economic' groups were the Employers Association, the Chamber of Commerce, and a few other business organisations. Or, in other words, the same French and *demi* activists who had protested against the sales tax at the beginning of the year by attacking the Territorial Assembly. To top it all, as Bouvier and Millaud had also found out, these business leaders knew the exact form their participation in the local community life was to take: They were all to sit as *appointed* members in the Territorial Assembly. Needless to say these prospective candidates easily outnumbered the existing, elected representatives of the Polynesian people. Bouvier and Millaud even had in their possession copies of the replies sent to the secretary-general by these businessmen who, of course, were all enthusiastically for a regional reform of this Fascist, corporative type.

The Territorial Assembly immediately asked the secretary-general to appear in person and explain how it came about that de Gaulle's regional reform, tending to decentralise and democratise the administration of the French provinces, had been perverted into a veiled attempt to infiltrate and paralyse the only parliamentary body in French Polynesia. The secretary-general was very sorry but he was so terribly busy that he did not know when he could find time to discuss the matter with them. As it eventually transpired, the poor secretary-general had simply been the front man for the Gaullist delegate for the Pacific, René Tomasini (recently promoted to ministerial rank), who had visited Tahiti at the end of January and explained how the reform was to be implemented locally. So as not to leave the slightest doubt as to where they stood, Bouvier and Millaud produced a second report, simply pointing out that the best and fastest way to achieve a similar decentralisation and democratisation in French Polynesia consisted of granting the territory the form of self-government that the Autonomist parties had been clamouring for since 1948. In the same positive and constructive spirit, they enclosed the detailed fifty-page draft of the desired statute, as it had been elaborated long ago. This motion was adopted on 18 February 1969, by 18 votes against 8.

Two weeks later a successor to Sicurani was appointed. He turned out to be General Billotte's secretarial chief of staff, Pierre Angéli, who had been such an efficient doorkeeper the year before when the Pacific Autonomist delegations had besieged the colonial ministry in Paris. By then the day for the referendum about de Gaulle's regional reform had been set by special decree for 27 April; the opening of the campaigns for or against it were not to begin earlier than 14 April. Nevertheless the first thing the new governor did was to transgress this electoral decree by making a strong appeal to the Polynesian electorate in a TV and radio speech on 4 April, inviting it to vote YES.

He began quite discreetly, saying that although he had just arrived, he was already sure of one fact: that nobody in French Polynesia wanted to sever the existing bonds between the territory and France. 'For her part the mother country considers dear Polynesia to be her favourite child, on whom she is lavishing loving care, aimed at educating her and making her prosperous and happy'. As an example of what France was doing for Polynesia, the governor mentioned the new airstrips recently built on Hao and Mangareva. He could hardly have chosen a worse example, as these airstrips had been built by and for the nuclear striking forces and were closed to all civilian traffic.

Suddenly changing subject and using a style of rhetoric worthy of a Roman pro-consul steeped in Cicero's orations, in the next breath Angéli asked: 'Would it be possible for the Government to fulfil its task without the participation of the elected representatives of the people, without the local population?' Of course the answer was a resounding NO. 'Without the participation of the citizens, the authorities would be helpless. Without the participation of private associations, the administration could do nothing.'

Apparently surprised at the new direction his carefully planned written speech was taking him, the governor made a pause for effect and exclaimed:

Well, it seems that I have let a word of great topicality slip out: participation! As a matter of fact that is what the forthcoming referendum is all about. All citizens are to be consulted and I shall therefore tell you briefly what the real issues are. But do not make the mistake of thinking that I am trying to influence you. Each citizen is to decide freely how to vote. My only intention is to inform you.

Whereupon he launched into an explanation of what the referendum was *not* about: 'As far as the overseas territories are concerned, it is useless to follow the metropolitan model in all respects. In France this so-called "regional reform" implies first and foremost a decentralisation of the administration. Of course such a reform is meaningless in an overseas territory where decentralisation is already a fact.' In other words what the governor was telling us was that French Polynesia had already been given self-government – without its having been noticed by anyone.

Quite logically, he immediately dropped this subject and dealt henceforth with the only local issue: increased citizen participation in the administration of the territory. Just as the assemblymen had feared, this 'participation' was strictly limited to stuffing the Territorial Assembly with a huge number of 'social and economic' representatives, appointed by the governor. The sole aim of this thinly veiled manoeuvre was no doubt to stop the assemblymen once and for all from adopting such obnoxious resolutions as when they had condemned the nuclear tests, asked for an impartial investigation of the radioactive pollution, and insisted on the right of the Polynesian people to run their own affairs.

Quite happy with these prospects, the governor concluded his illegal campaign speech with this poetic but far from intelligible vision:

On the other side of the earth our mother country is sweeping aside the mist and cold. Spring is smoothing out the wrinkles brought on by winter, and nature is coming back to life. But here in Polynesia we are living in the midst of a generous nature, continuously and spontaneously reborn. And everywhere man is striving; but to sustain his efforts, man must have hope, and here in our territory this hope is personified in the fifty thousand children for whom it will be springtime when winter has come for us.

27 DO YOU APPROVE?

The Autonomists strongly disagreed with the governor and felt his speech to be particularly out of season. But there was nothing they could do until 14 April when the campaigns for or against the proposed regional reform officially opened. It then appeared that the question which all French citizens were to answer by a YES or a NO was formulated thus:

Do you approve of the new law proposed by the President of the Republic, General de Gaulle, and aiming at creating new regions and modifying the composition of the Senate?

The text of the new law in question took up more than a dozen pages of fine print and was written in such technical language that only a lawyer could make any sense out of it. As it happened a great number of prominent French jurists protested that it made no sense at all, and a steadily growing number of political leaders (foremost of whom was Giscard d'Estaing) declared themselves openly hostile to this vague and elastic law which, in their opinion, de Gaulle could use in almost any way he liked, if he won. However this might be, it was absolutely certain that it was a grotesque swindle to put an identically worded question up to the poor Polynesians without explaining the very special and peculiar character of the reforms threatening them.

The Autonomists sent Bouvier to the governor's office to investigate what had been done to enlighten the Polynesian voters and these are the key portions of the report he read to his fellow assemblymen on 17 April:

According to decree number 69–296 of the 2nd April, 1969, determining the procedure to be applied during the referendum, the local administration is bound to supply the voters not only with ballots marked YES and NO, but also with the complete text of the proposed bill, in the French and Tahitian languages.

To begin with the local authorities have exceeded the powers conferred upon them by this decree by having printed in French and Tahitian a leaflet entitled *General de Gaulle's explanation of the reasons why he would like to create new regions and modify the Senate*. This is blatant government propaganda, the sole aim of which is to persuade the electorate to vote YES. When I asked the head of the department responsible whether it was

141

possible to have similar propaganda leaflets expressing the opposite view distributed, he replied that, contrary to the usual practice, the local political parties are not allowed to intervene in this campaign. Since we are not allowed to explain to the voters in the remote islands why we think that it is in their interest to vote NO, I propose that we request, of the local administration, the immediate destruction of all of de Gaulle's propaganda leaflets, illegally printed and not yet distributed.

Secondly the administration has been too negligent and restrictive in another respect. The decree clearly stipulates that the complete text of the new law has to be distributed in French and Tahitian. In fact only the French text is supplied and the locally printed edition of it takes up thirteen pages. The corresponding Tahitian translation, however, has shrunk to only *one* page. To top it all this page deals exclusively with the reform of the Senate which is of no interest or importance to us. In other words the Tahitian voter is left completely in the dark as to the true meaning of the 'regional reform', that is that the Territorial Assembly will be swamped with government appointees, to the detriment of the elected representatives of the Polynesian people.

I therefore recommend that the Assembly:
(1) immediately send a telegram to the Council of State protesting against the planned distribution of de Gaulle's 'explanation' to the Polynesian voters.
(2) at the same time inform the Council of State that it is lodging a written formal appeal, based on the failure of the local administration to supply a complete translation of the projected law or bill, as prescribed by law.
(3) ask the governor to see to it that the whole law text be translated at once into Tahitian and distributed throughout the territory, and that the distribution of de Gaulle's 'explanation' be stopped.

The Territorial Assembly did not lose any time in adopting this resolution and a telegram was dispatched to Paris the same day. But the person mainly responsible for these abuses and best placed to correct them, Governor Angéli, was no longer accessible, having just departed along with the secretary-general on a tour of the principal islands in the other groups. Of course, this tour was not designed to distribute any illegal campaign propaganda, but simply to remind the islanders everywhere of what a great leader General de Gaulle was. Thanks to him thousands of millions of francs had flowed into the territory enabling everybody to live better. And had he not recently shown his benevolence by freeing Pouvanaa?

The only civil servant the irate Autonomists managed to catch in the labyrinths of the administration building was a trembling underling who swore that he would do all in his power 'to correct these terrible and quite involuntary mistakes'. Of course it was too late to do anything, there being only one day left before referendum day.

Although the majority of the Polynesian voters on the outer islands never learnt what the issues were and voted YES without knowing what they were doing, those living in Tahiti were better informed thanks to the many meetings organised by the Autonomist parties, and they comprised more than half of the population of French Polynesia. Therefore the final figures were 53 per cent NO and 47 per cent YES votes. As usual their destiny was determined by the outcome of the referendum in France. Luckily the same number of voters there, 53 per cent, rejected de Gaulle's curious reform, and the general had to step down.

In the ensuing presidential elections, Governor Angéli, far from being deterred by this defeat, waged a vigorous campaign for the Gaullist crown prince, Pompidou. Against all odds the Autonomists managed once more to reach a sufficiently large portion of their electorate to ensure a clear victory in French Polynesia for the other candidate, Alain Poher. But this was to no avail since the majority of the French voters cast their ballots for Pompidou. The only gain on the local level was therefore that the new president very wisely threw the ill-conceived regional reform project into the wastepaper basket.

28 HIGH-LEVEL EXPLOSIONS

Those foolish enough to expect a change in France's military objectives with de Gaulle's disappearance from the political scene were quickly undeceived when the new president, Pompidou, appointed Michel Debré, the foremost champion of the nuclear striking force, to the post of minister for defence. During a press conference on 13 November 1969, a jubilant Debré declared that his aim was to catch up as fast as possible on the time lost that year, when no tests had been made for financial reasons.

With his usual pluck, he promised to realise the ultimate goal – a serial production of operational H bombs – in five years. Provided that he was immediately given the money he needed. Pompidou obligingly set aside 27 000 million. (The officially admitted costs of the embryonic striking force so far were 55 000 million French francs – $A1000 million.) The most indignant protests arose from some of the army generals, who bitterly complained that as a result of this option there was not enough money left for the conventional defence forces to protect France's borders.

Although fewer warships than usual were dispatched to Polynesia in 1970, the number of military personnel stationed there quickly reached 10 000 and that of technical personnel 4500. Inclusive of their dependants, this meant an invasion of more than 18 000 persons. According to an official communiqué, not less than eight tests were to be made, including the detonation of one 'experimental hydrogen bomb', and due to this heavy schedule the test series was to begin six weeks earlier than in previous years, – around 15 May. Of course the new minister for defence was coming out in person to witness the big hydrogen blast.

In the past the French authorities had surrounded all testing with a heavy screen of secrecy, which was quite meaningless considering the careful observations made of each test at close quarters by the three 'spy' ships – one Russian, one American, and one British – posted in the waters around Moruroa and Fangataufa. However this year Debré generously invited a dozen French correspondents, representing the most conservative magazines and newspapers, those most likely to produce highly favourable accounts of the great national enterprise towards which the French people had hitherto remained completely indifferent. Thanks to these press reports, we who had been living in the shadow of the atomic mushrooms for five years were gratified to get a few extra details about the perils to which we were constantly being exposed. For instance, the one megatonne hydrogen 'device' to be detonated this time, on 3 July 1970, was suspended sixty metres up in a huge balloon filled with 14 000 cubic metres of helium. At the last minute the 3700 men who had prepared the test were evacuated from the atoll on various vessels. The specially protected warship on which the reporters had been embarked hove to fifty kilometres away. As soon as the thermonuclear charge had been exploded, they were invited to come up on deck and admire what one of the journalists described as 'a stupendously beautiful pillar of fire piercing a perfectly symmetrical mushroom'.

Six hours later the whole party returned to Moruroa and landed at the base camp. The first thing Debré did was to take a swim in the lagoon, a very cheap trick to make the reporters believe the atomic bombs to be harmless, whereas the crucial question is: what happens to people who are exposed to radioactive fallout and eat contaminated food over a long period of time? For instance Debré had nothing to say about how the fifty Tureians, long since back on their island, were faring. According to the *Figaro* of 7 July 1970, when he eventually mentioned the radioactive dangers it was solely to explain how well the fallout behaved under the watchful eyes of the military specialists:

It cannot be denied that these atmospheric nuclear tests increase the radioactive pollution of the air in Polynesia. The problem is to determine the exact amount. This task has been entrusted to the *Service mixte de sécurité radiologique* (SMSR) [*Amalgamated radiological safety service*]. Well in advance of each blast, and taking into account its specific characteristics, this service determines the ensuing level of radioactive pollution and its effect on the population. After an explosion it measures the actual amount of fallout and makes a forecast as to the size of the area over which it will spread. The method used is the following: Before the blast the SMSR specialists are given certain data as to the strength of the bomb and the exact time of the scheduled explosion. Simultaneously they receive a stream of weather reports, which start to become reliable forty-eight hours in advance. With the help of all this information, they determine the geometrical form of the nuclear cloud and the amount of radioactive fallout it will contain. In the present case they have predicted that the fallout will take place at an altitude of 30 kilometres and within a rectangle 2100 kilometres long and 1500 kilometres wide.

Like all French ministers to pass through Tahiti before him, Debré seemed little interested in informing the members of the Territorial Assembly about what was happening and what he had in store for the colony. So once more they took the initiative and invited him to come over when convenient to him for 'a discussion of topical problems'. The day after the big bang, Debré replied in keeping with the standard formula used by all of his predecessors to the effect that unfortunately his many previous engagements prevented him from attending a regular session of the Assembly; but they were all cordially invited to meet him in the governor's residence on 5 July just before his departure.

Of course, what was said during an informal 'encounter' was never recorded. Being well aware of this regrettable oversight several Autonomist assemblymen made discreet notes of their own and published a full account afterwards in number 78–79 of Teariki's magazine, *Pupu here aia,* of which there was still no Tahitian edition. These are the essential portions:

The 'encounter' began at 10.40 a.m. in the presence of some thirty persons, among whom were a dozen assemblymen, several high ranking civil servants, some members of Debré's entourage, and a few CEP and CEA bosses. Aside from a photographer who took three pictures before disappearing, the press was not represented. To offset this the secret police had been invited. The encounter was very brief, lasting not more than an hour and ten minutes, from which twenty minutes are to be deducted for Debré's opening speech.

The Autonomists' spokesman was Henri Bouvier, who began by regretting that the meeting did not take place publicly in the Territorial Assembly and then went on to examine Debrés assertions point by point. The first one concerned the minister's statement that the whole population of French Polynesia – with the possible exception of a few separatists – was strongly attached to France. 'Personally I have never encountered any separatists among the assemblymen', replied Bouvier. 'But to speak truthfully, Monsieur le ministre, a current is moving in favour of independence, and it is quite a strong one.'

Next Bouvier contested Debré's version of how and why the French striking force had been created. The minister had stated that, during the 19th century, France had had the largest population in Europe, which explained its being so powerful that no other country alone had been able to conquer it. During the present century, however, the population had declined, mostly due to a falling birth rate; therefore it had become necessary to compensate for this numerical inferiority in troops by having recourse to qualitatively superior weapons. This was why General de Gaulle had decided to use atomic energy for military purposes. Debré had concluded: 'Today our striking force is so powerful that no other country on earth dares to attack France'.

Bouvier retorted that a nation's military might was still basically determined by quantitative factors. What counted yesterday was the size of armies. What counts today is the number and size of the atomic bombs a nation can muster. A deterrent exists when two powers, such as Russia and America, have attained a balance of terror, but such is not the relationship existing between France and one or the other of these two powers. And Bouvier added, textually: 'We do not believe, Monsieur le ministre, that France will ever be able, now or later on, with a few atomic fire crackers at her disposal, to prevent the Russian or the American superpowers from attacking France, and we are convinced that it would be sheer suicide on the part of your government to use an atomic weapon against these enemies'.

These objections had an explosive effect comparable to a thermonuclear blast in the megatonne range. Debré began to tremble, his face became convulsed, and he shouted angrily at the top of his voice: 'Monsieur Bouvier, I forbid you to speak like this and I warn you that, if you continue to talk about our defence in this manner, I will put an end to this meeting and leave the room'.

Without stopping to breathe, he next began to enumerate all the benefits French industry had derived from nuclear research, mentioning as an example the heart stimulator. Bouvier was ready with his answer, based on a recent report of the French National Research Centre, criticising the stupid waste of money and brain power resulting from the French military technicians' attempts to rediscover processes invented twenty years earlier by atomic scientists in other countries. Not only had they failed in their main task but this concentration on military programmes had hampered more utilitarian scientific research in France.

Debré declared that this was a childish way of reasoning and mentioned as an example of a nation that was lagging behind France because it was not developing a nuclear striking force – Germany.

Bouvier smiled but deemed it more useful to change the subject and asked Debré what had been done to protect the people of French Polynesia against radioactive fallout. If the dip he had taken in the lagoon was meant to show that the tests were completely harmless, he should draw the logical conclusion from this and make them henceforth in France. This excellent suggestion's being received with sullen silence by the minister for defence, Bouvier next wanted to know why the French National Radiation Laboratory was not allowed to extend its activities to Polynesia. Why, instead, had the important task of probing air, sea, soil and food for radioactive matter been entrusted to the so-called *Service mixte de sécurité radiologique (SMSR)*, consisting of army personnel? Furthermore, why had the French government never replied to the Territorial Assembly's repeated request to allow an international control commission to visit French Polynesia? If, as the French government insisted, no dangerous radioactive pollution had occurred, was it not in its own interests to let impartial radiologists furnish incontrovertible proofs?

Somewhat surprised by all these insolent questions, Debré appealed to the CEA and CEP directors sitting in a corner. But these had nothing to say, and seemed scared to death. It was eventually one of the other Autonomist leaders, Daniel Millaud, who broke the long, embarrassing silence. He regretted with convincing sincerity that de Gaulle's regional reform had come to nothing in France and declared that in French Polynesia there was still a majority for a thorough decentralisation and democratisation of the administrative system. Visibly relieved by the discussion's new orientation, Debré assured his flabbergasted audience that, in his opinion, it was 'perfectly normal in a territory in rapid economic and social evolution such as French Polynesia to confer upon the elected representatives of the people all the powers they needed to solve their own problems themselves'.

Of course, as Debré explained, he could not do much personally to promote such a reform, since it was the responsibility of the minister for overseas territories. The fact that the Basque Autonomist Inchauspé had been sacked and replaced by the UDR whip in the National Assembly, Henry Rey, had not affected the open door policy that was the hallmark of the Pompidou government. The new minister had decided to visit French Polynesia in the near future and Debré was convinced that he would listen attentively and sympathetically to their complaints and suggestions.

29 HOW TO CATCH A MINISTER

Three weeks later, on 1 August 1970, a short dispatch from the official French news agency, AFP, appeared in the local press informing us about the date of arrival of the new minister for overseas territories, Henry Rey and the programme during his visit. He was to fly out on a UTA plane on 11 September and embark the same day on a warship bound for the remote and isolated Marquesas Islands, 700 nautical miles north-east of Tahiti. From the Marquesas he was to return to Tahiti by military plane late in the afternoon of 16 September. The next day he was to conclude his visit by inaugurating a school and a swimming pool in Tahiti and by making a quick trip to the neighbouring island of Moorea for an unspecified purpose.

The members of the Territorial Assembly were greatly surprised by this unusual programme which did not include any meeting with them. Francis Sanford expressed the common opinion in the following angry statement distributed to the press:

I accuse the French government of treating the Polynesian people and us, their elected representatives, with disdain and mockery . . . Other Polynesian and Melanesian peoples have obtained self-government (witness the Cook islands) or become completely independent states such as Nauru, Samoa, and Fiji! The French government is making a terrible mistake by refusing to negotiate with the Polynesian majority parties, and its prestige will suffer, not only here but abroad as well. By acting in this manner President Pompidou shows that he intends continuing with the policy followed by ex-President de Gaulle and that he has already forgotten the lesson of the referendum. Yet the fact that the majority of the electorate in both metropolitan France and French Polynesia voted NO proves that most people are tired of Gaullist rule.

The minister for overseas territories will be visiting Polynesia in three weeks' time. Why does he want to spend several days in the Marquesas Islands? Is it to see whether they can be used for underground nuclear testing? I should not be too surprised, for we are often confronted with an accomplished act. Furthermore it seems that he will not be able to spare a few minutes for a meeting with us. There is a limit to what we can accept, however, and this limit has now been reached.

Paris sensed that Sanford was speaking for the vast majority of Polynesian leaders. So, in a face-saving manoeuvre the minister for overseas territories dispatched a 'final and detailed version' of the schedule for his forthcoming visit in which figured a hitherto unmentioned 'encounter' between the minister and the elected representatives of Polynesia.

But as he stepped off the plane on 11 September, a ridiculous quarrel arose over a simple question of protocol. Should the assemblymen come over to the governor's residence to greet the minister, or was it up to the minister to walk over to the brand new Territorial Assembly building and greet them there? The governor maintained that the first alternative was the only proper and acceptable one, whereas of course the assemblymen were of exactly the opposite opinion. Minister Rey settled the matter in the most offensive fashion: he let the assemblymen wait in vain and sailed off to the Marquesas Islands.

The next thing they heard from him was that he had made a speech in the small village of Taiohae on Nukuhiva, a speech ending in a firm refusal to make any reforms whatsoever. This did not create much of a stir among the few Marquesans who had gathered, for they were exclusively interested in such practical problems as copra prices and inter-island communications. But this oblique manner of dialoguing with them made the sorely tried assemblymen in Papeete see red.

However they had to wait until 9 a.m. on 17 September – the date and hour set by Rey himself for an encounter – to tell him face to face what they thought about these elusive tactics. But when they arrived for the meeting, with briefcases bulging with their detailed proposals for a new statute granting the territory full self-government, they found no minister in the meeting room but only the following letter:

Papeete, 16th September, 1970

Mr Speaker:

During my present visit to Polynesia the assemblymen representing the majority parties have been absent on all occasions, even though they had personally approved of the programme in advance.

Consequently I have decided not to attend the 'in committee' discussion planned for tomorrow. A minister representing the French government cannot tolerate constant changes for unacceptable motives in a programme relating to an official voyage being undertaken by him in a territory belonging to the Republic.

To show my eagerness to work hand in hand with the genuine representatives of the Polynesian people for the general good I invite all assemblymen to attend the previously agreed upon meeting tomorrow in the governor's residence.

Sincerely yours,

Henry Rey

The meeting in question was of course to be a non-committal 'encounter' which moreover coincided with their own deliberations; so the assemblymen preferred to stay and debate the problem that was the main item on their agenda: the urgency of replacing the old colonial statute with a completely new system of government. Looking out through the window Francis Sanford saw the three recently installed flagpoles and hit upon an excellent idea: Why not hoist the three flags symbolising their political dilemma? The first one was the French tricolour, meaning that they wished to keep certain ties with France. The second was the United Nations flag, recalling the promise contained in the charter to grant all dependent peoples their freedom. The third and last was the Tahitian red-white-red flag, a beautiful reminder that their aim was to rule Tahiti in keeping with Tahitian custom.

Sanford's suggestion was immediately adopted with great enthusiasm. Thus it happened that a little later on, right in the middle of a press conference, Minister Rey's eye was caught by the sight of an unknown red-white-red flag fluttering from a pole between the governor's residence and the Territorial Assembly. He tersely told the governor to put an end to this abominable spectacle. It proved more difficult than expected, for no matter how hard he and his staff searched through the *Journal Officiel* they could find no laws or decrees forbidding display of the century-old Tahitian flag. But never at a loss when it came to twisting the law, Angéli eventually had recourse to a decree from 1932 forbidding the use of political emblems – and what was a flag if not an 'emblem'? Without losing any more precious time, the governor phoned over to the speaker of the Assembly and enjoined him to haul down the two foreign emblems, leaving only the French tricolour.

The speaker politely reminded him that, in keeping with the tenets of the existing statute, all official communications had to be made in writing. Just as soon as they had received and duly recorded a letter from the governor, the whole matter would of course be put on the agenda. However, the speaker said, he very much doubted himself that the 1932 decree in question applied in the present instance – Au revoir, Monsieur le gouverneur.

30 PORTENTOUS OVERSIGHT

Since the minister for overseas territories was so much in favour of brief, informal, improvised encounters, the Autonomist assemblymen decided to show up for a last chat with him at the airport on the day of his departure, 18 September 1970. To make sure of getting in at least one word, they put on their specially made T-shirts in the Tahitian colours, across the chest of which was printed in big letters AUTONOMIE INTERNE (internal self-government). The local Gaullists parried by dispatching a group of militants dressed in tricoloured T-shirts marked POLYNESIE FRANCAISE. Alarmed at this sudden invasion of the airport, the governor ordered out not only the gendarmes but also the regular troops in combat dress, to occupy all strategic points. When Minister Rey and Governor Angéli arrived at 7.15 a.m. the crowd waiting for them in the terminal building had grown to such proportions that the gendarmes had a hard time keeping a narrow opening clear through it. Sanford and Teariki had taken up positions at the farthest end of this corridor, flanked by party members carrying both Tahitian and French flags.

Looking straight ahead with jaws defiantly thrust out, Rey and Angéli marched quickly through the crowd and stopped not far from the spot where the Autonomists were standing. At the same moment the head of the Thought Police (*Renseignements Généraux*), Arrighi, leaned over towards the captain of the gendarmes, Pigaglio, and whispered something into his ear. It was evidently an order, for Pigaglio marched right over to the nearest Autonomist holding a staff with a Tahitian flag in his hand, grabbed it, broke it, threw it on the ground, and trampled it under his feet. Before anybody had time to react, he gathered up the flag again and began walking towards the public toilets, loudly asking: 'Where is the W.C.?' Rightly furious, a Tahitian bearing a French flag threw it on the ground and began to trample it under his feet. Several other Tahitians followed his example, while many more tried to push their way up to the front rank, with threatening gestures. They were stopped by Francis Sanford and Teariki who shouted to them that the whole incident was a planned provocation and warned them not to attack the well-armed gendarmes. At about this point, the minister, his staff, and the governor discreetly slipped through a side door out to the fenced-off tarmac.

Upon Teariki's and Sanford's insistence, the Autonomists eventually consented to drive back to town where they gathered again around the three flagpoles outside the Assembly hall. They first hoisted the Tahitian flag and as it unfurled and began to flutter in the wind, it was greeted with a tremendous roar from the crowd. After a short silence a familiar voice began to express the pent up anger everybody felt. The speaker was a short, plump, grey-haired man whom nobody had seen in public for two years – Pouvanaa! Since he had been sent home to die in 1968, he had slowly recuperated, and was now ready to do battle again. He was more eloquent than ever and harangued the crowd for half an hour. What he and all the succeeding speakers asked for was the exemplary punishment of the two French police officers. The same demand was repeated a few hours later in a formal manner by the Permanent Committee of the Territorial Assembly.

By then the governor was counterattacking on two fronts. To begin with he sent over a police detachment to the now empty courtyard of the Assembly hall, equipped with a brand new decree, forbidding the hoistening of any flag other than the French tricolour on public buildings. The offending Tahitian and UN flags were consequently hauled down and confiscated. At the same time a long letter was handed to the Permanent Committee contesting the version of the events it had given. The governor wrote:

You are pretending that these events took place in my presence and that of the minister. In other words you are insinuating that the minister and I remained passive spectators while this incident occurred. I categorically deny this accusation. It is true that I noticed a certain agitation when the minister and I entered the terminal building, but at no time did I witness a 'flag incident' of the sort alleged. This leads me to believe that many of the other allegations made by your Permanent Committee are likewise of the same doubtful veracity.

With tongue in cheek the president of the Permanent Committee replied:

We have asserted that the incident took place in your own and the minister's *presence*, but we have never said or insinuated that you actually *saw* it since in order to have done so you would have had to be looking in the right direction, which was not the case. In keeping with my own observations and those of all the witnesses I have talked to, both the minister and you yourself stared straight ahead, without the slightest doubt, I suppose, in order not to see us Autonomists standing on your left. Nonetheless the 'certain agitation' you mention was in fact caused by this flag incident, and this allusion to it proves that both you and the minister were present.

The governor maintained that the assemblymen's act of accusation was based mainly on hearsay and that there was no justification whatsoever for sanctioning the two police officers. All five of the elected members of the Government Council had witnessed the incident and insisted that the version made public by the Permanent Committee was correct. When the governor still refused to discuss the matter, they angrily walked out, slamming the door behind them. Unfortunately that was all they could do; for, according to the existing rules, the governor was sole master of the agenda. Therefore the outcome of the whole affair was that both Arrighi and Pigaglio carried on as before.

On the same day that the local newspapers reported the governor's cover-up, they also printed on the first page a statement made by Minister for Overseas Territories Henry Rey upon his return to Paris. He had told the metropolitan reporters that 'there are no political problems in French Polynesia. I have carefully explained this to the local leaders and also stressed how scrupulously the French government has kept all its promises.'

31 COMMISSIONER ARRIGHI'S LAST BATTLE

With these subversive elements in the Territorial Assembly, Commissioner Arrighi considered it his duty to keep a more careful watch over them and ordered two of his most able agents to attend the parliamentary debates thenceforth. The utility of this measure is not immediately apparent as all of the debates in the Assembly are public and recorded in mimeographed minutes, available on request. However very little brainwork is needed to see that these printed records are very unsatisfactory documents inasmuch as they say nothing, for instance, about the wry faces and deprecatory gestures that a speaker may have made. Neither do they indicate whether a speech was made in an insinuating or offensive tone of voice. Evidently only trained agents in the audience could furnish this sort of valuable information. Unfortunately for them, most of the time Arrighi's men happened to make up the whole of the audience in the section reserved for the public, and were therefore spotted at once. Not even when they cleverly tried to disguise themselves by putting on dark sunglasses did their true identity escape the assemblymen.

These latter were definitely more amused than angered by these childish antics and, just for the fun of it, decided to play the shamming game to the hilt. Consequently they asked Arrighi on 30 October 1970 how it came about that two policemen attended the debates in the Assembly during their working hours. It was of course out of the question that, in a free, democratic country, they did so on orders from their boss. So the only possible explanation was that they were neglecting their beats or offices in order to satisfy their personal curiosity about the functioning of the democratic system. Although greatly flattered by this evident desire for self-improvement displayed by these agents, the assemblymen nevertheless felt compelled to draw the police commissioner's attention to this flagrant dereliction of duty.

The two agents promptly disappeared. But the assemblymen were never able to find out whether the reason was that, in spite of all appearance, the police commissioner possessed a certain sense of humour, for not long afterwards he left the territory himself. It looked like a solid victory for the Assembly, but just the opposite was true. Arrighi had been rewarded for his excellent work – with

156

a two-month holiday in France. The Assembly was no longer amused. Upon his return in February, 1971, its Permanent Committee adopted the following motion:

It is widely known that the Head of the Thought Police (*Renseignement Généraux*), Commissioner Arrighi, after leave of absence, has now come back for the express purpose of preparing the forthcoming election campaign of the pro-governmental candidate for the office of Mayor of Papeete. The aim of the present motion is to try to shed some light on the political activities of the administration. Towards realising this goal, we request that Governor Angéli inform us about:

(1) the true character of his own and Commissioner Arrighi's political roles,

(2) the laws and decrees permitting or obliging them to intervene in local politics.

Of course nobody expected the governor to give a frank answer. As it was, he replied in the usual manner, simply saying that he was not accountable to the Assembly, but only to the minister for overseas territories.

It was easy to understand why the Paris government took – to put it mildly – such a keen interest in the elections for the renewal of the Papeete city council scheduled for 2 May 1971. The outcome, important in itself, would also determine the senatorial elections to take place later in the year. French senators are elected for nine years by a limited number of qualified electors, mostly town and county councillors. At this time there were only two towns in French Polynesia, Papeete and Uturoa, and two municipalities, Pirae and Faaa. Therefore, if the incumbent senator, Alfred Poroi, were to be re-elected, he must first recapture the Papeete town council that he had lost in 1966. The outlook seemed quite good, for the number of French troops, technicians, civil servants, and businessmen living, working, and voting in Papeete had greatly increased during the past five years and they were all strongly inclined to vote for the openly 'pro-French' candidate, Poroi. The great question mark lay with the thousands of Polynesians who had migrated to Papeete from the outer islands during the same period, either recruited by the CEP-CEA or tempted by all the fabulous stories they had heard about life in the big city. Living in miserable corrugated iron shacks in fetid slum areas, they were more likely to vote for the pro-Tahitian list of Teariki and Sanford. Therefore the main task of the propaganda machine set up by the governor and Arrighi was to persuade these rootless and ignorant new voters – whose exact number nobody knew – to go to the polls and cast a ballot with Poroi's name. The result was an even more resounding defeat for Poroi than during the previous election. The Autonomists took all the twenty-seven seats in the town council, and the incumbent mayor, Tetua Pambrun, remained in office. It was hardly a coincidence that Arrighi was ordered to return to France for good, less than a week after this defeat.

This meant that Poroi might just as well give up for lost his seat as senator. Very wisely he did not even try to stand again and on election day, 26 September 1971, the choice stood between a Gaullist councillor, Emile Le Caill and Pouvanaa. It did not take the 111 electors more than five minutes to cast their ballots, and when they were counted, Pouvanaa had won with 74 votes as against 37 for Le Caill. The senator made the following brief declaration:

I continue to demand a re-trial to prove that I was framed in 1958. The fact that the people's representatives have elected me senator does not constitute a rehabilitation, for I was not condemned by the people, but by the government. My political career began fifty years ago, on the very day that I got back from the Great War. I had discovered that there existed a greater liberty and democracy in our home-country, France, than in Polynesia. The reason why I stood as candidate in this election, in spite of my age and my impaired health, is that the freedom for the Polynesian people that I have been fighting for all my life has not yet been won.

32 MASS MEDIA FOR THE FEW

By then the vagrant and elusive Henry Rey had been sacked and the ministry for overseas territories entrusted to the firm and hardhitting Pierre Messmer, a former army officer and minister for defence. In Tahiti this change was generally interpreted as a bad omen, a sure indication that Pompidou was going to use tougher methods against the recalcitrant Autonomists. Against all expectations Messmer began with a public declaration that it was high time to give the Polynesians the constitutional means to run their own affairs. It soon appeared, however, that what the new minister had in mind was not at all the reforms for which the Autonomists were clamouring, but rather an innovation with the effect of diminishing the powers of the Territorial Assembly in favour of a huge number of communal or county councils, to be created according to rules laid down by the French government!

When the new law was obligingly enacted by the Gaullist majority in the French National Assembly, the Polynesian assemblymen immediately appealed to the State Council to have it invalidated, arguing that articles 40 and 74 of the constitution had been violated. The only result was to postpone its application for two months. Therefore it was not until 16 March 1972 that the governor was able to convene the Territorial Assembly to an extraordinary session to announce the great news that he had a free hand to impose the hated 'liberal reform law'. He took this opportunity to inform them about another important decision of the French government: they were to be allowed to participate in the great national referendum being organised by President Pompidou to find out what the French people thought about the entrance of Great Britain, Ireland and Denmark into the European Common Market. Instead of feeling greatly honoured the Polynesian assemblymen received this news with marked coldness. The only portion of the governor's speech that brought forth a favourable reaction among them was the word 're-ferendum', and several of them formally requested that the Polynesian people be allowed to express, through a referendum, whether they were for or against the proposed law creating new counties, which concerned them a thousandfold more than the organisation of the Common Market in Europe.

Before receiving a clear answer to this request, Pompidou's meaningless referendum was imposed as per the original scenario, not only in France but in Polynesia as well. Since the inclusion of Great Britain, Ireland, and Denmark had already been accepted by the Common Market Commission in Brussels, Pompidou actually used this referendum as a sort of popularity test, without admitting to doing so. As a result few Frenchmen understood what it was all about, and fewer still cared to go to the polls. The Polynesians, who had hardly heard of the Common Market at all, were even less interested in Pompidou's strange political manoeuvres. The poor governor appealed desperately to their civic sense, as well as to their bellies, by claiming that many imported goods would become cheaper; but he failed utterly this time. Fifty-six per cent of the local voters stayed home and the pro-European votes cast represented only 30 per cent of the total electorate. The corresponding figures in France were 40 and 35 per cent.

During all these elections and referenda, the Tahitian leaders bitterly complained about the tight government control of the official radio and TV station, which prevented them from communicating with the electorate in the other island groups. Although the existing laws guaranteed all political parties free and equal access to these important communication media, the governor invariably managed, as we have seen, to ban the Autonomists from the studios year after year. Not until 19 December 1967, however, when the local Gaullists, too, found reason to complain about the governor's high-handed policies, did the Assembly unite and attack in force. The motion unanimously adopted on this occasion read:

Article 40 of decree number 57–812 of the 22nd July, 1957 stipulates that 'an agreement concerning the use of the radio station within the territory is to be signed between the Territorial Assembly and the State'. To this end we hereby request the Government Council to submit such an agreement for the approval of our Assembly, setting the terms and conditions determining which elected bodies are to be allowed to use the radio and TV to inform the population about their activities.

It is likewise our opinion that the political parties should be allowed to use these modern mass media during each election to inform the voters about their programmes. Why not also organise radio and TV debates on the French model with political leaders and journalists grouped together around the same table? We see no reason why we French citizens of Polynesia should be denied these means of expressing our opinions, freely available to our fellow citizens in France. Who has determined that we Polynesians are unable to debate our problems in a peaceful and dignified manner? Possibly to start with our programme may not be formally perfect, but we shall soon learn the technique. Everybody who is for progress must share our conviction that the realisation of our proposal would provide the population with impartial information and promote interest in public affairs.

The motion was signed by all five parties represented in the Territorial Assembly.

With unusual speed the governor replied on 12 January 1968, but only to say:

Mr Speaker,

You recently forwarded the text of a motion adopted by your Assembly on the 19th December, 1967, concerning the utilisation of the local ORTF radio and TV station.

I immediately dispatched the whole file to the Minister for Overseas Territories, asking him to contact the general board of the ORTF in Paris, which alone is competent to conclude such an agreement concerning the utilisation of the local station in Tahiti.

Jean Sicurani

Six months later the general board in Paris had not even taken the trouble to acknowledge receipt of this request. The assemblymen unanimously adopted a new motion reminding the authorities in considerably less polite terms about their wilful neglect. And since the Government Council had not produced any draft of an agreement, they decided to draw one up themselves. It was duly forwarded to the governor who quietly buried it in his special drawer for embarrassing enquiries.

The assemblymen were so disgusted that they did not make another try for four years until the end of 1972, when the Assembly came to term and had to be renewed. This territorial election was of far greater importance than all preceding presidential elections and referenda, which had little or nothing to do with local problems. Thus the battle for control over the broadcast media was resumed with new vigour. The Autonomists, who had a majority in the Assembly and consequently had selected the five members of the executive Government Council, ordered this latter to present a motion asking for daily time on the radio and TV for all local parties for the duration of the campaign. They did this on 16 August, twenty-five days before election day, which by then had been set for 10 September. The governor retorted that the director of the local station had no power to grant the request. It must be addressed to the general management of ORTF in Paris. Of course no reply had arrived by the time the Government Council next met a week later. To top it all, the governor told them that he had been called to Paris 'for consultations' – which meant in clear language that he was going to receive instructions from his bosses in the colonial ministry as to how to 'handle' the forthcoming elections. This time these instructions included strict orders to ban *all* local political leaders from radio and TV.

This might appear a bit more fair to the Autonomists, considering that they alone had been banned in the past. But although the Gaullist leaders were no longer admitted into the studios, their propaganda got through nevertheless, with the help of the governor and other officials who suddenly felt an urge to 'inform' the population over the air about everything France did for Polynesia. On the other hand Senator Pouvanaa and Deputy Sanford were not allowed to say anything about the same issue. As a matter of fact they were not allowed to say anything at all. Several times they tried to get around the ban by calling press conferences. But each time their long speeches were reduced to one-minute summaries delivered by an ORTF reporter. On the TV screen, as a rule, a still portrait accompanied these official digests; or, if on some rare occasions motion pictures were shown, they were silent and the necessary comments were again supplied by an ORTF reporter. In the outer islands the government radio propaganda was reinforced and supplemented by the many CEP and CEA agents who had fast ships and aeroplanes at their disposal and could thus visit and explain to the voters the tremendous benefits they reaped from de Gaulle's nuclearisation of Polynesia. The army officers and technicians were moreover allowed to vote in these local elections, as well as the more than 10 000 civilian Frenchmen who had settled in Polynesia since 1963, attracted by the wonderful opportunities of making money by working for the army and selling goods and services to the troops. Last but not least the creation of new counties weakened the position of the Autonomist parties, which suddenly found themselves confronted by six 'apolitical' lists, put together by the new mayors and county councillors.

As a result of all this government propaganda, the considerable increase in the number of French electors, and the secret manipulations of the new 'grass-root' politicians, the Gaullist parties won two seats, reaching a total of nine. Three winners were independents, who had the new mayors and county officials to thank for their victory. Charles Taufa and two other trade unionists also secured seats in the Assembly. This left fifteen seats won by the two Autonomist parties *Pupu here aia* and *Te ea api*. When shortly afterwards one of these Autonomist assemblymen changed sides following a dispute with a party colleague, a jubilant governor took to the air to announce that the election had furnished clear proof that the Polynesian people had rejected for good the Autonomist' dangerous policy leading to a separation from France.

33 SANFORD IS 'MESSMERISED'

President Pompidou was legally bound to call for new general elections not later than March 1973 and he preferred waiting until the last minute, in the hope that by then the French voters would have forgotten about all the financial scandals involving prominent Gaullists that had shaken popular confidence in his government. With the same purpose in mind in July 1972, he dismissed his prime minister, Chaban-Delmas, who had outraged public opinion by his clever use of legal loopholes to avoid paying any income tax at all for several years in a row.

To replace Chaban-Delmas as prime minister Pompidou chose Foreign Legion officer Pierre Messmer, the complete antithesis of all the smart politicians who had given the party such a bad reputation. Messmer's whole bearing and appearance testified to his rectitude. His back was like a ramrod and his gaze unblinkingly straight ahead. When he moved about he did not walk or stroll but marched in perfect time. His most relaxed position was a stiff standing at attention. No doubt this was all reassuring. Unfortunately Messmer suffered from a rather serious handicap: he was completely devoid of the intellectual qualities required for the difficult job with which he had been entrusted. In view of the impending elections Pompidou's choice seemed even more inappropriate, for Messmer was such an inept speaker, always sounding as though reciting a text learned by heart, that his audience rarely listened for more than a few minutes and never remembered a word of what he had said.

During the territorial elections in French Polynesia in September 1972 the Autonomist candidates had polled 14 949 votes as against 13 359 for all the other candidates taken together. How then to assure the victory of the approved Gaullist candidate Flosse over the arch-Autonomist Sanford during the forthcoming election? As he had been minister both for defence and for overseas territories, Messmer was thoroughly familiar with the political situation in Polynesia and soon came up with a seemingly perfect answer: the thing to do was to increase the number of Gaullist voters. How? Very simple: the 3000 Chinese who had become French citizens following de Gaulle's recognition of Communist China in 1964 had all shown their gratitude by regularly voting for the Gaullist candidates; but there was still a residue of 1600 Chinese who had obtained their citizenship papers too late to be entitled to vote yet. Nobody, not even the Chinese concerned, had ever criticised this as being unfair. But in November 1972 the Paris government suddenly discovered 'that the populations in the overseas territories were still being ruled by anachronistic colonial laws and decrees for which there was no longer any justification'. This was exactly what the Polynesian Autonomists had been saying for years. But it soon became apparent that the only unfair law the minister for overseas territories wanted to change was the one setting a five-year limit to the voting prerogative of new French citizens of Chinese extraction. Sanford and many other deputies strongly objected to this blatant attempt at increasing the Polynesian electorate by 1600 new Gaullist voters just in time for the general election in March 1973. However their protests were in vain since, as usual, all the Gaullist deputies to a man voted in favour of the bills proposed by the government.

Shortly afterwards, by a seeming coincidence that deceived nobody, the Chinese Embassy in Paris dispatched several advisers to Tahiti. This was the first time since the establishment of diplomatic relations in 1964 that the Peking regime had taken any notice of the Chinese community in Tahiti, an easily understandable lack of interest considering that the Chinese there had either acquired French citizenship or remained faithful followers of Chiang Kai Shek. So why send out this diplomatic mission now to a French colony where there were no citizens of Communist China? The only possible explanation of this enigma was the promptitude with which these 1600 Tahitian Chinese registered their names on the electoral records.

Sanford protested against these unsavoury manoeuvres and predicted that the Polynesian people would soon become so fed up that they would come to prefer independence in spite of the high price they would have to pay for their freedom. This made the governor furious, and upon orders from Paris he threatened to impose two slightly contradictory sanctions:
(1) the French government was ready to suppress with force all independence movements, and
(2) all French economic aid would be cut off immediately upon Polynesia's becoming independent.

As usual the government campaign for the Gaullist candidate, Gaston Flosse, began long before the official opening date. This time the main propagandist was the minister for overseas territories in person, who, since Messmer's promotion to prime ministership, was a colourless, ungainly bureaucrat endowed with, for Polynesians, the complete tongue-twister of a name of Xavier Deniau. Though visibly afflicted by the heat, Deniau doggedly made a complete tour of the principal islands dressed in a woollen suit and gloves to tell his scanty audiences about the huge sums of money that France would be lavishing on the islands if they remained French.

Likewise, in keeping with a long established pattern, on his return from the islands Deniau gave a glowing account of his visit:

Nobody has in any way criticised the nuclear tests. Nor have I heard anybody talk about independence. This word is taboo and was never mentioned during the many discussions I had with various groups, representing both left and right. There may be a current in favour of certain political reforms, but there are no separatists in the islands. Quite the opposite – and my conclusions are based on my recent personal contacts – I have a feeling that the peoples in our overseas territories are above all afraid that France will abandon them.

Quite unexpectedly the person who objected most strongly to this falsification of the facts was Pierre Messmer. The reason for his dissatisfaction was obvious to everybody except to the elephantine Deniau. The government's main strategy was to depict Sanford, Teariki, and Pouvanaa as anti-French separatists leading their people towards impending disaster. Therefore, within hours, the French government news agency AFP broadcast the following 'clarification': 'The true significance of this election is clear. The electors must make up their minds whether they want to belong to the French Republic or not. The Communists and the Autonomists are striving for the same goal: they want the overseas territories to secede from France.' Of course the identification of Autonomists with Communists was motivated by the general dislike among the Christian Polynesians of godless Communist tenets. As a matter of fact the only Communists in French Polynesia at that time were a few French servicemen and French technicians working for the CEP and CEA.

When at long last the election campaign was officially opened, Francis Sanford stood again with John Teariki as his proxy. As expected the Gaullist party presented their chairman, Gaston Flosse, and at the last minute the young trade union leader,

Charles Taufa, also decided to run. The issues at stake were few and very simple. Sanford was as bitterly opposed as ever to the nuclear tests, whereas Flosse was all for them on the grounds that they brought prosperity. Taufa wisely avoided the issue altogether. As for the perennial problem of the statute, there was a difference of degree. Sanford wanted effective self-government, Taufa took up the old RDPT cry of Polynesia for the Polynesians, while Gaston Flosse made several statements that might be interpreted as an approval of Taufa's stand.

Still banned during the campaign from radio and television studios, the three candidates had to depend on their luck in finding ships and planes to take them to the outer islands. As so many times before, Gaston Flosse and his lieutenants had the greatest luck, repeatedly being given free passage by the administration and the navy. Of course Francis Sanford was the least successful candidate in this respect and got no further than the Leeward Islands.

On election day, 4 March 1973, the French officers, soldiers, sailors, technicians, civil servants, settlers, and businessmen as usual cast their votes massively for the Gaullist candidate. The Chinese followed suit and in keeping with Messmer's scenario their number was swelled by the 1600 newly enfranchised voters. However, Sanford was helped by the demographic factor. Thanks to the high birthrate (4 per cent) among the Polynesians, this ethnic group had increased by about 3000 since the last general election and most of the new voters were Autonomists like their parents. This explains Sanford's easy victory in the first round, against many odds. He attained 17 240 votes, as against 12 513 for Flosse, and 5698 for Taufa. During the second round, required by law since no candidate had obtained 50 per cent of the ballots cast, Taufa stood down in favour of Flosse, but Sanford won nevertheless with a comfortable margin of 2500 votes.

In a message to the Polynesian people the re-elected deputy rightly pointed out that the outcome was above all a severe defeat for Governor Angéli 'whose official and secret manoeuvring to pervert the people's democratic free choice has utterly failed. To my way of seeing things Angéli is the most typical representative we have ever had in this territory of the totalitarian type of colonial system against which we are fighting.' Another firm supporter of the colonial system whom Sanford singled out for special mention was the director of the local television and radio station, Suhas, 'who was visibly shaken by the results of this

167

election when he announced them on the screen. A long rest in France will probably do him a lot of good and help him recuperate from the psychological shock he has undergone.'

The first thing Sanford did when the new parliament convened was to join Servan-Schreiber's liberal reform movement, which immediately sponsored his demand for immediate self-government in French Polynesia. A similar bill was drawn up and proposed by Pouvanaa in the Senate. Although the Gaullists lost 89 seats, they continued to rule with the help of other conservative parties, assuring them a majority of 275 seats against 215 for the opposition parties, which were far from united. The prospects for a prompt adoption of Sanford's reform bill by the National Assembly were therefore extremely slight.

34 OUT OF THE ORDINARY SAFETY MEASURES

In between all these more or less unwarranted elections, the French technicians kept on as discreetly as possible with their nuclear testing programme at Moruroa. The 1971 blasts numbered five, one of which was produced by a thermonuclear charge in the megatonne range. In 1972 three more explosions occurred, bringing the total number of atmospheric tests made to date up to twenty-nine.

As related earlier, from the outset the French government had tried to calm public opinion in French Polynesia with a categorical statement to the effect that 'not a single particle of radioactive fallout will ever reach an inhabited island'. These were the exact words used by Governor Grimald on 28 March 1963. Identical claims were made by the CEA engineer, Cavard, on 14 June 1965 and by the head of the French Atomic Energy Commission, Francis Perrin, on 20 July 1965. Therefore, these specialists assured us, no anti-atomic shelters had to be built, and no islanders were ever to be evacuated.

The extensive radioactivity blow-back that occurred during the first tests in 1966 showed how ill-founded, if not deliberately misleading, these soothing declarations had been. What made a particularly bad impression was the fact that this blow-back, affecting islands as far west as Samoa, Fiji and the Gilberts was revealed, not by the French authorities, but by the New Zealand National Radiation Laboratory. Even then the CEA-CEP headquarters refused to divulge any figures about contamination from fallout in French Polynesia.

Shortly afterwards rumours began to circulate that foreign legionaries were hurriedly building anti-atomic shelters on islands east of Moruroa and lying outside the narrow, well-defined paths along which all ministers, governors and admirals had always sworn that the radioactive clouds would obediently travel. These rumours were soon confirmed and substantiated by inhabitants from these islands who had fled to Tahiti. That the authorities were seriously concerned is shown by these printed instructions distributed among the people of Mangareva:

When you are asked to go to the protective shelter [*abri de prévoyance*] these instructions will help you to remember the precautions you must take:

1. Before leaving your home:
(a) Remember the animals. Attach them so as to prevent them from doing any harm. Leave enough food and water within their easy reach to last for three days.
(b) Likewise protect some of the things that you leave behind. Carefully close all windows and doors. Wrap up in vinyl tissue (which will be distributed when needed) your boats, household utensils, crops and food products. Extinguish all lamps as well as the burners of your kerosene refrigerators. Stop all motors.
(c) Prepare one or more parcels containing your valuables and important documents such as identity cards and land deeds, linen, and particularly for your babies, silver ware and such things as rubber teats, thermos bottles and the formulae to which they are used. Whatever happens, you will be allowed to keep these parcels provided that their weight does not exceed 20 kilograms. You can also take along games, guitars, plaited mats, and blankets. But no animals.

2. When the time to leave comes:
You must proceed to the shelter within two hours after the church bells have rung.

Keep all family members together so as to facilitate checking in.

A motor vehicle will assure a shuttle service for the sick and the aged and for pregnant women.

It can of course be argued that all these measures do not merely reveal that the authorities had been mistaken or lying about the health hazards, but also more positively show that they were really trying to protect the population, at least on some islands. Unfortunately we have no proof whatsoever that the protection offered was adequate. Quite the opposite, in fact. There is every reason to remain sceptical when we know, for instance, that, before the islanders' return to their homes, these were 'decontaminated' by the army simply by sprinkling them with water, which as often as not found its way into the soil of their yards and vegetable gardens. Of course another pertinent question is why no shelters at all were built on the islands lying in the immediate vicinity of Moruroa, of which Tureia must receive first mention. The fact that the authorities, having loudly proclaimed that no islanders would ever be evacuated, suddenly dispatched the Tureians to Tahiti in 1968 for a three-month 'holiday', can hardly be taken as confirmation of a well-planned, efficient security policy.

Incidentally serious fears for the fate of the Tureians had already been expressed the year before by a French military helicopter pilot, Philippe Krynen. His testimony may be found in a book *La bombe ou la vie* (Fayard, Paris, 1969, pp. 55–6), whose author, Abbé Toulat, is a Catholic priest courageously trying to draw his countrymen's attention to the plight of the Polynesians. Here is the key passage:

In June and July 1967 three tests were made at Moruroa. The devices were small and therefore produced much less radioactivity than later A and H bombs. The first two had been detonated hanging down from a balloon. But due to a technical mishap the third bomb exploded at sea level, which of course was more dangerous. Two days later I flew to Tureia (126 kilometres north of Moruroa) to pick up two meteorologists who had been left there together with the population of about sixty persons at the time of the explosion. I was forbidden to wear the protective orange overall, so as not to alarm the population. But I put on my special boots and gloves. I spent three minutes on the atoll, just the time needed to take off the two meteorologists. For my part I was given a special shampooing, after which I could join my mates; but the two meteorologists had to remain in the hospital on board. However, before being allowed leave in Papeete, I had to submit to a special examination which revealed the existence of radioactive iodine in my thyroid glands. The amount was slight but I had to remain under observation for three days. As for the meteorologists, they were kept for a week in the hospital at Hao. This was a thought-provoking experience. Since I had had to be decontaminated after having spent only three minutes on Tureia and the meteorologists who had been there for a month needed more extensive treatment, how much more radioactivity must not the islanders have absorbed? They had not been evacuated and had received no instructions as to how to protect themselves. They continue to eat the lagoon fish and coconuts, to handle palm leaves and stones. In other words they are living and procreating in a radioactive environment.

Among the many reassuring statements that the civilian and military authorities repeated ad nauseam there figured right from the beginning a firm promise *to prevent* the islanders from eating contaminated fish. Here is how General Thiry, the person mainly responsible for the selection of Moruroa as a test site, explained his probably well-intended accident prevention policy in a letter dated 9 October 1963 to the Territorial Assembly: 'If the islanders frequently eat contaminated fish there is a risk that after a few years the number of cases of leukemia and cancer will increase. That is why the fish will be kept under observation in the areas where radioactive fallout is likely to occur so as to prevent the inhabitants from eating contaminated seafood.' Francis Perrin, the Atomic Energy High Commissioner, was even more specific in his letter of 16 May 1966 to Teariki quoted in one of the earlier chapters, for he envisaged 'temporary prohibitions against the eating of certain species of seafood', accompanied by 'economic compensations to the islanders for the losses incurred'.

Any person at all familiar with the topography of French Polynesia will immediately realise the utter futility of the proposed measures. Altogether there are 130 islands spread out over a surface almost as large as that of Europe. Many of them are of considerable size, as for instance most of the atolls in the Tuamotu group, each one made up of one, two, or three hundred small islets strung out along a circular reef between 80 and 300 kilometres in circumference. Furthermore the 7000 inhabitants are constantly on the move in quest of coconuts, fish and other seafood. To watch over them day and night all year round in order to prevent them from eating any contaminated fish is thus an enterprise of such magnitude that thousands of guards equipped with hundreds of speedboats would be required. This clearly explains why the CEA-CEP bosses never have tried to carry out Perrin's solemnly proclaimed watch-dog policy.

Confronted with their conspicuous failure to apply any of the safety measures that they themselves had proposed, the authorities resorted to more subtle tactics: They opened up to the public the new radiation laboratory built a few kilometres east of Papeete at Mahina, and invited all worried citizens to come out and see for themselves all of the thorough checks and investigations being undertaken there by a host of white-coated scientists manipulating complicated instruments and machines. Right from the beginning the Autonomist leaders showed how taken aback they were at the fact that the Mahina laboratory was not staffed by personnel from the French National Radiation Laboratory but rather by military doctors without any special qualifications, belonging to the so-called SMSR, created especially by the very CEP-CEA organisations carrying out the tests. As the Polynesians saw it, this was tantamount to letting the accused be his own judge – and it is hard not to share their opinion. Moreover they suggested that the easiest way for the

French government to prove that the nuclear tests did not endanger the health of the population was to let an international team of radiobiologists visit French Polynesia. But as we have seen, this reasonable request, made repeatedly by the Territorial Assembly, always ran up against the same stony silence in Paris.

Neither was the Papeete town council any more successful in 1966–67 when it asked the civil and military authorities not less than four times to be given the facts and figures concerning radioactive pollution of the air, the sea, the soil and the water. The only answer the town councillors ever received was a stern admonition from the governor to read the laboratory bulletins published in the local newspapers. Since these bulletins simply proclaimed after each nuclear blast that it had been perfectly clean and innocuous it is easy to forgive the Polynesian leaders for continuing scepticism. As a matter of fact they boycotted the Mahina laboratory until 7 April 1971, when Henri Bouvier, president of the Assembly's Permanent Committee accompanied a group of visiting French senators there out of courtesy. Here is the report he subsequently published in *La Dépeche de Tahiti*:

Before visiting the premises Dr Roger, the director of the laboratory, explained to us in the lecture theatre how the nuclear tests are made, what effects they have, and how the laboratory carries out its radiobiological studies. In my opinion this account contained some very rash assertions about the innocuousness of the tests and was at the same time remarkable for its failure to mention their possible harmful effects on our environment. Since it did not seem to me that these omissions were solely in the interests of being brief, due to the shortness of our visit, I asked Dr Roger to be kind enough to answer some questions that I wished to put to him in order to make his account more complete. He agreed to do so but declared that this exchange would have to wait until the end of our visit, giving as an explanation for this that it would be better to see first how the laboratory functioned.

In one of the last rooms that we visited, I noticed two small bottles on a worktable on whose labels I could read the signs *Sr 90*. I asked Dr Roger on the spot what these bottles contained. He answered that it was strontium. When I pressed him for further details he explained that it was indeed strontium 90. On our return to the lecture theatre, we were served champagne. I took advantage of this opportunity to ask Dr Roger the questions he had previously promised to answer. But before he had time to open his mouth, Mr Pujol, the government administrator, took over and shouted: 'Gentlemen, let us make haste to drink up our champagne as we

173

are in danger of being late for our dinner with the admiral'. The Gaullist counsellor Jacques Teuira immediately fell in, almost shouting: 'Yes, yes, hurry up, or we shall be late'.

Infuriated by these bullying methods, I asked the senators and the other visitors to take careful note of how obvious the colonial servants and their accomplices were in their bad faith and bad conscience and I declared where I stood face to face with the directors of the CEA that I was not too surprised and that this was the very reason why I had hitherto refused to visit the laboratory and listen to their explanations, because I knew that no free and open discussion would be allowed. Then, reminding Dr Roger of his promise, I asked him firmly if he intended to keep it and answer the questions I wanted to put to him. He then accepted.

'Dr Roger', I said, 'could you tell us where you found the strontium 90 in the two bottles that we have just seen?'

'It was found in the natural environment.'

I narrowed down my question: 'Could you tell us exactly where and in which natural substances it was found?'

He protested: 'But strontium has always existed everywhere in the natural environment'.

I insisted: 'Dr Roger, don't try to hide the truth. You know as well as I do that I was asking about radioactive strontium 90. You know perfectly well that this type of strontium is produced by the fission of uranium and that it has *never* existed in the natural environment until it had been introduced by the explosions of atomic bombs. For this very reason it is considered to be the best means of tracing fallout resulting from these bombs. The discovery of such traces *always* constitutes proof of radioactive fallout. Will you therefore, please, tell us in which substances you found it.

This forced Dr Roger to admit the obvious truth that the strontium 90 we had seen came from food samples taken in Tahiti and analysed in his laboratory.

We thus had under our own eyes definite proof that the nuclear tests made by the CEP, far from being 'clean', seriously pollute our natural environment, which means everything that we eat. Of course I pointed out all the consequences of this fact, particularly stressing how impossible it is to prevent such pollution. Dr Roger had to admit that it was completely impossible to 'recapture' the cloud of radioactive particles after the explosion of a bomb so as to avoid their falling down all around the world and with the help of wind and rain indiscriminately poisoning the oceans, the earth, the plants, the animals, and the human race.

Therefore, even in the most favourable circumstances, the 'precautions' taken by the CEP – which according to the French government's assertions result in perfectly 'clean' tests – can only reduce the dirtiness of these explosions, and at the most avoid *direct* accidents caused by instantaneous exposure. But these so-called precautions can in no way eliminate the risks of a slow and continuous poisoning of the human race produced by long-life elements such as strontium 90, caesium 137, and carbon 14 emanating from the explosions of atomic bombs.

35 NO SCIENTIFIC PROOF WHATSOEVER

As an excuse for not furnishing any precise quantitative data on the perils of radiation, the civil and military authorities in Polynesia have consistently told local critics of the tests that all facts and figures could be found in the detailed reports that the French government sent every year to the United Nations. These reports were carefully examined, so the story went, by eminent UN experts who again and again fully exonerated France. The following bald statement made by Minister for Defence Michel Debré on 10 June 1972, typifies the official French view:

Our tests have in no way been harmful to the environment. The UN Scientific Committee on the Effects of Radiation has just released a report declaring them to be innocuous. The real reasons behind the criticism levelled at France are political. The French Atomic Energy Commission has taken all the necessary measures for the protection of the population and the environment. No scientific proof whatsoever exists to back up the accusations made against the French government.

One might have expected the governor or the CEP-CEA bosses to have freely distributed these UN reports to the Polynesian Autonomists so as to bring to a stop once and for all their ill-founded, politically motivated criticism of the nuclear tests. Strangely enough they have done nothing of the sort, and all requests for copies addressed to the director of the Mahina laboratory – who allegedly had supplied the data contained in the reports – have always resulted in the even more surprising admission that none is available. The French government has been equally reluctant about quoting any facts and figures from these reports when answering foreign critics.

All UN documents are public, the only difference being that some are printed and sold at the headquarters and in selected bookstores throughout the world, whereas others are mimeographed and distributed only to delegations. The six French annual reports about the nuclear tests in Polynesia belong to the second category, but many hundred copies exist and can be consulted in New York as well as in many national and specialised libraries. Yet, to our knowledge, nobody has ever taken the trouble of reading and analysing these precious documents for the benefit of the general public. It is a pity, for we have found a perusal of them extremely rewarding, not to say revealing. Considering that all reports are made on the same model, we have selected one of them for more detailed comment, which we believe to be generally valid. Its title is 'Radio-active Fallout after the Nuclear Explosions in Polynesia, May-December, 1970'. It is marked Distr. Limited, A/AC.82/G/L.1381, 23 June 1971 and comprises 140 pages. It is above all remarkable for the preponderance of data having no relevance whatsoever to the subject matter.

Thus the first twelve pages are taken up with a quite unnecessary description of the well-known techniques of measuring radioactive fallout. In the next twenty-two pages we are told by text and maps how the radioactive clouds produced by the eight explosions undertaken in 1970 travelled around the world. However all the facts had been made known by the radiation laboratories in New Zealand, Australia, Africa, and South America long before the publication of the French report. For some unaccountable reason the only measurements given in this section show the *average annual* amount of strontium 90 in the milk as calculated by unnamed scientific institutions, *mainly in Africa and South America*. (This discretion is motivated by the fact, nowhere mentioned, that these observations have been made by French government scientists or local scientists in Africa and South America hired by the French government.) Admittedly the annual average is also given for Tahiti, which is of no interest whatsoever compared to the wholly lacking figure for the radioactive contamination of the milk *at the time when nuclear tests took place*. We are also compelled to ask why the anonymous authors are exclusively interested in *milk*, a beverage that can be found only in Tahiti and even there is of extremely limited use. Another six pages are devoted to an abstruse discussion of the possible sources of contamination of the milk in South America and Africa – and that brings us to the last page of the text!

The rest of the report is taken up with two appendices containing tables and graphs that at first glance seem to supply some of the basic information that the desperate reader has been searching for so far in vain. Thus the first table of Appendix I, entitled 'The Radioactivity of the Atmosphere', shows the beta radioactivity in pCi/m^3 in five 'stations' in French Polynesia. But the few figures given are again the *averages* for successive *ten-day periods* and all 'stations' are located at maximum distance from

Moruroa in the Austral Islands, in the Society Islands, and in the Marquesas. Nor is it anywhere explained just what is meant by the word 'station'. The only thing certain is that it cannot refer to a building or an observation post, whose existence could hardly have escaped the islanders. Moreover the extent of the military scientists' geographical knowledge may easily be judged from the fact that, of the five names of the islands where they had been 'stationed', two are spelled incorrectly.

Still more discouraging, this first page of Appendix I is the *only one* offering any data from French Polynesia, for all of the following twenty-nine pages deal with air pollution *in South America, Africa, and Europe!* Once more a considerable amount of padding may be observed, for the same data are presented twice throughout, first in tabular form and then graphically. Although the figures are few, they are not reassuring. For instance, in Lima, the average beta radioactivity rose from 0.041 before the first test to 34.115 during the ten-day period when the explosion of the megatonne thermonuclear device observed by Minister Debré took place. If instead *the exact daily figures* had been given, the magnitude of the pollution would have come out even more clearly.

The second and last appendix contains sixty-four pages of tables and graphs (meaning further unneeded padding) dealing at long last with the only subject of any real interest to us, 'The Radioactivity of the Biosphere'. The question that immediately arises is whether the bookbinder has not made a terrible mistake and wrongly inserted a chapter intended for a report on pollution problems in Africa and South America. Let us only say in passing that whoever took these samples ought immediately be dismissed for incompetence and laziness. Some of the tables list as few as two samples for the whole year of 1970! The reader with enough patience to wade through all this irrelevant material will be rewarded in the end, however, by the discovery of thirty pages of tables devoted to the contamination problem in French Polynesia. Alas, the value of this belatedly supplied information is out of proportion compared to the space it occupies, for it can easily be summarised in the following, more succinct manner:

In the Austral Islands, at unspecified dates, during the third or fourth quarter of 1970, *one sample* was taken of each of six vegetables, six fishes, and six pieces of meat.

In the Marquesas Islands, visited by the observers at the

beginning and at the end of 1970, again not more than *one sample* was taken of about ten different food items.

In the Society Islands, a slightly larger number of vegetables and animal food items were sampled, but *only once,* and in most instances the samples were taken long before or long after the tests.

In the Tuamotu Islands, where the health hazards were greatest, the number of samples taken is the smallest. No exact dates are given and only three out of eighty islands were visited by the military doctors of the SMSR.

Under these circumstances it is not so surprising that the few strontium 90 and caesium 137 figures listed give no cause for alarm. But why are they so few? Over the years the Mahina laboratory has produced and distributed to the local press numerous news bulletins describing in loving detail the incredibly thorough and comprehensive studies being undertaken by its field-workers and radiobiologists. For instance on 3 July 1970, on the day of the big thermonuclear display observed by Michel Debré, the following reassuring account was published:

Since France began testing nuclear bombs here, more than 35 000 samples of fish, crustaceans, fruits, and vegetables have been taken in the territory of French Polynesia and analysed in the radiobiological laboratory at Mahina . . . Every week the laboratory receives two hundred samples of fish, spiny lobsters, pawpaws, mangoes, bananas, etc. To start with they are dried and calcined. The ashes are crushed, pulverised, and pressed into pellets which are put into a lead chamber where their radioactive contents, if any, are determined.

By the end of 1970, the period covered by the UN report under scrutiny, the laboratory must have accumulated more than 40 000 samples. Therefore one may rightly ask why, out of this enormous number, only a small number have been included each year in the reports sent to the UN committee on atomic radiation. Another splendid opportunity for confounding the critics has been missed.

Not surprisingly the members of the UN Scientific Committee on the Effects of Radiation have never been much impressed by these reports, as the minutes of their meetings clearly show. Again and again they deplore 'the paucity of the data' and declare themselves unable to reach any valid conclusions. Or, to quote (A/SPC/SR. 903, p. 9) the excellent formulation of the New Zealand representative, Mr Templeton, who regretted in 1973

179

that 'his delegation could not accept a resolution which sought to base complacent conclusions on a partial picture of incomplete data'. It is also of some interest to note that when the UN Conference on the Human Environment, held in Stockholm in June 1972, condemned the French nuclear tests in the Pacific, the resolution was motivated precisely by the unsatisfactory character of the French UN reports. On 29 November of the same year, the most representative UN forum, the General Assembly, took exactly the same stand. Not less than 105 nations voted against France, whose only allies were Portugal, China and Albania!

Minister Debré had asserted six months earlier that 'no scientific proof whatsoever exists to back up the accusations made against the French government'. As we have just seen, an analysis of the very documents on which Debré relied forces us to conclude instead that no scientific proof whatsoever exists to back up the French government's contentions that the tests are harmless.

36 MORE MISSED OPPORTUNITIES

If the members of the UN Scientific Committee on the Effects of Atomic Radiation had known French Polynesia better, they would certainly have found much greater reason for concern. For us living in the islands, it is obvious that the anonymous authors of the French annual reports have not only used outrageously unscientific sampling methods, but which is even worse, also omitted most of the information essential to a correct evaluation of the health risks.

To begin with there are no data of any sort from the most exposed islands, of which of course Moruroa and Fangataufa deserve first mention. More than fifty thousand French technicians, conscripts, sailors, professional soldiers, foreign legionaries, and Polynesian workmen have lived for longer or shorter periods at Moruroa and Fangataufa. We can take it for granted that the soil, the vegetation, and the lagoon and sea organisms are highly contaminated on any island where dozens of nuclear devices have exploded. Besides this, thanks to the unintentional indiscretion of a military doctor, we know that the first tests were particularly dirty. The doctor's name is Leguen and this information somehow slipped out in 1971 when he was talking to a reporter from the *Dépêche de Tahiti*, which published the following interesting account on 18 June:

A few days after the first explosion (Aldebaran) of the 1966 testing series, it actually became necessary to prohibit the eating of all lagoon fish because they had become so contaminated that they were no longer fit for consumption. This explosion took place at sea level on board a barge. In spite of its feeble strength, it seems to have been quite poisonous for the submarine fauna. It caused massive destruction at point zero and various fission products led to secondary contaminations. Three explosions of this type occurred in 1966 and 1967.

The UN reports have nothing to say about these dangerous blasts and their consequences. Next to the test sites themselves the most exposed islands are Tureia, Marutea, Matureivavao, Mangareva, Vahitahi, Pukarua, and Reao – inhabited by populations varying between 50 and 500 persons. None of them figures in the reports either, an oversight that cannot be pure coincidence but must be ascribed to their having been left out deliberately. And what are the criteria for having selected Anaa, Makemo, Rangiroa, and Pukapuka in their stead? Could it by any chance have been because these atolls happen to be situated *well outside* the path or corridor usually followed by the radioactive clouds? As for the remaining groups in French Polynesia: the Society, Austral, and Marquesas islands – the geographical distribution of the few samples taken there is equally spotty and capricious.

Considering the wealth of information contained in these reports about the negligible amount of milk consumed in French Polynesia, the authors' total lack of interest in the potential health hazard inherent in drinking water, moreover, is very curious. With the exception of Papeete, where the water is pumped up from below, everywhere else it comes from the sky in the form of rainwater. The group worthy of the closest attention, of course, is the Tuamotus, where there are no rivers. The 7000 inhabitants thus depend entirely on rainwater collected from the corrugated iron roofs of their homes and preserved for weeks and months in concrete tanks.

When a nuclear explosion is followed by a heavy downpour, the radioactive particles adhere to the raindrops, producing a higher than usual concentration in the water tanks. This is why the New Zealand National Radiation Laboratory regularly includes in *its* reports on 'Fallout from Nuclear Weapons Tests Conducted by France in the South Pacific' a wide range of drinking-water samples from more than twelve stations, the easternmost of which is Aitutaki in the Cook Islands and the westernmost is Funafuti in the Ellice Islands. As these reports clearly show, a significant and sometimes dangerous increase in the amount of fission products and beta activity in the rainwater catchment tanks has occurred every year in connection with the French tests. Incidentally the highest figure of 135 000 pCi/litre was recorded in Apia, Samoa, in September 1966, after the 'inaugural' blast witnessed by General de Gaulle during his eventful visit to French Polynesia described in an earlier chapter. There are only two possible explanations for the omission from the UN reports of all data on the contamination of rainwater in French Polynesia. Either the radioactive particles originating at Moruroa obligingly jumped over all the French islands, or the military doctors in the Mahina laboratory are afraid of revealing the truth. Until it has been scientifically proved that the French radioactive particles possess special jumping propensities not found in their Russian and

American counterparts, our only regretful choice remaining is to opt for the second explanation.

Turning next to the islanders' dietary habits, there is again a marked difference between the Tuamotu atolls and the mountainous islands in the other groups. Due to the aridity of the soil, no vegetables or tubers can be grown on the atolls. Nor is there any feed for pigs and fowl. Consequently the islanders have to rely on seafood and imported foodstuff such as rice, flour, and canned meat. With commendable foresight the CEA-CEP bosses commissioned a team of French scientists from the Museum of Natural History in Paris to make a survey of the little known flora and fauna of the Tuamotu Islands in 1964 and 1965 BEFORE THE BEGINNING OF THE TESTS. The results of their thorough and extensive investigations, wholly financed by the CEA-CEP, have been published in successive issues of the *Cahiers du Pacifique*, the well-known journal of the Singer-Polignac Foundation.

In a preface (volume 12, pages III–IV), the director of the Museum of Natural History, Professor Maurice Fontaine, describes his scientists' task in these moving terms:

When the biologists who have signed the following papers dealing with Moruroa – where they all toiled together harmoniously during their field work – agreed at the outset to participate in this long-range biological research project in the nuclear testing area, I am certain that they did so fully aware of their responsibilities and feeling that they had a moral obligation to contribute to the success of this joint project deriving from humanitarian considerations . . . After several years of sustained efforts, they may now happily conclude that they have fulfilled their mission, having realised their twofold aims of making scientific discoveries and of achieving complete mastery of the environment. In this volume, about which we previously knew only one thing, that it existed – they marshall all basic data required to undertake radiobiological studies.

In another preface to a paper by the malacologist, Bernard Salvat, Professor Fontaine confirms that the military high command wanted above all for the scientists to find out 'which marine species were best suited to serve as indicators of radioactive contamination'. Consequently the islands surveyed were those most likely, if not certain, to receive radioactive fallout: Tureia, Matureivavao, Marutea, Reao, Pukarua, and Mangareva. In this paper *(Cahiers du Pacifique,* number 11), Professor Salvat is categorical: The marine animals that absorb the greatest quantities of radioactivity are the turbo shells, tridacna clams, and squid. He also stresses the great dependence of the atoll dwellers on these very food items. His fellow scientists add to the list of easily contaminated species: sea turtles, spiny lobsters, tuna, and bonito – but consider them less of a health hazard solely because of their secondary importance as. food items. Of the few land animals, the coconut crab, which is regarded as a great delicacy in the Tuamotus, is singled out as the greatest potential threat to the health of the islanders. Sea birds and their eggs, eaten in season on most atolls, are also on the blacklist. The greatest danger here is that birds contaminated on the sites could and would fly over to the other inhabited islands in the group.

With this fine groundwork laid by the scientists from the Natural History Museum, it should have been no problem at all for the military doctors of the SMSR to make a proper selection of food samples for a record and study of the spread of radioactive fallout through the islands after each test. Therefore it is extremely puzzling, to say the least, to discover that they have failed to do so year after year. Or, if they have regularly sampled shellfish, clams, and squid, who decided, and for what reasons, to omit from the UN reports all information of such vital, or rather lethal character? And why has Professor Fontaine never denounced this shocking disregard of the noble moral and humanitarian spirit in which the field surveys of the Natural History Museum had been undertaken?

The UN reports are no more helpful to us in forming an opinion about the extent to which the fish have been contaminated. True, here and there we can find isolated samples from marginal islands. But instead of an indication of the Polynesian or Latin names of the species sampled, these are simply listed as 'lagoon fish' or 'ocean fish'. Conspicuously absent are the promised data about the 2000 tonnes of fish sold annually in the central market in Papeete, where we have been assured 'a horde of dedicated inspectors from the Mahina laboratory have been taking samples with meticulous care ever since the detonation of the first bomb'. One would also have expected at least some information about the contamination of migratory species. On both Moruroa and Fangataufa the lagoons communicate with the surrounding sea through deep passes, six kilometres and nearly half a kilometre wide respectively. Therefore great quantities of lagoon fish are swept out through the passes and eaten by tuna and bonito, which can in their turn enter the lagoon to feed. As we all know, for each new link in the food chain the amount of radioactivity increases exponentially. What one must also remember here is that the first link in the food chain is usually plankton, which is rapidly contaminated by the radioactive particles falling into the ocean. If any studies have been made of the plankton in French Polynesian waters, they too have been left out of the UN reports without any explanation at all.

The fishes with the highest concentration of radioactivity are, of course, big species such as tuna and bonito. The main problem confronting us is their migratory habits enabling them to carry the radioactivity they have absorbed to far lands and continents. Right from the beginning this was the danger uppermost in the minds of the Polynesian leaders opposed to the tests. As related in earlier chapters, a succession of ministers, governors, generals and admirals at once tried to assuage these fears with solemn promises to enforce 'temporary interdictions' against catching and eating tuna and bonito. When the absurdity of all such attempts became apparent, the emphasis shifted to the 'control' or check carried out by well-equipped oceanographic research vessels making annual cruises for the purpose of catching and measuring the radioactive contamination in all migratory fishes.

Once more the UN reports do not contain a single figure from which we can form an opinion on this important matter. What we do find is simply a series of maps showing various cruises of an odd assortment of navy ships and ordinary fishing craft plus the following standard formula repeated word by word year after year: 'The studies of deep-sea fishes and species caught by trolling around the islands prove that, as in the past, the international fishing zones are practically untouched by radioactive contamination other than that existing everywhere on earth'. Even if it can be proved – which seems extremely doubtful – that all contamination in French Polynesian waters stems from tests made by the ugly Americans, Russians and Chinese, it would nevertheless be extremely useful to know the exact amount of radioactivity in the fish we are eating every day. Another point that remains far from clear is how the anonymous authors of the report can know that *the international fishing zones* are practically untouched when, according to the maps, all cruises have occurred within the territorial waters of French Polynesia.

Of course the contamination problem can also be examined from another angle, simply by regularly subjecting a representative cross section of the population to thorough medical

185

examinations. Year in and year out, one of the proudest boasts of the director of the Mahina laboratory has always been that this is exactly what his staff has been doing – and that no anomalies or diseases attributable to the nuclear tests have ever been discovered! To take just one example: in the famous communiqué issued on the big H bomb day, 3 July 1970, it is explicitly stated that 'two hundred individuals have been selected and are being examined regularly. The result is quite surprising. The Europeans who come from the northern hemisphere are three times more radioactive than the Polynesians, and on the high islands the natural radioactivity is six times higher than on the atolls.' Those of us who did not have enough faith in the bomb people to blindly accept such flat statements and also wanted to know the amount of *artificial* radioactivity on the atolls were, as usual, told more or less politely that all facts and figures could be found in the UN reports.

The uncomfortable truth is that they contain next to nothing about these medical checks. For instance, in the 1970 report all we can learn is that for 22 men and 10 women of unspecified age, race, and geographical origin, the *average* content per gram of potassium was 30 pCi of caesium 137! As for the date when these observations were made, all that is said is that it was 'after the 1970 tests'. Since 200 persons were being examined in the laboratory in July, are we to conclude that at the end of the year there were only 22 men and 10 women left? By not accounting for the fate of the remaining 168 persons, the Mahina staff leaves the door open to the most frightful suspicions. Incidentally, the impression we get from the successive bulletins issued by the bomb people is that the persons examined are not the same from year to year but rather that the researchers' net is, as it should be, cast in many different directions. Therefore, by now, many thousands of French Polynesian inhabitants must have undergone a medical checkup. How come then that we have never met a single person who has participated in the vast and comprehensive health survey?

The Health Department in French Polynesia shows a similar reluctance about releasing documents allegedly tending to exonerate the bomb experts. Up until June 1963, statistics, listing among other things the number of deaths and their causes, were published every month in the *Journal Officiel*, and detailed information about diseases and epidemics was readily available. From the date when the CEP established its headquarters in Polynesia, however, and down to the present time, public health statistics have no longer been published. What is more, if anyone is bold enough to make an enquiry about this taboo subject, he is immediately reported to the secret police.

The existence of a special army hospital in Papeete, whose apparently very busy doctors are under the strictest obligation to observe secrecy, is also very hard to understand, if there is nothing to hide. By the way, in keeping with old colonial practice, the civilian hospital in Papeete is also staffed exclusively with army doctors. These little-publicised facts should be kept in mind when trying to appreciate at their true value statements such as those made, for instance, by the colonel in charge of the French Polynesian Department of Health at the 1973 regional meeting of the World Health Organisation in Wellington. Not only did he repeat the official French claim that the nuclear tests at Moruroa were harmless, but furthermore quoted as a definite factor of proof that he had serving under him 'fifty doctors who had never reported to him any detrimental effects on the health of the population in the territory that might be ascribed to the nuclear tests'.

Finally let us see what the highest French authority, the minister for public health, had to say in the eighth year of the nuclear testing programme about the health risks in French Polynesia. The minister in charge at the time was later the number-two man in Giscard d'Estaing's government, Michel Poniatowski. Here is the complete text of the written question remitted to the French National Assembly by the Polynesian deputy, Francis Sanford, along with Poniatowski's belated reply:

Question number 1711, 25 May 1973:
Mr Sanford asks the minister for public health and social security: (1) if he is able to indicate the exact number of deaths due to cancer that have occurred in French Polynesia during the last ten years, and (2) if he can undertake an evaluation of the amount of radioactive contamination existing in the following three French Polynesian islands: Hao, Tureia, and Mangareva.

Reply, dated 15 September 1973:
The minister for public health and social security informs the honourable member of parliament that he has no direct responsibility for the territory of Polynesia. He is nevertheless able to state: (1) that the frequency of cancer and leukemia has remained unchanged in Polynesia during the last ten years, and (2) that the radioactivity in the islands of Polynesia, taken as a whole, has stayed within the limits of the fluctuations of the natural radioactivity.

187

37 THE BIG MEETING OF MINDS

More convinced than ever by all these clumsy official attempts to hide or deny that the nuclear tests represent a real danger to the health of the present and future generations of Polynesians, Francis Sanford and Pouvanaa decided in May 1973 to draw attention to their desperate plight by sending out mimeographed copies of the following open letter to the French people to not less than 200 newspapers and magazines:

Dear compatriots,

You may find this appeal somewhat unusual. In fact it is quite uncommon for parliamentarians to try to get directly in touch with their fellow citizens outside their constituencies, at a time when there are no elections.

This procedure may appear even stranger when the parliamentarians who make this appeal are not the leaders of a big national party and the problem to which they want to draw your attention seemingly concerns only persons living at the antipodes.

Though such is the situation, we nevertheless trust that you will understand us, particularly as the explanation we can offer you is quite simple and will bring to your mind many issues with which you are already familiar.

Why we are reaching out to you today is above all because the government obstinately refuses to listen to us, although the problem is too serious to be hushed up by those in responsible positions. This is why you must listen to us.

For many years the French government has created and perpetuated in French Polynesia a state of affairs such as you, citizens of metropolitan France, would never have endured. And the government has been able to do this to us in your name, because we are a small people of no more than 120 000. But do you find this acceptable as democratic method? We refuse to believe so.

We, inhabitants of French Polynesia have a right to know what you, citizens of our mother country really think in this respect. You must show your feelings, either by silently approving of the present government policy, meaning that the strongest decide, or by protesting vigorously against the fate the government has reserved for us. It is up to you to say whether it is fair and good to use French Polynesia as a field for atomic bomb tests, thereby exposing your fellow citizens who live there to present and future dangers.

This is the question we should like to ask every mother, every father in metropolitan France: Would you have accepted the installation in France of a base for testing nuclear bombs of the type that every year since the 2nd July, 1966, have been adding new clouds of radioactive fallout?

If we are to judge by the official protests at long last emanating from all capitals in the countries around the Pacific rim (and whose inhabitants are no less courageous than you are), it would seem to us that you will reply in the negative. Considering that the President of the Republic, following the example of his illustrious predecessor, favours direct democratic consultations, we hereby request him to organise a referendum, putting the following question to the people of France: 'In order to be able to retort to the ill-founded protests of the governments in the southern hemisphere, do you accept our demonstrating how perfectly harmless our atomic bombs are by exploding them henceforth in metropolitan France?'

Since 1963, first the former deputy, John Teariki, and then we the undersigned, as well as the Territorial Assembly, have been continually protesting against the nuclear tests and requesting that an international control commission study the radioactive pollution of our environment. With great scorn the French government has turned a deaf ear to all these requests.

Each time that we have demanded explanations from the government, the only answer worth mentioning has been the cynical but quite logical statement that if an accident happens during a nuclear test, the number of victims will be much smaller in French Polynesia than in metropolitan France! So this is the true reason leading the government to build its nuclear testing bases at the antipodes of Paris. What a singular benefit for Polynesia to derive from belonging to France!

We will never accept this. Since becoming French, we Polynesians have twice demonstrated [by sending a batallion to fight in Europe during both the first and the second world wars] that we are ready to make the greatest sacrifices to save our mother country. In return we demand to be no longer treated as guinea-pigs for these lunatic experiments which, if they ever achieve their purpose, will only result in the total destruction of France, through massive retaliation by a far superior atomic power.

Your compatriots in the Pacific ask for your help in stopping this madness.

Pouvanaa a Oopa
Senator of French Polynesia

Francis Sanford
Deputy of French Polynesia

French newspaper and magazine editors are forever publishing glowing accounts of Tahiti the last paradise on earth, knowing from long experience that this subject is of perennial interest to the stressed and distressed city dwellers making up the bulk of their readers. The accompanying glossy pictures invariably show voluptuous hula girls dressed in little more than flower leis, either dancing teasingly in front of goggle-eyed male tourists, or invitingly stretched out on a sandy beach. As often as not there are also a few pictures of athletic, brown-skinned men elegantly casting a fishing net into the water or, for the benefit of their European guests, opening an earthern oven filled with baked pigs, lobsters, breadfruit, and other native delicacies. As explained by the text, this is how the happy, carefree Polynesians spend their days. At night, of course, they all make love in some sweet-scented glade or in their charming little grass huts, but rarely with the same partner two nights in a row.

In this open letter, however, the legendary South Sea paradise seemed more like hell – and the fact of its being signed by two authentic natives did not help much, since they insisted on relating only unpalatable truths. So naturally, under these circumstances, the editors preferred filling their columns with material of more immediate and proved concern to their readers, such as political scandals, royal romances, wars and revolutions, the private lives of movie stars, fortunes won and lost, football matches, hold-ups, and horse races. In the end only one of the 200 newspapers and magazines published Pouvanaa's and Sanford's open letter.

Not unexpectedly the magazine daring to go against the current was the *Express*. In taking once more an independent stand and espousing an unpopular cause, it reflected the views and personality of its owner, Jean-Jacques Servan-Schreiber, commonly called JJSS, who is the only genuine maverick in French politics. For instance, in the darkest days of the Algerian war, he did not hesitate to denounce the torture practised by the French army, a subject carefully avoided for 'patriotic' reasons by all political parties and the whole French press. And when the colonels in Greece began sending their opponents to concentration camps, JJSS even went so far as to dispatch a special commando in a chartered plane to Athens to rescue the singer Theodorakis. He had also, right from the beginning, severely criticised two of de Gaulle's most cherished projects: the

Concorde aeroplane and the nuclear striking force as being too costly and serving only the very doubtful end of enhancing French 'prestige'. Of course his enemies have always been quick to point out that JJSS can well afford to display the craziest ideas, being a multi-millionaire. But what they forget to say is that JJSS has earned every cent of his considerable fortune himself, by founding and administering a series of successful newspapers and magazines. And again and again he has been proven right. Having been elected deputy for Lorraine on the ticket of the small Radical Socialist Party – which in spite of its name is a middle of the road liberal party – JJSS rapidly gathered around him a motley group of other independent-minded deputies, who have become known as the reformers, because of their common strong conviction of its being high time to modernise the whole French economy and society. Of course, they are less unanimous when it comes to methods most likely to attain this end. As for JJSS, he makes no secret of his admiration for the American democratic free-enterprise system. Francis Sanford had eventually adhered to this loose association because he felt less of an outsider there than in any other parliamentarian group. After all, was not he himself fighting for far-reaching reforms in Polynesia?

Having not only published but also read and liked Pouvanaa's and Sanford's letter, JJSS immediately wanted to translate his indignation into action, just as a knight, during the middle ages, used to draw his sword and gallop off to slay the dragon. With due regard for the actual circumstances, he did something almost as audacious. He proposed forming a 'peace commando' corps and attacking the enemy in his main fortress in Polynesia.

This was the first time any Frenchman of national stature had offered Pouvanaa and Francis Sanford his active help and, as soon as they had caught their breath after the initial surprise, they gratefully accepted. True to style, in less than two weeks JJSS had rounded up two socialist deputies, a female reform deputy who was a medical doctor by profession, one famous Catholic theologian, a leading Protestant churchman, two environmentalists, a non-violent philosophy professor, a Catholic anti-bomb writer, and last but not least, a pacifist French army general with the aristocratic name of Paris de Bollardière. Half of the crusaders were flown out to Tahiti by JJSS to be the main speakers at an anti-bomb rally organised by the Autonomist parties in Papeete for 23 June 1973. In true commando style, the remaining members were to attack the ultimate enemy bastion at Moruroa. Of course for chief they had General Paris de Bollardière.

To take to the streets, to participate in protest meetings are foreign methods, distasteful to the polite and gentle Polynesians. Accordingly the few street demonstrations to occur in Papeete in the past had always been organised by Europeans and *demis* with for targets Pouvanaa and the other Polynesian leaders. Therefore it was far from certain in advance that enough Polynesians would attend the meeting to transform it into the meaningful event the Autonomists were hoping for.

However, by sunrise on 23 June, it was obvious that all such doubts were ill-founded. Bus after bus rolled into town from the country districts, disgorging batches of men and women in black and white Sunday attire. From the slum areas on the outskirts of Papeete a steady stream of working people came walking barefoot along the tree-lined roads. All converged on the old two-storey Town Hall. When JJSS and his five companions arrived and took their seats on the upper balcony shortly before 8 a.m., the crowd filling the garden and overflowing into the adjacent street numbered more than 5000 persons, of whom only about ten were Europeans and none Chinese. The first aim had been achieved: it was the biggest political meeting ever held in Tahiti.

Like all Autonomist meetings, this one began with a long prayer by a native pastor, after which the metropolitan speakers, one by one, more or less forcefully, more or less eloquently, explained how and why they had become determined opponents of the nuclear tests in Polynesia and the French nuclear striking force. Sentence by sentence their speeches were translated into Tahitian by Francis Sanford. The resounding applause that greeted them showed that the various and varied arguments advanced by the speakers were well understood by their audience. Yet there is no doubt that what most impressed the five thousand Polynesians gathered that bright Saturday morning was the simple fact that six metropolitan Frenchmen had taken the trouble to come all the way from Paris with the exclusive purpose of supporting Pouvanaa, Teariki, and Sanford. Accustomed as they were to having all Frenchmen passing through the islands staunchly defend the tests and the colonial system, it was an inspiring experience for them to discover that there existed other men in France who were on their side.

This imbued them with so much fresh courage that, after the

meeting, they did not hesitate to form a procession and march through the streets, brandishing hastily painted boards inscribed with slogans such as:

> Stop the Tests
> We Want Self-Government
> No More Criminal Tests
> We Refuse To Be Guinea Pigs
> Our Children's Blood Is Not for Sale
> Test the Bombs in France

Needless to say, when Sanford asked them to do so, the whole crowd dispersed peacefully. Those of the many gendarmes charged with the easy task of maintaining order, who had previously served in such metropolitan provinces as Brittany and Corsica or in such overseas departments as Martinique and Guadeloupe, where bombings, street fights, armed attacks, and even murders are quite common, were amazed at the calm dignity of these Polynesian demonstrators. But for the very reason that they possess these admirable qualities, the French government, of course, continued to treat them as perfect non-entities, even after this mass meeting.

38 MORE WHITEWASH

Luckily for the Polynesians they were no longer alone in their desperate fight. In fact the number of protesting nations had grown from one, Japan, in 1963, to more than 100, as shown by successive condemnations of France in the various UN bodies. Although the French government was very much concerned by the adverse votes of many of its traditional allies among the Arab and African states, as so many other offenders in the past, it had the sweet consolation that the United Nations was completely powerless to enforce any effective sanctions. In fact its first serious setback did not occur until 1972 when some of the Pacific peoples at long last resorted to more forceful means of persuasion. We are referring, of course, to the extensive boycotting of French planes, French ships, French goods and even mail and telephone communications with France that year, on the part of New Zealand and Australia. This action was a result of a growing awareness that the tests might be responsible for a gradual increase of leukemia and cancer over the next five or ten years. What the Paris government found particularly annoying was the rapid spread of these boycotts to important trading partner countries in South-East Asia.

Reluctantly Pompidou, Debré and Messmer began to ponder the easiest and cheapest way to placate the foreign protest movements. To everybody but them the obvious solution was to stop the nuclear tests altogether. After all, de Gaulle had been dead for two years so there was nothing to prevent them from burying his impossible dream of nuclear grandeur along with him. In point of fact, there was every reason for *doing* so. France had already spent at least 100 000 million francs ($A1000 million) on this megalomaniac attempt at competing with the big powers. Even after seventeen nuclear tests in the Sahara, followed by twenty-nine more at Moruroa and Fangataufa, the results were still pitiful. According to the surely well-informed Defence Committee of the National Assembly, the French nuclear striking force still consisted of a few small A-bombs – some of which had to be delivered by Mirage planes – with a total fire power of not more than 20 megatonnes, while Russia and America each possessed highly sophisticated thermonuclear weapons with a total fire power in the neighbourhood of 25 000 megatonnes. Moreover France lacked early warning systems and anti-missile defence lines. 'This being the situation, how can we deter the enemy from attacking us? If we have the temerity to use our bombs, the only result will be that a quarter of an hour later France will be erased from the map.' The Frenchman who spoke this simple truth in 1972 was none other than Professor Francis Perrin, the head of the Atomic Energy Commission, who had just resigned in protest against the suicidal foreign policy of his government.

The next best solution would have been to go underground. There is no lack of desert and mountainous regions in France where such tests could be made as safely as in Nevada or Siberia. But France was inhabited by 52 million people, of whom 32 million vote, and who have an intense dislike for the idea of having to suffer the consequences, however small, of radioactive seepage and accidental leaks. Whereas in French Polynesia there were only 120 000 people, not fully aware of the dangers and of a more fatalistic turn of mind. This explains why, in 1962, de Gaulle had decided to undertake atmospheric tests there. Now, for the same reason, ten years later, Pompidou ordered the army to find a suitable place for underground testing somewhere in the islands. The whole project was to be kept strictly secret.

As usual the secret soon got out. The first hint was furnished in early August of 1972 by an extraordinarily large number of boxes and crates piled up on the wharf in the middle of Papeete in full view of the thousands of people driving by each day. Shortly afterwards a big warship docked and began loading them. Each box and crate was marked in big block letters EIAO, the name of a small, uninhabited island (or rather rock) in the Marquesas group. Only one year before, the local newspapers had had a great deal to say about this little-known island which, according to a couple of French scientists who had just surveyed it, had preserved its original flora to a much greater extent than any other island in French Polynesia. Consequently the Territorial Assembly had followed the advice of these enthusiastic scientists and voted a law declaring Eiao a protected national park. There was no doubt that this was the island that the bomb people were illegally going to ruin now. The fact that some of the crates contained billiard tables and movie projectors clearly indicated that they were to stay there for a long while. A wealth of drilling equipment bore equally eloquent witness to the nature of their task.

The governor hurriedly put out a story that the expedition was organised by the French Geological Service (BRGM) with the aim of mining the huge deposits of titanium located in the central core of the island. But he singularly failed to explain how the geologists could know anything *in advance* about these titanium deposits. Nor did he comment on the well known fact that there is an abundance of titanium in Europe at prices far below those that any mining company in the antipodes would be able to offer.

During the next six months the local press continued to keep us informed about the work of these uniformed 'geologists'. It consisted of drilling several holes down through the basalt rock to a depth of 1000 metres. No minerals were found, which did not seem to bother them much; but on the other hand they seemed saddened by the fragility of the basalt rock and it was impossible not to ascribe their sadness to the fact that this made Eiao unsuitable for all nuclear underground tests.

It is not unlikely that this failure or general mix-up had something to do with Debré's elimination from the 'new' government formed by the badly shaken Messmer after the half-lost general election in March 1973. Debré's departure was all the more significant as most of the other ministers stayed on after having simply changed portfolios. His successor as minister for defence was Robert Galley, who up until then had been minister for scientific research, and as such had worked hard to promote the nuclear striking force. One of the few new faces in the post-election cabinet was that of a 43-year-old deputy, Bernard Stasi, who became minister for overseas territories. For a change he was not a member of the Gaullist party but belonged to a conservative splinter party hiding under the grand label *Centre Démocratie et Progrès*. However these cabinet changes did not matter much since all powers were concentrated into the hands of the president, whose name was still Pompidou. As could be expected the latter's aversion to making underground tests in metropolitan France was as strong as ever. He now decided, therefore, to resume the atmospheric tests, at the same time ordering the disguised CEA-CEP 'geologists' to continue their drillings somewhere else in French Polynesia.

It was this retrogade decision that had prompted Pouvanaa and Sanford to publish their open letter and that had eventually led to the mass meeting in Papeete. With an incredible lack of imagination the 'new' French government parried by publishing a White Book (in French) that simply repeated these same old lies (pp. 6–9):

(1) The explosions take place only when the weather conditions are absolutely safe, which they are during the southern winter, when the wind blows from west to east at all altitudes – towards an uninhabited zone measuring 6000 kilometres.

(2) There is a network of monitoring stations in the immediate vicinity of the tests, as well as elsewhere in French Polynesia. Numerous samples of the air, the seawater, the marine animals (fishes, shells, plankton) and the food products consumed on the atolls are systematically collected and then analysed in laboratories possessing the most modern equipment. In addition other monitoring stations have been established in more remote parts of the world, beginning with the French Overseas Departments (Réunion and Guiana), but also in many other countries.

(3) The results of our researches and those made in foreign countries are transmitted to the UN Committee on the Effects of Atomic Radiation *thus making it possible to verify the harmlessness of our tests*. The radiation produced by our testing is actually *so insignificant that it may be completely disregarded*.

The only new data concerned the health hazards represented by migratory species of fish contaminated in the waters around Moruroa. But the main aim was to rebut Peruvian complaints that tuna and bonito caught along the west coast of South America had been poisoned by the nuclear tests. This was impossible, declared the White Book, for these species never cross the intervening ocean in a straight line but always travel in a wide circle, first toward the Society and Cook Islands, then southward down into the roaring forties, which they follow eastward until they reach the tip of South America, then swimming north with the Humboldt current. According to the authors of this White Book, it takes the bonito and tuna at least eighteen months to make this enormous circuit. As a result they have lost all of their radioactivity upon eventually reaching the coastal waters of Peru. But what guarantee do we have that such highly contaminated fish are not caught shortly after having left Moruroa – let us say in the Society or Cook Islands? The White Book had nothing to say about this danger.

Not surprisingly this piece of science fiction was completely overlooked and ignored, both in the Pacific countries and elsewhere in the world. On the other hand the new Labour governments in New Zealand and Australia had in the meanwhile devised new, spectacular methods of drawing world attention to France's stubborn refusal to stop polluting the southern hemisphere. To begin with they made a joint petition to the

International Court of Justice in the Hague, requesting it to issue forthwith an interim injunction against the tests, and the fact that the hearings dragged on for several weeks only contributed to keeping the case in the public eye. Equally effective in this respect was the dispatch of a New Zealand frigate to Moruroa. But by far the most courageous and successful actions were the protest cruises of the *Fri* and *Greenpeace III*, which doggedly kept up their watch against heavy odds outside the forbidden zone, until the French high command had no other choice but to board the vessels in international waters and seize them and their crews by force. The presence on board the *Fri* of General Paris de Bollardière and his peace commandos, as well as the eye injury inflicted on Skipper McTaggart of the *Greenpeace III* by the French boarding party, were highlighted in the universally adverse reports published in the world press.

It was now obvious, even to Pompidou and Messmer, that they could not go on forever flouting international opinion. Therefore another site suitable for underground tests had to be found in a hurry, or the whole nuclear programme abandoned. Very conveniently the government 'geologists' who had made the unsuccessful test drillings at Eiao declared at this critical stage that they had found the ideal site. The new minister for defence, Robert Galley, flew out to Tahiti to announce the good news, primarily for the benefit of the Australian and New Zealand governments and people. To the stupefaction of the foreign journalists attending his well-prepared press conference on 30 August 1973, the site chosen for future underground tests was none other than the atoll of Fangataufa, often used for atmospheric tests until it became too heavily contaminated by the 2.5 megatonne thermonuclear blast on 24 August 1968. How was it that nobody had previously understood that the ideal place for blowing up atomic bombs is a tiny atoll? Why had the 'geologists' wasted six months drilling holes in a brittle rock like Eiao when this splendid alternative existed? These were the two key questions that the journalists wanted Galley to answer. He responded in his own way by promising, with a big smile, that a group of journalists would soon be taken on a conducted tour of Fangataufa, but declined any further comment. After all, there were certain military secrets that could not be revealed.

The promised press visit took place at the end of October 1973. Of the eleven carefully selected journalists, two worked for the French government agency AFP, two were employed by the

French government Radio and Television System (ORTF), while the remaining seven all represented solidly conservative French newspapers. Servan-Schreiber's weekly *Express,* which had shown the most active interest in the tests, was not allowed to send a correspondent. After much feasting in Tahiti, the members of the party were flown out to Fangataufa, where they were met by the top technician in charge of the testing programme, Claude Ayçoberry. He took them to a derrick of the ordinary type used by all oil men, and proudly explained that his crew had drilled through the 500-metre-thick top layer of soft coral as 'full of holes as gruyère cheese', and had just reached the hard rock below. One of the reporters wanted to know what kind of rock it was. Well, it was basalt, admitted Ayçoberry, without specifying that Eiao was formed of the same rock which the same 'geologists' had found so brittle that all plans for using that island for underground tests had been abandoned.

It soon became apparent that the only thing that seriously worried Ayçoberry was how to measure the effects of each underground blast. The atmospheric tests had been easy to study from observation towers and aeroplanes had always been able to collect radioactive particles, which quickly supplied all necessary information. In order to obtain any data at all when the tests were made underground, instruments had first to be lowered into the pit and samples brought up to the surface after the blast by drilling new holes at an oblique angle. Even if and when these delicate techniques had been mastered, it was far from certain that the data retrieved would provide all the answers. Ayçoberry made no secret of his opinion that it was sheer folly to abandon a technique of proven efficiency in favour of a less reliable one, exclusively in order to placate a handful of wild and woolly political agitators. But of course on the other hand, it was an exalting task to be a pioneer in an entirely new domain, for up until then nowhere in the world had anybody ever tried to detonate atomic bombs in the core of a small coral island.

Some of the approved French newspapers published not only the factual accounts of their correspondents but also editorials. In these the French government was unanimously congratulated for the elegant and diplomatic manner in which it had solved the stupid international conflicts resulting from politically inspired protests against the clean French tests. None of the reporters had cared to ask the Polynesian leaders what *they* thought of this· solution. But Pouvanaa, Teariki, and Sanford did not have to wait long for an opportunity to speak their minds. It came in January 1974 when the new minister for overseas territories, Bernard Stasi, came out to Tahiti to take stock. During a mass meeting they repeatedly and angrily condemned all forms of nuclear tests in Polynesia and asked for immediate self-government. Each time they were wildly applauded by the 4000 people attending the meeting.

Stasi, who incidentally was the twelfth minister in as many years, turned out to be a handsome man in his early forties, with agile mind and body. In pleasant contrast to his slow-moving and formal predecessor, he mingled freely with the crowd and literally jumped at every occasion offered to display his considerable talent as a dancer. He had previously manifested his liberal views by publicly criticising the fascist régime in Chile and the scandalous electoral frauds in the French overseas department of Réunion (earning him severe reprimand from Pompidou and the Réunion deputy, Michel Debré). In Tahiti Stasi justified his reputation to some extent by promising to repeal some of the old colonial decrees of 1932 which gave the governor dictatorial powers, and he definitely gave the impression of being capable of a certain sincerity and compassion. Of course he did not dare disobey his instructions to the point of engaging in dialogue with the Autonomists. But upon his return to Paris he took the unprecedented step of mentioning in a press release not only the government-sponsored meetings and the ghost-written patriotic speeches but also the Autonomist protests and demands. This was too much for his bosses. When for the fourth time in two years Prime Minister Pierre Messmer reshuffled his hapless cabinet on 1 March 1974, Stasi got the sack without ceremony. In order to avoid any similar blunders in the future, Messmer decided to assume direct responsibility for the overseas territories. To that end he installed a trusted non-entity of a man, Comiti, as a sort of executive secretary, in Hôtel Matignon, next to his own office. Without the faintest trace of irony in his voice, Messmer explained in front of the TV cameras this sudden disappearance of a whole ministry in the following terms: 'As everybody will surely realise, this new arrangement will make it possible to handle overseas problems with the special care and attention they merit'.

39 GISCARD'S NEW DEAL

Messmer's popularity continued to decline at such a rapid pace that it was only a matter of time before his turn to be dismissed would come. Or in more vulgar though equally accurate terms, he was in the state of a groggy boxer who had already lost the fight but was desperately trying to avoid being k.o.'ed. He was saved by Pompidou's sudden death on 2 April 1974, which allowed him to make a slightly more honourable exit. For the people of Polynesia Pompidou's death amounted to their being given an unexpected new opportunity of deciding their own destiny two years earlier than foreseen, since Pompidou had been elected in 1969 for a seven-year period.

Gaston Flosse and the other local Gaullists decided with touching faithfulness to support the only sure-loser amongst the presidential candidates, Chaban-Delmas. The two leaders of the small group of 'independent' members of the Territorial Assembly, Frantz Vanizette and Charles Taufa, were more clever, flying off to Paris without saying a word. On their return they were more talkative and declared that, exactly as they had suspected, the leader of the Independent Republican party, Giscard d'Estaing, was the candidate able and willing to do the most for French Polynesia. In all his speeches and manifestos, not only did he promise a new deal with far-reaching social reforms but had also, albeit a little more discreetly, declared that in the overseas territories this meant internal self-government. When it came to nuclear policy, Giscard was against further atmospheric tests and in favour of underground testing, without bothering to say anything about the delicate problem of where these tests should be made. For Vanizette and Taufa these declarations were quite satisfactory, since they pleased the Polynesian voters without scaring too much the Frenchmen and *demis* who derived much of their income from the CEP-CEA organisations and the troops.

For their part Pouvanaa, Teariki and Sanford had no confidence in any of de Gaulle's men and saw no difference at all between 'pure' Gaullists like Messmer and Chaban-Delmas and 'independent' collaborators like Giscard d'Estaing who had been de Gaulle's minister of finance for many years. Their only hope for salvation was, therefore, represented by the third candidate, François Mitterand, leader of the Socialist or Labour party. In the latter's campaign manifestos there figured a clear promise to let the inhabitants of the French overseas territories decide for themselves, through a referendum, the sort of government they wanted. As for the nuclear tests, they were to be suspended at once, and in the unlikely event that they would have to be resumed, the new government promised to consult the Polynesian people first.

Back in 1965, Teariki had managed with difficulty to persuade the Polynesian electorate to vote for Mitterand. Since then the Socialist party had formed an alliance with the Communist party, which made it even harder for the Autonomist parties to defend his candidacy. Both the Protestant pastors and the Catholic priests had instilled in the deeply religious Polynesians a profound aversion to the godless Communists, and they were therefore reluctant about a candidate who was allied with the devil's disciples. Pouvanaa, Teariki and Sanford retorted, of course, that whatever the repercussions might be in metropolitan France, a victory for Mitterand was the only way for the Polynesian people to achieve their goals.

Their adversaries did not hesitate to play on the religious prejudices of the Polynesian voters, and even exploited them to the limit after the elimination of Chaban-Delmas on the first round when it became apparent that Mitterand had a good chance of beating Giscard d'Estaing. They rapidly covered the buildings with posters and filled the local newspapers with full-page ads in both French and Tahitian, warning the gullible Polynesians against the persecutions that would befall them if Mitterand won. (Incidentally, Mitterand was a good Catholic, even though he did not attend mass every Sunday.) As a typical example of the Red terror, it was mentioned in big type that in Russia, *in one single year*, 66 bishops and 8100 priests had been murdered. The year was 1922, but that was mentioned in much smaller type. Another time, the local propagandists for Giscard succeeded with an astonishing accuracy in counting all the Russian churches that had been closed by the Reds between 1917 and 1939. They numbered no less than 53900! For the more sophisticated Polynesians and *demis* working in the administration or for private business firms there was another series of posters and ads, spreading the equally terrifying news that a Mitterand victory meant higher taxes, a devaluation of the currency, and general unemployment. As for the last category of voters, the French settlers and merchants and the CEP-CEA personnel, no special terror campaign was needed: they all knew for whom to vote.

The campaign rules were as unfair as ever. For instance Giscard d'Estaing's and Mitterand's recorded speeches addressed exclusively to metropolitan voters were retransmitted by the local radio and TV station, but the local political leaders were forbidden from explaining in French and Tahitian why they were for one or the other of the candidates and what his victory would mean on the local level. Neither were they allowed to embark on the navy and government ships which made the circuit of all the inhabited islands to distribute the ballots and the approved metropolitan propaganda. Because election day was so near they were unable to visit the outer islands on other vessels. Nor could they reach the electors on time with circulars mailed through the post office. Thus, as usual, the only persons present and able to wage a campaign in the outer islands were the French missionaries, administrators and CEP-CEA personnel.

In spite of all these tremendous handicaps, Mitterand won in French Polynesia, with 51.23 per cent of the votes as against 48.76 for Giscard. Revealingly enough, the only archipelagos where Giscard obtained a majority were the Marquesas with a 90 per cent Catholic population and the Tuamotus with 70 per cent Catholics. In the south-east corner of the Tuamotus, the combined efforts of the Catholic missionaries and the officers of the nuclear forces – who of course all preached the same gospel – produced particularly impressive results. Take for instance Tureia with a total population of sixty persons, where the following unbeatable score was officially recorded and accepted:

Registered voters	Ballots cast	Valid ballots	Giscard d'Estaing	François Mitterand
45	45	45	45	0

Nevertheless the votes cast for Giscard as a result of 'friendly persuasion' were much fewer than those cast by the French colonial servants, technicians, officers, soldiers, sailors, and temporary civilian residents whose number certainly exceeded 10 000. If their ballots had been counted in their home constituencies in France, as they in all fairness should have been, and not used to bolster the total figures for French Polynesia, Mitterand's victory here would naturally have been much greater, not to say crushing.

Giscard d'Estaing had a narrow victory over Mitterand in France as a whole, and the first thing he did after acceding to the presidency and appointing a cabinet was to vow solemnly on 8 June 1974 to make underground tests only, from 1975 onwards. Unfortunately the impact abroad of this excellent resolution was greatly spoiled by his simultaneous admission that a last series of atmospheric tests had to be made at Moruroa during the forthcoming months. The new minister for the defence, a retired colonel named Soufflet of whom nobody had ever heard, explained the importance and urgency of these farewell blasts by saying with a straight face that the bombs to be tested were for fighter planes, and the aim was to find out how they behaved when dropped. Consequently it was not possible to make such tests underground. Although the logic of his conclusion was faultless, his premise seemed altogether wrong. Why use fighter planes for dropping small atomic bombs in 1974 when all nuclear powers delivered their bombs with the help of missiles, some of which had a range of 10 000 kilometres? Little by little the truth came out. In order to compensate for their failure to produce operational thermonuclear bombs within the prescribed time, the French military technicians had put together some 25-kilotonne tactical A-bombs to be used by Jaguar fighter planes for destroying 'limited targets' during a conventional war. Already, earlier – in their spare hours, so to say – they had produced even smaller, 10-kilotonne tactical bombs for thirty-six tanks. According to figures published by NATO headquarters, the American troops stationed in Europe by then possessed 7000 such tactical A-bombs, whereas the Russians probably had more than 10 000. Therefore it is extremely hard to understand why it was so urgent for the French bomb people to poison the Polynesian skies once more during the summer of 1974 in order to realise such an insignificant goal. The most likely explanation was that what mattered most was to soothe the ruffled feelings of a growing number of jealous and furious high army and air force officers who, year after year, had seen all military budget allowances spent on missiles and nuclear submarines.

Servan-Schreiber, whom Giscard had appointed minister for reforms, with wide powers, proposed as a first reform, aiming at both making certain economies and improving the relations with the Pacific peoples, the immediate suppression of these scheduled and completely senseless aerial tests. With his usual outspokenness he blamed Messmer for having presented a *fait accompli*.

According to JJSS's version, Messmer, who had stayed on as prime minister until Giscard's election, had used this respite – and the weakness of the interim president, Poher – to set in motion the whole CEP-CEA bomb machinery in French Polynesia, which had then moved on so smoothly and fast that it was too late for Giscard to stop it when he eventually discovered what was going on after his election. In confirmation the first bomb exploded only a few days later on. These unwelcome revelations made the numerous Gaullist ministers so furious that they told Giscard that he had to choose between them and JJSS. The new president, whose own party did not hold more than seventy seats in the National Assembly, could not govern without the support of the 173 Gaullist deputies, so JJSS had to go.

The first explosion on 16 June was quickly followed by seven others. When the last poisonous cloud drifted out over the ocean on 16 September, over a period of nine years France had detonated a total of forty-two nuclear devices in the Pacific skies. At least two were 150 kilotonnes, and the last one probably as much as one megatonne in strength – figures hardly tallying with the declared purpose of testing only small tactical weapons.

40 MIRV-Stirn

The mystery surrounding the first nuclear tests of Giscard's reign was soon dispelled. Even better, various spokesmen for the new government suddenly vied with each other with proud declarations about the accomplishments of the CEP-CEA technicians. To be sure they had indeed tested some small tactical A-bombs at Mororoa, but that was only half the story. For they had also launched out in a completely new direction, hopefully leading to the very pinnacle of military might. What they had done was nothing less than to test some experimental MIRV's, or at least some sort of gadgetry with multiple warheads. 'The chances are excellent that France will be able to update her whole nuclear arsenal by 1982', declared a happy general. The minister for defence was also optimistic, albeit a bit more cautious: 'We must keep up with the general evolution. It is always possible to perfect existing weapons. That is why the Russians and the Americans continue with their underground tests year after year. Consequently 1982 will only be the first stage in our progress along a road whose end we cannot yet clearly discern.'

It was at exactly this time, in September 1974, that President Ford and Secretary Brezhnev met in Vladivostok to discuss their MIRV problem, which was of just the opposite kind – they already had too many highly sophisticated thermonuclear MIRV's and were trying to limit their meaningless overkill capacity. Their tremendous achievements – Russia had developed missiles with eight independently targeted thermonuclear warheads of two megatonnes each, whereas America had preferred making smaller MIRV's with a superior aiming precision – were the result of ten years of research and gigantic investments. And now France with its limited technical and economic resources had just initiated a similar over-ambitious programme. It was hard to believe the news, but it was confirmed by Giscard d'Estaing in person in a televised address to the nation at the beginning of 1975 in which he said: 'I have been pondering the defence problems for some time, and I have finally arrived at the same conclusion as General de Gaulle, that our independence can only be assured by a mighty nuclear striking force'. But how mighty was it actually? Giscard admitted that America and Russia had a tremendous advance. 'But France is the third nuclear power in the world, which is a remarkable achievement for a country of our size.' The only thing that can be said of this way of reasoning is that few runners participating in a long-distance race in a sport stadium would be very proud of arriving in third position after having been overtaken several times by the winner and the number two man. Giscard also conveniently overlooked Great Britain, which surely had a more valid claim of being the number three nuclear power. Of course it was not long before the French nuclear champions had to eat their own words. Only a few months later the defence ministry let it be known that the programme had already been slightly revised: The first MIRV's were not to be operational until 1985!

Giscard had waged his campaign mainly on a promise to give the French people a new deal. Admittedly, within a short time after his election he managed to push a few long overdue reform bills through the National Assembly which, for instance, legalised certain abortions, lowered the voting age to 18, and simplified the medieval divorce laws. But at the same time his decision to pursue de Gaulle's and Pompidou's policy of nuclear grandeur excluded, as far as the Polynesian people were concerned, any hope of significant changes in their colonial status. For in order to carry out the new long-range MIRV programme, continued French domination of the islands was of course an absolute pre-requisite.

It was therefore urgent to find a new minister for the overseas territories, shrewd enough to hide this unpleasant truth as long as possible from the Polynesian leaders. Giscard's choice was one of the youngest and most handsome of the Gaullist deputies, Olivier Stirn. The son of a highranking civil servant, he chose the same career as his father and at the age of twenty-three became the right-hand man of the then minister for overseas territories, Louis Jacquinot, infamous in Polynesia for having solemnly promised in 1962 that no French nuclear tests were ever to be made in the Pacific. Stirn chose the right moment to enter politics – the summer of 1968 when the student revolt in Paris produced a conservative backlash in the provinces – and was easily swept into the National Assembly together with 357 other Gaullist candidates. Having been re-elected in 1973 after a mud-slinging campaign against strong left-wing contenders, he was rewarded with a cabinet post where his urbane manners, diplomatic finesse and persuasive tongue were put to good use; he became liaison minister between the government and parliament. All the while he continued to keep in touch with events in the overseas territories and with his many friends in his former ministry. The pay-off came even a little bit faster than expected, for he was only thirty-eight when Giscard made him a full-fledged minister, responsible for executing the government's policy in the five territories and four departments beyond the seas.

As far as French Polynesia was concerned, the fact that the new minister was well informed about colonial problems was even more disastrous than the total ignorance of his predecessors. It meant that he knew exactly where all the local leaders stood, and that he was able to forge in advance all the weapons he needed to combat and confound them. Having been repeatedly delayed by the vexatious problems in two other overseas territories, the Comoros Islands and Somaliland, whose inhabitants had a deplorable tendency towards rioting in protest against the government's refusal to give them independence on their own terms, Stirn eventually came out on his first official visit to French Polynesia in March 1975.

During his ten-day stay he behaved like an American presidential candidate, travelling about and shaking hands with everybody within reach. Now and then he even took a long walk on foot so as to be able to meet and talk to 'the people'. His headquarters in the governor's residence was open to every individual and organisation. During the numerous receptions, feasts and parties he attended, he chatted in a friendly manner with the local leaders, both Autonomist and Gaullist. Of course he also made many speeches in which he carefully avoided all controversial subjects. The avowed reason for this shyness was the political round-table conference to be held on the last day of his visit. When the local leaders were finally convened they did not waste any time about stating their wishes. There was also a surprisingly wide consensus; Autonomists and Gaullists alike wanted more power, and asked specifically for the creation of a government made up of local men, chosen by and responsible to the Territorial Assembly. This request cannot be considered revolutionary, being simply the sort of democratic system in existence in France and most other countries in Europe. Stirn listened attentively, asked polite questions, and said that he was going to take their wishes under consideration to the largest extent possible. In other words, nobody could have personified Giscard's new liberal reform deal better than this suave and charming young minister.

Addressing himself especially to the peoples of Australia, New Zealand, and the other Pacific islands, Stirn was even more explicit in an article published by the *Pacific Islands Monthly* in June 1975. He wrote:

In a somewhat curious way our tests have led some to question France's presence in the Pacific and in other regions of the world. Some, probably lacking adequate information, depict France as a country living in the past, preoccupied with preserving the last remnants of her colonial empire and with constraining against their will the populations of these territories within a system of exchange and relations directly inherited from colonialism. What a mistaken and unfair view! France has probably done more than any other country to emancipate people and respect their dignity. Where there is a wish for independence, France is granting it. Not as some powers have done, abandoning everything from one day to the next, thus exposing the newly independent countries to a long period of anarchy, but by leading them progressively to the full exercise of the responsibilities of national sovereignty.

The same month that Stirn publicly confessed to these liberal views, another round-table conference was held in the ministry for overseas territories in Paris, with a representative delegation of Polynesian political leaders whose travel expenses were all paid for by the French government. Once more they were kindly invited to express their ideas about how this progressive transfer of government responsibilities should be made, and they all responded by presenting concrete, detailed proposals. Though Stirn was remarkably unwilling to make any firm commitments – arguing that he was basically a sort of co-ordinator – the Polynesian leaders were quite hopeful about the final outcome.

Their anger and disappointment were, therefore, all the greater when, at long last, two months later, they received the text of the reform bill that Stirn had drafted on the basis of their consultations. All in all it was a thoroughly retrograde text that deprived the Territorial Assembly and the Government Council of most of the modest prerogatives they had hitherto enjoyed. Inversely the governor's position was greatly strengthened. Some assemblymen wondered half in earnest, half mockingly whether it was not an old nineteenth-century colonial statute which, after gathering dust in the ministry for several generations, now had been dispatched to Tahiti, due to some clerical mistake.

Stirn's own explanation – expounded in several radio and

newspaper interviews – for having presented a bill that disregarded all the demands made by the senator, the deputy, and the assemblymen, was that he knew better what the Polynesian people wanted, since he had personally consulted the people in question. How and where? Of course, during his short, hand-shaking tours of a few islands in March . . .

41 OPERATION OPEN ATOLL

While Stirn was 'consulting' the Polynesian people in his own curious way, the army 'geologists' were hard at work at Fangataufa drilling deeper and deeper down through the coral layer, encountering more and more unforeseen difficulties. The small group of hand-picked journalists who had visited the atoll in October 1973 had been told that the first experimental underground explosion was to take place 'within a year'. In February 1975, the commanding admiral issued a warning to foreign ships not to pass closer than 30 miles (48 kilometres), a sure sign that everything was ready for the big event. But month after month went by without any further news from Fangataufa.

In May it was rumoured in Papeete that the well-known French vulcanologist, Haroun Tazieff, had been asked by the CEP-CEA bosses to come out and examine the test site. The Autonomists, who were as concerned as ever about the dangers of radioactive contamination, tried to contact him, but his hosts cloaked all his movements in such complete secrecy that nobody managed to get even a glimpse of him. However it was not possible to keep him from talking if he wanted to once he was back in France, and an enterprising reporter from one of the Tahitian newspapers who looked him up there actually had no difficulties at all in obtaining an interview. Tazieff began by stating categorically that he was 'firmly opposed to all forms of nuclear tests', in the same breath adding: 'The fact that I accepted an invitation from the army to visit Fangataufa therefore does not mean that I approve of the tests made there'. As he told the story, the bomb people were anxious above all that there might be cracks in the volcanic base of the atoll and fissures in the surrounding sea bed. Unfortunately the data gathered by the army 'geologists' were so limited that Tazieff had been unable to draw any valid conclusions. It was nevertheless his considered opinion that 'certain rocks are so porous and lacking in shock-resistance that there is a risk of radioactive leakage'. And he concluded: 'As the tests will be made in spite of all this, the best solution is to request an impartial scientific organisation to supervise them.'

While Tazieff's cautious views and mild warnings were still being pondered in the islands, the Australian government announced on 7 June 1975 that its seismographic observatories had registered an underground explosion in the south-east corner of the Tuamotu group. Two days later the French ministry of defence admitted that a small eight-kilotonne bomb had indeed been exploded in the core of Fangataufa at a depth of 623 metres. The pro-government French weekly *Le Point* followed up on 16 June with the following enthusiastic bulletin:

EUPHORIA AT FANGATAUFA

Since the first explosion occurred at Fangataufa, the anxious mood prevailing there until then has given way to general euphoria. Everything went exactly according to plan, and the test was entirely successful. This first test will be followed in quick succession by four others. The reason for the previous anxiety was fear that the atoll might crack, leading to pollution of the ocean.

This sounded too good to be true – and unfortunately was not. The 'geologists' had definitely not had time to undertake the numerous drillings all over the atoll which alone could have permitted them to find out whether or not any cracks and vents had occurred at the inner base of the atoll. Neither did they possess the necessary diving apparatus to examine it from the ocean side all the way down to the bottom, 4000 metres below the surface. Even if somehow this first minuscule explosion had not produced the slightest cracks and fissures, it was still extremely doubtful that the coral conglomerate and basalt rock forming the atoll would resist future and much more powerful explosions.

Very few persons in South America, Australia, New Zealand, Fiji, and other Pacific countries shared the euphoria of the CEP-CEA team at Fangataufa. There seemed nonetheless to exist a general tendency in all foreign government circles to believe that a new era had dawned in France with the election of Giscard, and in the absence of the visible symbols of their hatred, the atomic mushrooms over Moruroa, most of the protest movements lost their ardour, too. The French government did all in its power to foster these illusions, and mounted clever diplomatic, trade and press offensives aimed at soothing residual resentment in those countries.

One of the most important propaganda manoeuvres consisted of organising a new press visit to Fangataufa in September 1975, called 'Operation open atoll'. As a measure of the tremendous progress towards liberalisation made since the last visit in 1973, the party this time was made up of not less than sixty journalists representing practically the whole political spectrum in France, and even included a few newspaper and radio reporters from New Zealand, Fiji and Australia. Furthermore all three dailies in French Polynesia were for the first time allowed to send their best staff writers who were of course infinitely better informed about local conditions than their metropolitan and foreign colleagues. The following account of this quite interesting press visit is, by the way, based on their accounts.

After the usual feasting and sightseeing in Tahiti, the reporters were received at Fangataufa by the same technician who had been in charge in 1973, Claude Ayçoberry. However they were a little more curious than their predecessors, for they immediately established through a quick cross-examination that he was neither geologist nor nuclear physicist, but simply a former navy officer who had obtained a degree in electrical engineering. The radiological security service was likewise not headed by a specialist but by a military doctor who had probably been chosen for the job because of his name – Lavie.

Their next discovery was the incredibly tiny size of the atoll, roughly five by eight kilometres, and the narrowness of the coral ring or rim, which rarely exceeded 200 metres. In many places the sea washed constantly over the low reef, and the little vegetation there consisted of low bushes. Ayçoberry and his men took the party to the southern portion of the reef ring where the first bomb had been detonated at a depth of 623 metres. The site of the test pit was marked by a concrete slab with a crack across it. One of the reporters was nasty enough to ask whether the bomb had not caused similar cracks in the coral conglomerate and basalt rock in the inner part of the atoll and whether as a consequence some radioactivity might not have leaked out into the ocean. Ayçoberry denied this very energetically without revealing how he could know anything about possible leakages at great depths. Lavie came to his assistance with the deadpan assertion that he had 'scientifically' calculated that it would take 1500 years for the encapsulated radioactivity to seep out into the ocean. By that time, he added, it would of course be harmless. This brilliant demonstration left his audience speechless with admiration. Lavie used this pause to inform them about the annual reports to the UN Scientific Committee on the Effects of Atomic Radiation which constituted definite proof that the forty-one bombs exploded in the skies above Moruroa and Fangataufa had not polluted the environment in the slightest degree. For some unexplained and unexplainable reasons, however, he did not distribute any copies of these reports among the reporters.

Next stop was on the northern rim of the reef where an oil rig marked the site of the next test hole, being drilled at that time. The hole was 2.5 metres across at the surface but gradually decreased in size to about one metre at a depth of 500 metres. When completed, steel tubes were to be sunk into the hole and welded together section after section. The bomb could then be lowered, together with all sorts of measuring instruments attached to long cables. Finally the 600-metre-deep hole was to be filled with special concrete plugs so as to prevent poisonous gases and radioactivity from escaping.

Unfortunately, said Ayçoberry, the observations that could be made with the help of these instruments embedded in the test pit were inadequate for precise determination of the success of the blast. Therefore, after each explosion, it was necessary to drill another hole at an oblique angle down to the cavity formed by the melted rock in order to bring radioactive samples up to the surface. One of the visitors wanted to know how the technicians went about preventing gas and radioactive particles from escaping through these new openings, but before a satisfactory answer was forthcoming another reporter shouted: 'But the hole is full of water! Where does it come from?'

Of course it came from the surrounding ocean. But Ayçoberry was quick to refute the obvious conclusion that if it had seeped *in* through the coral and basalt rock before the explosion, it could just as well seep *out* the same way after it. In his opinion that was simply not possible because all the water was transformed into steam when the bomb went off. Not everybody was satisfied with this answer, which left out the whole problem of continuing seepage after the explosion. But they were all tired, thirsty and hungry and perfectly willing to leave matters there and drive off to the officers' mess where a sumptuous meal was awaiting them.

Later on, the party was flown over to Moruroa and taken to one of the two gigantic concrete pyramids used as watch towers or observation posts during the atmospheric tests, and now of course empty and abandoned like the fortresses in the Maginot line. Here they were given another lecture about the reorganisation of the CEP-CEA. After these first two experimental blasts on Fangataufa all further underwater tests were to be made on Moruroa and, to save money, all troops were to be brought over from Tahiti and stationed there. Their number had been reduced to 3000, which meant an additional saving. On the other hand it cost 80 million French francs ($A1 500 000) to drill a small test pit, and the cost would increase as bigger bombs had to be detonated at gradually greater and greater depths. Of course each pit could be used only once. How many tests were to be made each year was a great secret, so let us only add here as an indication that the number of American underground tests has averaged about thirty a year since the Partial Test Ban went into effect in 1963, and that the corresponding Russian figure is fifteen.

This time a couple of the visiting reporters also went to see the principal critic of both atmospheric and underwater testing, Francis Sanford. He was ready, and gave them the following text of a written question that he had addressed in the French National Assembly to Prime Minister Jacques Chirac and Minister for Defence Yvon Bourges on 24 May 1975:

Considering that the island first chosen for undertaking underground tests, Eiao in the Marquesan group, had to be abandoned, Mr Sanford should like to know whether any scientific studies have been made of the geological formation of Fangataufa and Moruroa and if so, whether they clearly prove that there is no risk that the lagoons and the surrounding ocean may become contaminated and that its flora and fauna may eventually absorb concentrated doses of radioactivity. He asks furthermore if it is not to be feared that repeated nuclear explosions in the base of these atolls may result in an accumulation of radioactive elements and their gradual diffusion into the ocean environment through the porous rock of which they are formed. In view of the scientific, non-military character of these alleged geological studies, the deputy requests moreover that the CEP-CEA be immediately authorised to publish them.

Exactly three months later, on 24 August, the minister for defence replied:

The most suitable sites have been surveyed, and Fangataufa and Moruroa have been chosen. The extensive studies that have been undertaken make it highly improbable that any radioactivity will leak out into the lagoons or into the ocean. However if for some unforeseen reason a leak should occur, nothing more than gases containing low concentrations of short-life nuclides, completely harmless for the environment, would then escape. All radioactive matter will moreover be encapsulated in the vitrified lava produced by each blast. At any rate the composition of the rocks is such that the radioactivity emanating from an explosion would only filter slowly through them. During this slow process even long-life fallout would lose its radioactivity and this to such an extent that when it might eventually reach the marine environment the radiation dose would be below the measurable level!

Sanford waited patiently until his guests had stopped laughing and then showed them a small cylindrical object. It was a core from one of the test pits at Fangataufa, smuggled out by a Polynesian workman. The brownish core was full of holes. Of course the geological studies cited by the minister for defence as the ultimate proof of the solidity of the atoll rocks have never been made public. There is every reason to believe, therefore, that the underwater tests at Moruroa will continue to pollute the environment as badly as did the previous tests, and that the plankton, fishes, shells, clams, and squid, regularly eaten by all Pacific islanders, will also absorb in the future dangerous doses of both short-life and long-life radioactive fallout.

Naturally the most exposed region will be, as in the past, eastern Polynesia; but we must not forget that strong and stable ocean currents exist which may carry contaminated plankton and fish all the way to the shores of New Zealand and Australia. Thus the only difference now is that whereas, in the past, the radioactive contamination could be detected immediately by the New Zealand monitoring stations in the islands, from now on it will take months and years before unsuspecting victims of this more insidious form of poisoning will become aware of what has happened to them. If they ever do.

42 SHALL WE HAVE TO USE AFRICAN METHODS?

With the bulk of the CEP-CEA personnel and material thus transferred from Tahiti to Moruroa and Hao, it was of course sorely tempting for the French government to repeat a dirty trick it had just pulled off in another overseas territory, the Comoros Islands in the Indian Ocean, at the time when they won their independence. One of these islands, Mayotte, happened to have a good harbour, badly needed by the French navy. The population was therefore encouraged to ask for continued French protection, and Paris obligingly responded by separating and isolating Mayotte from the other islands with the avowed aim of transforming it into a French overseas department.

There was no doubt that the same tactics could be applied with equal success in French Polynesia, considering that the Catholic population of the Tuamotu and Marquesas islands always had solidly voted for the Gaullist party. All that was needed was to create a new constituency, comprising these two archipelagos and entitled to elect its own deputy – who would then ask Paris to transform it into a department, making it French forever! If such a manoeuvre caused the Autonomists in Tahiti and the other remaining islands to opt for independence, Paris would only be too glad to abandon them to their fate. For, as the French ministers, admirals and generals saw it, this meant simply an end to the troubles fomented by Autonomist agitators, and an end to useless give-aways to recalcitrant voters.

Little by little, another consideration prevailed, however, and eventually made Paris abandon its plan to balkanize French Polynesia. As we all know, the Pacific Ocean contains a tremendous, unexploited wealth in the form of food, metals and oil, and the more islands a government owns, the greater its share will be. The utter failure of the 1975–76 UN conferences on the sea to reach an agreement encouraged all maritime nations to extend unilaterally their territorial waters and economic zones as far as possible, and France was no exception. Its biggest grabs could obviously be made in eastern Polynesia with its many far-flung islands. These glittering economic perspectives explain why in the end Stirn's much-heralded statutory reform bill, when transmitted to the Polynesian Assembly in October 1975, turned out to be a blue-print for transforming the *whole* of French Polynesia into a French department.

As usual, the first and loudest protests came from Francis Sanford. By a lucky coincidence, he was even able to make himself heard in Paris, since this was the time of the year when the budget of the overseas territories was discussed in the National Assembly. In consequence, he had for once a guaranteed right to intervene, and the time alloted to him on this occasion was fully five minutes... To save time and money, he dispatched a written message to Paris and asked the deputy for New Caledonia, Roch Pidjot, to read it in the Assembly, on the appointed day, November 5. In this strong plea for a more decent deal, Sanford began by placing the basic problem in its proper geographical and historical perspective:

Whereas practically all former British, Australian and New Zealand territories in the Pacific are now independent states, here in French Polynesia all our attempts to modernize the old colonial statute, dating from the era of the sailing ships, have consistently been thwarted in the most categorical and brutal manner by first General de Gaulle and then President Pompidou.

After having briefly recalled some of their most repressive actions, Sanford went straight to the heart of the matter:

What counts today, however, are not the words and deeds of those who are dead, but what you who are still alive think and do, particularly those of you, wherever you are sitting in the hemicycle, who proclaim that you are in favour of profound changes and reforms. I was filled with new hopes when I listened to the inaugural message from President Giscard d'Estaing, read from the tribune of this Assembly, on May 30, 1974. The words which I appreciated most were the following: 'France definitely opts for an increasingly liberal policy and will henceforth everywhere in the world work for the cause of freedom and the right of the peoples, I specify all peoples, to be their own masters'. I wondered of course whether this noble principle applied solely to the peoples under English, Dutch, Portuguese and Spanish rule, or also to us. To my great satisfaction, the new minister for Overseas Territories, Olivier Stirn, shortly afterwards dispelled my doubts by solemnly declaring that he planned to grant French Polynesia a new statute of such a liberal character that it was to be just one step removed from independence. Our colleague Roch Pidjot, the deputy for New Caledonia, was present at this meeting and can easily confirm that such were the terms of the promise then made.

Later on, Monsieur Stirn came to see us in our islands in order to listen to our complaints and wishes. The words reoccurring most often in his pretty speeches were 'dialogue', 'consultation' and 'change'. At the end of his stay, he made another shining promise: this 'freedom charter', opening a new era, was to be introduced in the parliament during this Fall session.

But what do we see today? With a delay of several months, we have just received the draft of a bill which represents such a step backward that I can well believe that it is a text from the imperial days of our grandparents dug up in the archives at Rue Oudinot. The only person in our territory who gets more power is the governor who will become a high-commissioner! I should like to ask you, dear French colleagues, if you would consent to have your country ruled by a civil servant who is at the same time president and prime minister and who is furthermore dispensed with the obligation of having his actions approved by the parliament? This is nevertheless the system of government in our country. Worse yet, Monsieur Stirn intends to strengthen his hold on us. Whereas we simply ask for your democratic system, meaning a government made up of responsible, elected ministers.

Sanford concluded his message with this warning:

During our twenty year long fight against the colonial system, we Polynesians have hitherto respected the established law and order. But I now begin to realize that this may be the very reason why the French government consistently has disregarded our aspirations. I am confirmed in this belief when I see, for instance, that each time there are disorders and blood flows, in Somaliland, the French government always promptly accedes to the demands of the people. This is how they have long ago obtained the sort of genuine self-government with an elected cabinet, headed by a prime minister, that we have vainly been asking for in Polynesia. Do we really have to resort to African – or Corsican – methods to make ourselves heard?

The few MPs who had cared to show up were of course thoroughly bored by this silly speech about matters of no immediate concern to themselves and their electorate. No debate ensued therefore, and as they were used to, the Gaullist and Giscardian deputies automatically approved all government proposals on the spot. Yet, the fate of French Polynesia was entirely in their hands. True, according to the constitution, Stirn's reform bill had first to be sent to the Territorial Assembly in Papeete, but this requirement was sheer mockery, considering that this body was only permitted to express 'an opinion'. Whereupon – whatever that opinion was – the government majority in the French National Assembly could, and certainly would, make it into a new law, without further ado.

Of course, it would look better – especially to the countries in and around the Pacific – if the National Assembly did not impose the new statute against the will of the elected representatives of the Polynesian people. Stirn and his local henchmen therefore applied some particularly persuasive methods, accompanied by liberal dispensations (existing libel laws do not permit a more precise wording), to win over two Autonomist assemblymen in financial difficulties. Their first reward was a free trip to Paris to see the sights and hobnob with leading Gaullist and Giscardian politicians. This tipped the balance in the Territorial Assembly slightly in favour of the Gaullist-Independent coalition.

Outraged by this betrayal, the Autonomists hit back in a much more honest and ingenious manner. They took advantage of the temporary absence of the pro-government fellow travellers – five altogether and convened (as they could easily do, having the speaker on their side), an extraordinary night session at such short notice that it was materially impossible for the jolly tourists to return to Tahiti in time. Having thus temporarily regained their former majority, the Autonomist assemblymen quickly formulated an extremely unfavourable opinion of the proposed retrograde 'reform' bill. As soon as Stirn learnt about this truly extraordinary night session, he peremptorily ordered Governor Videau to send in a company of gendarmes to stop the proceedings. The latter objected that this was illegal, an objection which so infuriated the overseas minister that he sacked the governor. To succeed him, Stirn sent out a sterner man named Charles Schmitt (an Alsatian), who had been a sort of political superintendent in the police department during the repressive reign of de Gaulle's hated Minister of the Interior, Marcel Marcellin.

43 NO OTHER CHOICE

The Autonomists were by then loudly clamouring for the dissolution of the Territorial Assembly, on the quite justified grounds that it was no longer representative. When this demand was rejected by Stirn, the Speaker refused to convene it further, thus blocking the whole parliamentary machinery. Next, in an unprecedented move, the French Prime Minister Jacques Chirac, stepped into the act by issuing an authoritarian decree declaring the famous night session illegal. But so was probably also his decree, and the Autonomists promptly appealed to the State Council to have it quashed.

While waiting for its verdict (it may take the Council several years to reach it), Senator Pouvanaa, Deputy Sanford and Speaker Vanizette jointly published a manifesto, warning the French government that its high-handed methods left them no other choice but to resort to extra-parliamentary actions. Their manifesto began thus:

If the present relations between Paris and Tahiti do not improve, Polynesia will not remain French much longer. When will the French government learn something from all its missed opportunities to decolonize? When will it stop using stooges, whose only interest is to make money, to maintain for a short while a rotten system which is a disgrace to France and for which there exists no moral justification whatsoever? When will the government at long last accept the world as it is and take into consideration the will of our people instead of stifling it?

After having related the main episodes of their recent struggles, they concluded in the same vein:

Nothing else can be more dangerous in Polynesia, or elsewhere, than to refuse the irresistible march of the colonial peoples towards greater freedom and democracy. The present government condemns itself by trying to arrest this movement with quickly forgotten promises, legal infringements and threats against our persons. This is a much too fragile dam against the torrent of freedom that will rapidly destroy it and sweep away not only the rotten structures but also those which might have been worth preserving.

The French government is keeping its control over Polynesia in order to avoid having to undertake unpopular nuclear tests at home, and because these 4 800 000 square kilometres of ocean contain enormous mineral resources, coveted by French mining companies. But these desperate efforts will come to nothing. Polynesia will remain French only with the consent of its inhabitants. A prerequisite is that we have good reasons for wanting to remain French, and the best reason France can give us is to acknowledge our right to run our own affairs. Instead of offering us, as Mr Stirn does, a statute comparable to the beads used for barter trade in the past. The colonial period is over, Mr Stirn. It is now 1976!

This strongly worded manifest was published at the beginning of May, barely one month before the expiration of the 1975–76 parliamentary session of the Territorial Assembly. According to the rules, the new 1976–77 session was to be convened not by the speaker but by the governor, who, on order from Paris, let it be known in advance that if necessary he was going to use troops to re-open the doors of the Assembly. True to his words, on the appointed day, June 10 1976, the governor dispatched an impressive number of gendarmes, equipped with automatic rifles, tear-gas grenades, helmets and face-shields. To their consternation they found the gates locked and the building occupied by two thousand Polynesians.

When the governor arrived under police escort in his official DS car, the demonstrators surrounded both the car and the escort. Trapped as he was, the governor had little chance of escaping unhurt if he ordered the gendarmes to intervene. They were too few anyway to disperse the angry crowd. So after having vacillated for about an hour, the governor slipped out of the car and set out on foot for his office. With a remarkable and typically Polynesian generosity, the demonstrators let him escape completely unscathed. Then, by a show of hands, they decided to continue their occupation of the Assembly building for an indefinite period. Calmly, quietly and peacefully. But in order to be able to repulse any surprise attack, guards were appointed to keep watch around the clock. At the same time arrangements were made to satisfy both the material and spiritual needs of the live-in demonstrators: a supply and kitchen brigade was created and a daily prayer service instituted. With a fresh water source in the backyard the Autonomists seemed capable of holding out forever.

The manner in which the French government reacted to these events showed how right the Autonomists were in their contention that the only way to get a hearing in Paris was to use strong methods. For less than a week after they had occupied the Assembly, Stirn called a press conference and let it be known that he had second thoughts about his 'reform bill' and was now going to revise it, 'so as to make it conform closer to Polynesian realities'. This sounded fine to the Autonomists, who had always insisted on a realistic approach to their problems. The only remaining question was how different this new version was to be. It soon appeared that they were never to know until it was too late, because this time Stirn was going to send the bill directly to the French National Assembly. The justification for by-passing the Polynesian Assembly was, strangely enough, that it was basically still the same old bill, and that a second consultation of the elected representatives of the Polynesian people was therefore not needed.

As a measure of their new determination and aggressiveness, the Autonomists immediately devised an extremely simple but efficient method of forcing the French government to consult not only the assemblymen but the whole people of Polynesia. As Francis Sanford explained at a big meeting, all he had to do was to resign from the French National Assembly and then stand again as candidate during the ensuing by-election. If he then, as he had every intention of doing, waged a campaign on the single issue of internal self-government, the election would instantly be transformed into a referendum. Having adhered to the letter to this plan, Francis began a vigorous campaign well in advance of the election date, September 12.

His main contender was the chairman of the local Gaullist party, Gaston Flosse. This gave the voters a clear-cut choice, considering that Flosse during all these events had supported all Stirn's manoeuvres and aims. Even to the point of having his home-made majority approve, outside the plenary chamber of the Territorial Assembly, Stirn's retrograde draft bill. The young trade union leader Charles Taufa also decided to stand. He was as strongly in favour of genuine self-government as the Autonomists. A little more unexpected was the candidacy of a young, part-Chinese nephew of Pouvanaa, Charlie Ching, just returned from a French prison where he had served two years for stealing munitions in a Tahitian army camp, in protest against the atomic tests. His platform was based on immediate independence. Just for the record, there was a fifth, maverick candidate, Elisaia, who wanted God to rule Polynesia – with his disinterested help, of course.

Although Sanford had to fight against all the usual odds – exclusion from the radio and TV studios, lack of funds and strong government support for the Gaullist candidate – he won his hitherto biggest victory with 22 484 votes (55.37 per cent). Gaston Flosse was a poor second with 13 884 votes (34.19 per cent), and Charles Taufa third with 2933 votes (7.22 per cent). Charlie Ching, who had been disowned by all Autonomist leaders, including Pouvanaa, obtained 676 votes (1.66 per cent), and the theocratic prophet Elisaia a pitiful 340 votes (0.8 per cent). If the six or seven thousand metropolitan civil servants, technicians, officers and soldiers, temporarily stationed in Polynesia, had been disqualified to vote in local elections (as the Autonomists had always requested), the Gaullist candidate would of course have fared much worse.

To all people in French Polynesia – with one exception – the main lesson of this election was that two thirds of the voters, and perhaps as many as four fifths of the Polynesians, were for internal self-government (*autonomie interne*). The only person to arrive at a different conclusion was the governor who went on the air, late in the evening of September 12 to express his satisfaction over the results which, according to his very personal analysis proved only one thing: that 98.34 per cent of the voters (all those who had *not* voted for Charlie Ching) were against independence! Whereupon he smiled happily and said goodnight.

By then Giscard had sacked his Gaullist prime minister, Jacques Chirac, reshuffled his cabinet, and made the Minister for Overseas Territories subservient to the Minister for the Interior, Michel Poniatowski. Although this move can be interpreted as a disgrace for Stirn, its main significance was to confirm that Giscard's ultimate aim was to transform the remaining French possessions in the Pacific into departments – to be run, like those in metropolitan France, by the President's most trusted collaborator, Poniatowski.

44 GRIM OCCUPATIONS

The September elections had clearly shown that the overwhelming majority of the voters were in favour of Francis Sanford, and that Stirn's unswaying support of Gaston Flosse was unacceptably antidemocratic. The most embarassing thing (as the new Minister of the Interior saw it) was that Stirn, after the occupation of the Territorial Assembly, had allowed the setting up, in another building, of a rump parliament, with Flosse as Speaker. This was an illegal act, which the Supreme Court was bound to invalidate sooner or later, thereby nullifying also all the decisions adopted by Flosse and his fifteen complices.

Poniatowski, who could not fail to blame Stirn for this mess, reluctantly decided that the only course open to him was to deal with Francis Sanford. As the latter, after his resounding election victory, had flown off to Paris to attend the parliamentary autumn session, Poniatowski phoned the deputy and casually invited him to drop in one day for a friendly chat. When Sanford showed up, Poniatowski, all smiles, simply asked him to come back with his most trusted lieutenants to work out the final text of the new statute, as if there existed already a general agreement between him and the Autonomists on all major points.

Sanford decided, if not exactly to trust him, at least to accept his offer to enter into negotiations. A few weeks later, he was therefore back in Poniatowski's spacious office, accompanied by the Speaker of the House Frantz Vanizette and the two Autonomist Assemblymen Daniel Millaud (*Ea api*) and Henri Bouvier (*Here aia*). Also present were Stirn and Poniatowski's dog Ulysse, of whom the latter was definitely treated with greater love and consideration than the former by their common master. Poniatowski's attitude towards the Autonomists could not have been more charming and friendly but they, in their turn, remained quite reserved throughout the meeting and kept repeating that they would not be satisfied with anything less than full internal self-government. As a first proof that Poniatowski meant business, they wanted him to dissolve the divided and unworkable Territorial Assembly.

Poniatowski seemed sincerely pained that their reasonable demands had been waived aside in the past (he looked on this occasion in a very disapproving manner in the direction of the number one underdog, Stirn) and said that he was personally going to see that they got satisfaction. At the same time, he hinted that he expected, as a suitable manifestation of this new *entente cordiale*, an immediate evacuation of the Territorial Assembly. Fine, replied the Autonomists, but we want first to see all your splended promises in writing. Considerably miffed by this insulting lack of confidence in the spoken word of the number two French minister of state (who moreover was President Giscard's closest friend and most trusted adviser), Poniatowski nevertheless agreed to dispatch to them very shortly a full draft of the new, liberal, epoch-making statute.

The forty or so Autonomist militants, who with their wives and children occupied the Territorial Assembly, had even less faith than their leaders in Poniatowski's words, and showed it by strengthening their defences and putting up a few additional fences. These squatters had lived permanently in the building since 10 June 1976, sleeping at night in Polynesian fashion on plaited pandanus mats, spread out on the floor of the caucus rooms. For cooking their meals, they used both the Assembly restaurant and the lawn outside, where they had dug Polynesian style earth ovens. In between their guard duties the occupants gathered in the lobby and chattered, sang, danced, studied the Bible, or slept. Once or twice a week a sympathetic owner of a Papeete cinema showed a Western or religious movie in the well-equipped conference room. Every Sunday a Protestant service was held in the entrance hall, attended by all squatters.

Of course, this unarmed militia of volunteers had not a chance of holding the building against a well-organised attack of French soldiers and gendarmes. But a warning system (based on coded messages, and flashed by powerful electric torches and quickly relayed within a wide radius) would immediately have brought thousands of Autonomist militants to the scene, ready to throw themselves into a battle, generating even more dangerous disorders. For this reason mainly, Poniatowski preferred a negotiated solution.

Although the main spokesman for the Autonomists for some time had been Francis Sanford, their supreme guide was still Senator Pouvanaa. At eighty-one, he seemed outwardly very frail and old, and most of the time he had to use a wheelchair when moving about. His voice had also lost much of its former strident pitch. But his mind was still very alert, and all important issues were invariably brought to his attention, and his verdict was final, without appeal.

However, at the crucial time when his lieutenants saw Poniatowski in Paris, Pouvanaa was affected by some mysterious disease, which his family tried to treat in Polynesian fashion with herbs. As often happens, they did not resign themselves to taking him to a French clinic until it was too late. On 10 January, the old freedom fighter passed away, and the corpse was taken to a *lit de parade* in the Papeete Town Hall, which was immediately filled with flowers and crammed with weeping Polynesians. Ever since he had been released in 1968, Pouvanaa had demanded a retrial, so as to prove his innocence. But since the reopening of the case would have forced the court to sentence those mainly responsible for the wrongs done to him, that is, the governor and Minister for Colonies at that time—he was denied justice until his death.

At the very least, Governor Schmitt should have kept away from Pouvanaa's funeral, which took place the following day. Instead he chose the thoroughly hypocritical course of turning up for the religious service in the Evangelical Church in Papeete, where he stood dressed in goldbraided uniform in the front rank of mourners, next to the coffin. Or he acted, perhaps, on orders from Minister Poniatowski, prompted by the mistaken idea that this official homage would please the Autonomists. The governor's offensive example was followed by the CEP admiral in charge of the nuclear testing programme, which Pouvanaa had never ceased to condemn as 'a satanic enterprise'. He, too, looked very sad, and almost cried.

As if this had not been enough, Governor Schmitt inappropriately stepped forward, at the open grave, ahead of Teariki and Sanford, and delivered an *oraison funèbre* which was a masterpiece of wilful deceit that of course deceived nobody. According to Governor Schmitt, Pouvanaa had been a great French patriot—as proved firstly by his heroic act to enlist in the French Army during World War I, to fight for his beloved mother country in the Verdun trenches; and secondly, by his enthusiastic support of General de Gaulle during World War II. What Governor Schmitt left out altogether was thus Pouvanaa's struggle of more than fifty years for the freedom and independence of the Polynesian people, for which he had been constantly persecuted and harrassed by all French governors, including Schmitt.

Shortly afterwards, the promised draft of the new statute

arrived. It did not take the Autonomists more than a few minutes to discover that it was basically the same retrograde text concocted by Stirn in 1975, which had caused the still unbridged rift between him and them. And when scrutinising the draft more closely, they discovered that some of the powers guaranteed the Territorial Assembly and the Government Council by the existing statute had actually been taken away. The reform proposed by Poniatowski was indeed putting the territory on the slippery road to the total dependence, as represented by the French overseas departments Martinique, Guadeloupe, Guayana and Réunion.

What the Autonomists could not understand was why Poniatowski, after having been so positive and understanding during their discussions in Paris, had gone back on his promise to grant them full internal self-government. Our guess is that Poniatowski deliberately started with a low bid, so as to be able—during the continued negotiations—to impress his partners favourably each time he made concessions which he had been willing to grant all the time. In this manner it would be easier to draw a line, which the Autonomists were not allowed to overstep. Poniatowski may also have heard how eager they were to get back in power. He had therefore concluded that they were willing to accept a far from perfect statute, as long as this also meant dissolution of the paralysed Assembly and new elections, which they were sure to win.

Whatever the explanation was, the situation called for much more diplomatic finesse than Governor Schmitt possessed. For instance, when one of the Autonomists called Poniatowski 'an unashamed liar', the governor gave him a dressing down, as if he had been a naughty schoolboy. Within a few days, the Autonomists had delivered a highly critical six page analysis of the draft, which ended with the following ultimatum to Poniatowski:

What is urgently needed in French Polynesia is not a colonial pact of the sort you have sent us, but a statute guaranteeing a political evolution. If you continue to refuse our demands, we shall feel compelled to opt for independence.

45 PONIATOWSKI'S NEW DEAL

Poniatowski tried to undo the harm he had caused himself by inviting Francis Sanford to another round of friendly negotiations in his Paris office. The offer was once more transmitted by the governor in a tone befitting a master issuing an order to a servant. That was the last straw for the deputy, who fired off the following declaration of war:

Mr Governor,

In your letter dated 7 February 1977 you inform me that in order to make progress in the present negotiations concerning the statute, you deem it necessary for me to travel once more to Paris to meet the Minister for the Interior.

After having read, with sinking heart, the recent proposal drafted by the Paris government, I regret to say that I have completely lost faith in all the high-ranking representatives of the French government and their many promises.

As I have seen with my own eyes, the policy which the successive presidents—De Gaulle, Pompidou and Giscard d'Estaing—have applied to the overseas territories has only one aim, and that is to preserve their dependent status.

This is why, in my opinion, there is only one solution left, if we wish to break the institutional, economic, social and cultural bonds hampering us, and that is to achieve independence.

Consequently, a referendum should be organised in French Polynesia to ascertain whether the inhabitants want independence or not. Of course, only people born in the islands, that is, those who would automatically become citizens of a free Polynesia, should be allowed to cast a vote.

Having so clearly expressed my thoughts, I suppose you realise how useless it would be for me to make the proposed trip to Paris.

Sincerely yours,
Francis Sanford
Deputy of French Polynesia

Next, Sanford sent out a call to all precinct bosses of his *Ea api* party in Tahiti and Moorea, asking them to attend a caucus the following day in Papeete. His faithful ally and *Pupu here aia* party leader, John Teariki, did likewise, whereupon their troops showed up for a joint meeting in the lobby of the Territorial

Assembly. Sanford went right to the heart of the matter by reading the text of his letter opting for independence, which he immediately translated into Tahitian. He was again and again interrupted by loud cheers. A show of hands confirmed that everybody was for independence.

The precinct bosses then went back to their villages to spread the good word. A squad of discreet police snoopers reported, as they always do on similiar occasions. Their reports, of course, ended up on the desk of the French Minister for the Interior, Michel Poniatowski. To top it all, Francis Sanford had himself been interviewed by all local journalists, specifically in order to let it be known that he planned to travel to New York to ask the UN Committee on Decolonisation to put the case of French Polynesia on their agenda.

It is possible, and even likely, that Stirn (who, incidentally, by now had broken away from the Gaullist movement to form his own Social-Liberal Party), felt a certain malicious joy over Poniatowski's discomfiture. And it is quite certain that President Giscard was greatly grieved by the course the events had taken. Too many Pacific, South American and Asian countries were already highly critical of France, because of her determination to continue to test her nuclear arms in Polynesia—they were likely to start complaining now about France's non-compliance with the famous UN General Assembly resolution No. 1514 (adopted on 14 December 1960) about the rights of all colonial peoples to become independent.

The only bright aspect of this mess—from the French point of view—was that Pouvanaa was not there any longer to direct the battle and galvanise the Polynesian people. Poniatowski cleverly decided to concentrate his next offensive on the weakest links in the Autonomist chain: the French-born Speaker of the House, Frantz Vanizette; and the French-educated Senator Daniel Millaud, who after having been Pouvanaa's proxy for many years, had taken over his seat in the upper house after his death. As expected, they were both moderate and reasonable. The minister realised, however, that it was of no use to renew the negotiations, even with these men, unless he was willing to make them a better offer. So this was precisely what he did.

The first concession was easy to make. It consisted simply of giving up his previous attempt to reduce the existing powers of the local political bodies. The second was to officially recognise the right of the Polynesians to fly the red-white-red flag, which had long been in universal use throughout the islands. It was thus a face-saving measure on behalf of the French government, rather than a new gain for the Polynesians.

The third concession seemed to be more genuine, for it concerned the role of the executive Government Council, which Poniatowski now was willing to endow with two heads: the governor, restyled high commissioner, (presiding when state business was on the agenda); and an elected vice-president, (occupying the chair, when the matters dealt with were purely local affairs). The powers retained by the French government were still numerous and extremely important, for they included defence, police, justice, broadcasting, TV, foreign affairs, the monetary system, overseas trade, air traffic, scientific research and higher education. This left to the locals, as in the past, the worrisome task of raising revenues to pay for social welfare, medical care, primary education and public works.

As for the power to control immigration, which the Autonomists had been so eager to take over, Poniatowski proposed a compromise: it was to be left in the hands of the French police, but with the proviso that the local Government Council should be consulted. Although some of the Autonomists doubted that this would enable them to stem the mounting tide of French immigrants—which threatened to swamp at least the main island, Tahiti—Poniatowski left them no other choice but to trust him blindly.

The most tempting bait dangled before the noses of the Autonomist leaders, however, was article 62, containing the firm promise to henceforth let the Polynesians control and reap all benefits from the 200 mile economic sea zone. The high-faluting language in which this article was couched was not easy to understand, even for the two well-educated emissaries whose mother tongue was French. But Poniatowski's smart technocrats obligingly 'translated' it into more comprehensible colloquial French, so the good news could be passed on to the Polynesian people.

Although the gains on the whole were minimal, the Autonomists gradually became more and more inclined to accept Poniatowski's proposals—especially as he promised to dissolve the Assembly and call new elections, as soon as an agreement had been reached. It was this prospect of coming back into power, above all, which in the end broke down the last resistance to the proposed deal. The argument most frequently heard in the relative privacy of the caucus rooms was: 'It is better to take a few steps in the right direction than to stand still forever.' Or: 'Once we are inside, we shall find ways of taking over the whole government.' The last to give in was Francis Sanford, who in March 1977 signed a formal peace treaty with Poniatowski, spelling out the mutual engagements.

Incidentally, this 'new deal' also implied that Poniatowski had dumped the most faithful ally of a long succession of reactionary French governments, Gaston Flosse who was bound to lose the new elections, following the dissolution of the Assembly. It did not take Poniatowski long to find the perfect way to placate and console him—that is, by simply making him a deputy. But how? After all, Francis Sanford had beaten Flosse by a two to one majority during the deputy race on 12 September 1976, and was more popular than ever. Ponia knew the answer. He proposed to Flosse, that French Polynesia henceforth be allowed to elect two deputies to the French parliament, instead of just one, as had been the case up to now. And furthermore, he proposed that the territory be cut up into a western and an eastern constituency, in which case the first one would contain the majority of the Autonomist voters, and the second one a majority of *Tahoeraa* voters. The only inconvenience with this gerrymandering was that it was a little bit too blatantly unfair, as there would be only half as many voters in the eastern constituency than in the western constituency; or 25 000 against 50 000! Poniatowski's reassuring answer to this timid objection was: 'Never mind, politics are a dirty business and only the results count.'

Flosse immediately became an ardent defender of Poniatowski's new deal, which was given an official seal of approval by President Giscard, who invited Sanford and Flosse to come and have lunch with him in the Elysée Palace in Paris— separately—at the end of March 1977. A few days later, to their enormous surprise, Poniatowski was sacked in a reshufflement of ministerial portfolios. Of course, his sacking had nothing to do with his handling of the colonial problems, but was rather a consequence of the inept way he had handled the campaign of the UDF party during the French municipal elections that had just taken place. Giscard's arch-enemy, the Gaullist leader Jacques Chirac, had triumphed and become mayor of Paris.

At the Papeete end, the enthusiasm for the new deal was less noticeable. For instance the squatters in the Territorial Assembly, whose numbers had been augmented with two newborn babies, were so mistrustful that they refused to pack up and go home, until they had been shown the decree fixing new elections for 29 May. As expected, the Autonomists swept the country and obtained 13 856 votes and 16 seats, as against 8 409 votes and 10 seats for Flosse's *Tahoeraa* party. The remaining four seats went to politicians representing outer island constituencies who, as usual, preferred to be on the winning side, which gave the Autonomists an even more solid power base in the Assembly.

The greatest surprise of the election was the relative success of the young, little-known candidates of a new political party, *Ia mana te nunaa* (Power to the people), with a socialist programme. They stood in the Windward Islands. They polled 1 334 votes which, however, was not enough to secure any seats for them. The score of Charlie Ching's party *Te taata Tahiti tiama* was even lower than his own in the 1976 deputy race, down from 676 to 420 votes, mostly because there were several pro-independence candidates for the voters to choose among. The general significance of these 29 May territorial elections was therefore perfectly clear: the immense majority of the Polynesians were still behind the old Autonomist leaders. The foremost among them, Francis Sanford, was quite naturally entrusted with the task of forming and presiding over the slightly revamped local Government Council.

46 TE TOTO TUPUNA

Poniatowski's successor as Minister for the Interior, Christian Bonnet, showed in a number of ways that he had a better opinion of Olivier Stirn, who had been allowed to remain at his post as Minister for Overseas Territories. As a result Stirn came out to Tahiti as soon as the new statutory reform had been implemented, for no other apparent reason than to receive the homage of his now happily self-governing Polynesian subjects.

Before he arrived, Teariki, who had succeeded Pouvanaa as leader of the *Pupu here aia* party, announced that he and his party colleagues had decided to stay away from all receptions organised in Stirn's honour. The reason he gave was as follows:

We welcomed Stirn very warmly when he was here in March 1975. On that occasion he swore that he was going to give us a new, extremely liberal statute. But after his return to Paris he quickly changed his mind. Or he had perhaps never been sincere. I refuse therefore to shake hands with a man who does not keep his promises.

Stirn did not appear unduly upset by this boycott, and plunged with his usual zest into the festivities which filled up most of his waking hours during the next four days. He also found time for enlightening his Autonomist friend about the true significance of article 62. It was not the case, as they had been made to believe by Poniatowski, that they were the sole masters of the ocean wealth contained in the 200 mile economic zone. On the contrary, the correct interpretation of this ambiguously worded article was that the French government remained in full control.

Although it was certainly a sheer coincidence, the Polynesian dissatisfaction with this belated revelation exploded a few hours later. We use the word 'exploded' deliberately, and in a literal sense, because what happened shortly before midnight on 12 August was that a loud bang, produced by the detonation of some explosives, reverberated through the small colonial capital of Papeete. As the policemen who quickly arrived on the scene discovered, it had been caused by a dynamite charge placed in the telephone exchange situated opposite the High Commissioner's residence, across the main thoroughfare, Avenue du Général de Gaulle (named after the perpetrator of a long series of infinitely

234

more dangerous bombings).

The explosion had done very little damage to the building. Further investigations revealed the existence of three more dynamite charges, placed along the outer walls. These had failed to explode, due to some faults in the release mechanism, or simply due to the bombers lack of expert knowledge.

The obvious conclusion that the bombing was politically motivated was confirmed by the discovery of a message written in French: 'TAKE YOUR FLAG, YOUR PEOPLE, STIRN, AND GO HOME'. The only reason the bombers had tried to blow up the telephone exchange, and not the Residency where Stirn was staying, must have been that the latter building was heavily guarded by French gendarmes.

The police inspectors did not lose any time looking for indices but rounded up the same night the most notoriously anti-French locals—that is, Charlie Ching and the other pro-independence candidates from the most recent territorial elections. They were subjected to a rather rough questioning, but were all able to produce water-tight alibis.

Less than two weeks later, a much more serious political crime was committed. This time a former French navy officer, Pierre d'Anglejean, who long ago had left the service and gone into business, was shot dead in his home, during his sleep. The murderers who had managed to enter his conspicuous villa in the Lotus residential village on the west coast of Tahiti, unnoticed by his Chinese wife, had again left a message in French. It read: 'WE DO NOT WANT ANY MORE FRENCHMEN IN OUR COUNTRY'. And it was signed in Tahitian: 'TE TOTO TUPUNA', meaning 'The Blood of our Ancestors'.

What shocked the whole French community of 15 000 recently-arrived settlers was the fact that Pierre d'Anglejean had never been active in politics and had no declared enemies. The only possible conclusion therefore was that he had been chosen in a random fashion and murdered as a warning of what might happen to them all, if they stayed on.

The murderers had used a stolen car which had been spotted by several residents of the Lotus village, who all stated that they were four young Tahitians. When they abandoned the car a little bit further along the road, they were recognised by several Tahitians. It was therefore an easy task for the police to apprehend them. During the next few days, nine more Tahitians, all teenagers or in their early twenties, were arrested, accused of belonging to the same *Toto Tupuna* gang. Yet another suspect was brought back from Rarotonga, where he had believed himself safe from extradition. Although Charlie Ching once more had a clear alibi for the night of the murder, he too was arrested, charged with being the organiser and planner of all these criminal acts.

The four Tahitians who had been observed driving through Lotus village readily admitted their participation in the raid, and gave the same version about how Pierre d'Anglejean was shot with the only gun in their possession. They all explained that they considered themselves to be soldiers in a Tahitian army of liberation, and to prove the point they willingly told the story of how, prior to the murder, they had planned to sabotage CEP airplanes and ships, transporting personnel and equipment to Moruroa. But the military airfields and naval harbours were too well guarded, and they had therefore decided to kill Stirn, when he flew in from Paris at the beginning of August. Their totally unrealistic plan fell through, owing to the fact that none of them was a sufficiently expert shot to puncture the tyres of the airplane just before it landed, so as to make it crash on the tarmac. In the end, they had instead tried and failed to blow up the telephone exchange.

The remaining ten Tahitians had participated only in the theft of about 400 kilogrammes of dynamite from the Public Works Department and a private construction company, which both kept the explosives in unprotected warehouses. As for Charlie Ching, the *Toto Tupuna* commando members confessed great admiration for him and said that they had voted for him, but denied strenuously that he had participated in any way in these more or less successful commando raids.

The local French-language newspapers did not accept this version, and announced in big headlines that Charlie Ching and his followers were all certain to get a death sentence. The new High Commissioner, who was the old Governor Charles Schmitt, was in no way better or wiser than before his unmerited promotion. He decided after this series of violent deeds to share his responsibilities with the elected members of the Government Council. This is the text of the official bulletin issued on 15 September:

The Government Council devoted most of the time during its meeting yesterday to the Charlie Ching affair. Although the French Government is responsible for the maintenance of law and order, the High

Commissioner, who chaired the meeting, asked each councillor for his views about the latest events.

The councillors, in their attempts to determine the causes of all this violence, mentioned excessive drinking, idleness, broken families, debasing movies, growth of urban slum areas and even drugs. All the councillors agreed that the ensuing agitation was of political nature, and that special efforts must be made to enlighten young Polynesians, tempted to listen to the arguments advanced by the pro-independence factions. On the other hand, nobody knew how to tackle the basic social problems.

In other words, the 'solution' adopted by the High Commissioner was to forget the real problems, caused by the installation of huge military bases and the massive immigration of French settlers, and instead launch anti-independence in-doctrination courses. This scheme, which like all similar attempts by his predecessors, tried only to attack the symptoms, but not the causes of the manifold social evils, was, of course, doomed to failure. The only difference this time was that it came to an earlier and more abrupt end, for poor Charles Schmitt perished on 31 October 1977 in a strange accident.

The Alsatian-born High Commissioner, who had never been near the sea before his unexpected promotion to supreme ruler of a Pacific colony made up mostly of water, suddenly discovered the pleasures of aquatic sports. He even invented a new one: boat surfing. On stormy days he would go out in his outboard motorboat to the barrier reef, and then surf back on the waves rolling across the coral-studded lagoon, all the way to the beach. The problem was obviously how to avoid the coral patches, and this was precisely what poor Schmitt failed to do on this fateful day. When his boat was brutally stopped in its mad race, he was thrown out and landed headlong on a coral stone. His badly-injured wife kept shouting, until some fishermen heard her and came to her rescue. By then her husband was already dead.

To fill the vacant post, the government appointed an old colonial hand, who was at the same time an experienced police boss, Paul Cousseran. He had begun his career as 'information officer' in Vietnam, in those far-away days when it was still a French colony, albeit in open revolt. Next he had laboured mightily in Algeria to maintain French rule, until a new, atrocious colonial war ended with another French defeat. After serving as special troubleshooter and even ambassador in some of the former French African colonies, which now were independent,

Cousseran worked for several years as departmental head, first in the police division in the Ministry of the Interior, and then in the Ministry for Defence. Immediately prior to his appointment as High Commissioner of French Polynesia, he had been provincial governor in metropolitan France. With this impressive service record, Cousseran seemed to be the ideal man to handle the troubles brewing in Tahiti.

He arrived on 20 December 1977 and had to go into action almost at once, when a riot broke out in the territorial prison outside Papeete. The way he handled this new outbreak of violence made Schmitt's attempt to re-educate the pro-independence Tahitian youths look like an almost humanitarian enterprise.

47 MUTINY WITHOUT BOUNTY

With the arrival of the *Toto Tupuna* men in September, the number of inmates in the Nuutania territorial prison rose to 173. Out of these, two were foreign legionnaires; one an Italian burglar; and one a French embezzler; while all the remaining 169 were Polynesians, mostly sentenced to heavy terms for such relatively minor crimes as pilfering, burglary, robbery, wife-beating and sexual assaults. The preponderance of Polynesian inmates, most of them young men, reflected clearly the desperate social and psychological disarray of a whole lost generation. For after many years in the Papeete slums—where their parents had been enticed to settle in the early 1960s, when the French army needed an abundance of cheap labour—the children born there became gradually less and less Polynesian in their customs and beliefs, without being more at home in the strange European world of which they were thus made prisoners, long before they were actually sentenced and locked up.

It is easy to realise the contagious effect the exploits of the *Toto Tupuna* commando had on the inmates in the Nuutania prison. Especially as no great effort was made by the director of the prison to isolate them in a special ward. An audacious plot was soon hatched by some of the most hardened prisoners, mostly serving life sentences. Their aim was to take over the prison and then send out two separate commandos in captured police vans. The task of the first one was to kidnap the French High Commissioner and the CEP admiral in charge of the nuclear testing. The second commando was to steal provisions and arms for a long seige. The hostages were then to be locked up in the prison and released only after the French government had granted independence to the people of Polynesia.

On D-day, 14 January 1978, the conspirators, who were not more than a dozen, seized a warder. They beat him to death with broken table legs, took his keys, and began opening the cell doors. When the other warders arrived, attracted by the noise, they were locked up in the empty cells. One of the warders escaped, however, and managed to alert the Papeete police headquarters.

In the meantime, the prison director, returning from some business in town, found the main gates wide open and about fifty prisoners standing calmly in the yard inside. Among them were practically all the *Toto Tupuna* men, whereas the ring leaders had set out in various directions, in accordance with the pre-conceived plan.

The local-born director, who spoke excellent Tahitian, tried to persuade the prisoners to return to their cells, and declared himself willing to listen to any complaints they had. They chose as their spokesmen four members of the *Toto Tupuna* gang, who promptly delivered their demands. They were: 1) grant immediate independence 2) send home all Frenchmen 3) stop poisoning us with your bombs. The director, who had expected them to ask for better food, more frequent leave or perhaps a colour TV, could only promise to transmit their requests to the proper authorities.

More or less at the same time, the High Commissioner arrived at the prison gates, after having taken the precaution to send for a company of foreign legionnaires from Mororoa. His first act was to order the fifty available gendarmes to encircle the prison building.

The fifty or so prisoners who took an active part in the mutiny reacted by giving it an even more political character. First, they searched the prison until they found a Tahitian flag, then they took it up to the roof and stuck it up on a pole. Next they painted streamers, made of bed sheets, with anti-French and anti-bomb slogans. By then some of the mutineers had discovered the warders' beer supplies, and collected all the bottles of spirits they could find in the dispensary.

A Polynesian party without music and dancing is no real party, and a record player was therefore brought up. Soon everybody was wildly dancing and singing. But now and then shouts were heard, mostly in French, for the comprehension of the journalists and the gendarmes: '*Vive l'indépendance! A bas la bombe! Les Français dehors!*' The shouts were often accompanied by projectiles of various kinds aimed at the besiegers.

As a drawn-out and successful defiance of the French authorities would have far-reaching political repercussions, the High Commissioner decided (or had received orders from Paris) to use force. The first attempt, made at midnight, was preceded by a volley of teargas grenades. As soon as the first exploded, however, the mutineers brought up three hostages to the roof and threatened to throw them down to certain death in the courtyard, if the gendarmes advanced further.

Their choice of hostages was highly revealing of the rioters' anti-European feelings: they consisted of the Italian burglar and the two Spanish legionnaires. The fourth European prisoner, the French embezzler, had hidden himself so well that they could not find him, which was probably very lucky for him.

The only thing left for the High Commissioner to do was to wait for the mutineers to fall asleep, in good Polynesian tradition. By 4 a.m. only half-a-dozen men were still on the roof, and most were snoozing. The hostages had also been allowed to stretch out. At 4.30 the High Commissioner gave the order for the assault to take place. A truck smashed down the main gate, and fifty gendarmes with weapons drawn rushed into the compound and placed dynamite charges at all locked doors. As soon as the prisoners on the roof realised what was going on, two of them grabbed one of the legionnaires and began carrying him towards the edge of the roof. The next moment three shots rang out. One of the Polynesians staggered and fell, mortally wounded in the head and chest. The shots had been fired by two of the best marksmen among the gendarmes, posted on a hill behind the prison. To avenge the death of his comrade, one of the other mutineers slashed the leg of their Italian hostage with an axe, before disappearing into the building.

In the meantime, the gendarmes had advanced cautiously from block to block, throwing large numbers of teargas grenades into the rooms and corridors. Nobody tried to resist, least of all those prisoners who, during all these goings-on, had been sitting quietly in their cells, either locked or unlocked. Among them was, for instance, Charlie Ching. Two hours after the signal to storm the prison building had been given, the last of the coughing, sneezing prisoners came out with their arms over their head, or handcuffed behind their back.

While a heated public debate was still raging—whether it had really been justified and necessary to shoot one of the prisoners (who turned out to belong to a local branch of the famous Marsters family of Palmerston Island)—the High Commissioner called a press conference. The main point he tried to make was that the rioters were all vulgar criminals, who had just borrowed a few political slogans to dress up their break-out. As for the previous acts of violence, committed by the *Toto Tupuna* gangsters, they only demonstrated how desperate the foolish separatists had become, as a result of the total lack of public support. This point was to be driven home again, the High

Commissioner hinted, during the impending legislative elections on 12 March.

The aim of these elections was to renew the whole French National Assembly at the expiration of the regular five-year mandate of the 491 deputies. In accordance with Poniatowski's promise, French Polynesia was on this occasion gerrymandered in such a manner that Flosse was bound to win in the eastern constituency. The Autonomists seemed equally certain of winning in the western constituency by nominating the popular mayor of Papeete, Jean Juventin.

It soon appeared, however, that far from having been annihilated by the High Commissioner's anathema, the separatists were very much alive and ready to take an active part in the electoral campaign. Even Charlie Ching would take part—although not in the flesh, as he was still sitting in his cell in the severely damaged prison building. As long as he had not been sentenced after due trial, the law allowed him to stand as a candidate, and this was precisely what he did in the western constituency, where his broad face smiled for several weeks from all electoral boards. Three more candidates advocated immediate independence, while the *Ia mana te nunaa* party, which ran candidates in both electorates, preached the sensible thesis that the first aim should be to achieve economic independence. Because of this less extremist attitude, it was backed by the French Socialist Party.

Not less than 15 per cent of the voters cast their ballots in favour of these 'separatists', as the High Commissioner persisted in calling them. Charlie Ching's total was 1 714 votes, which was four times as many as he had won during the 1977 territorial elections, before his *Toto Tupuna* followers began resorting to violent protest actions. As a result of these marginal gains, the two main candidates—Flosse and Juventin—barely scraped in with respectively 52 per cent and 51.5 per cent of the votes.

In France, the govering coalition of Giscard's UDF and Chirac's RPR parties won 285 out of the 491 seats at stake. Quite naturally, most ministers were reappointed—with the notable exception of Olivier Stirn, who, however, was allocated another portfolio. His successor as Minister for Overseas Territories was a colourless mayor from a small town in southern France, with no previous colonial experience, Paul Dijoud. When he turned up in Tahiti, dressed in the same sort of Parisian winter suit as Stirn, and delivering the same message in the same pompous language, it was even more difficult to understand why he had been appointed.

If there existed a slight difference, it was solely quantitative: Dijoud talked longer and more volubly than Stirn. In fact, on his first visit to the islands, he was already haranguing the still invisible Polynesian nation as he walked down the steps from his plane at Faaa airport, and he kept talking in the same vein for four days, until he finally disappeared into the plane that took him back to Paris. His message? The same old, unwanted assurances that France was here to stay for the greater glory of France and the enormous benefit of the lucky Polynesians.

48 THE BAD CHOICE

All this local agitation and turmoil did not bother the French government unduly, as in the meantime it had won a total victory on another, more important battlefront. Since 1975, no more protests had been heard in Australia, New Zealand and the Pacific islands, due to the false belief that the switch over to underground tests at Moruroa had eliminated all health hazards for the populations living in the southern hemisphere. With the exception, of course, of the residual radioactive substances produced by the previous aerial tests and still suspended in the atmosphere, which would continue to sink down slowly to earth for many years to come. But the prevailing attitude in these countries seemed to be that it was meaningless to protest against this accomplished fact, however sad it was.

At the military base on Moruroa, the army engineers and technicians appreciated, above all, the invulnerability they had acquired against all further protest actions from Greenpeace and similar anti-nuclear groups. For these enterprising adversaries could no longer hold up the tests – as they had been able to do in the past, when the tests were made in the atmosphere – simply by patrolling endlessly outside the territorial twelve mile zone surrounding Moruroa.

If we are to judge from the recriminations voiced at a much later date, at least some of the CEP bombers had nevertheless at this early stage realised the very simple truth that an atoll is the worst possible place on earth for making underground tests. An atoll can best be likened to a tower of porous coral, resting on a foundation of brittle basalt rock. For this reason, the Americans had never for a moment envisaged using Bikini or Eniwetak for underground testing, but had as early as in the 1950s established a new centre for that purpose in the Nevada desert. The British government, which also had used a Pacific atoll (Christmas Island), for atmospheric testing in 1957-58, likewise estimated that it was a totally unsuitable site for underground explosions and gratefully accepted the American offer to share its testing facilities in Nevada.

There was still another serious drawback at Moruroa. The atoll was too small and consisted mostly of a lagoon, that is, water. In fact, the total circumference of the narrow reef was not more than fifty kilometres, and by 1975 half of it was covered with roads, air strips, bunkers, warehouses, work shops, housing units, community halls, and other buildings. There was also a four kilometre wide gap, or pass, in the reef, through which the lagoon communicated with the ocean. When the order came that year to switch over to underground testing, this left the technicians with a mere twenty-five kilometre long stretch of the reef for the whole future testing programme. According to the findings of the American geologists R. T. Butcovitch and A. E. Lewis (*Aids for estimating the effects of underground nuclear explosions*, University of California, L.A. 1978), a ten kilotonne bomb, detonated in the rock foundation of the sort that exists at Moruroa, hollows out a cavity 20 metres wide and 90 metres high, and fractures the rock within a 150 metre radius. The corresponding figures for a 150 kilotonne bomb are 55 by 220 metres and 400 metres.

The minimum interval between the test pits which had to be observed at Moruroa was therefore 500 metres for the smaller bombs and one kilometre for the bigger bombs. All available evidence indicates that the spacing for the next three years after 1975 actually followed this pattern. But because the shafts were all drilled along the edge of the atoll, they were always too close to the outer wall at their point of detonation – 600-1200 metres below the surface of the sea. Incredibly enough, the CEP lacked the necessary diving equipment to determine the nature and extent of the damage done to the foundation of the atoll, and the amount of leakage and seepage that occurred each time a bomb was detonated. As usual, this ignorance was taken advantage of by the CEP propaganda machine, for it said in several bulletins that 'no leakage and seepage had been observed'. They did not explain that the only reason for this non-observance was that no observations had been made.

Occasionally, there were signs, observable from the surface, that an accident had indeed occurred; and sometimes news of such accidents leaked to the local press, as for instance on 27 December 1976, when *Le Journal de Tahiti* published the following short notice:

According to persistent rumours, the last underground test, undertaken about a month ago, has been far from successful. In fact, the radioactive gas produced by the explosion did not escape along the predicted path, and the technicians are still trying to figure out what happened to it. The CEP officials refuse, as usual, to give any information, nor do they want to make any comments.

Another accident, which occurred in 1977, was not revealed until 1983. The source of this information is particularly reliable, as it was the Government Commissary for the Prevention of Natural Disasters, Haroun Tazieff, who spilled the beans in an official report. According to this interesting document, a huge tidal wave washed over a portion of the reef on 24 November 1977, after the explosion of a 150 kilotonne bomb. The only possible explanation is that the detonation had torn out a sizeable chunk of the flank of the atoll.

Although the CEP technicians took these accidents in their stride, they envisaged the future with serious apprehensions, as it was obvious that the limit for what the atoll could take might be reached much sooner than they had thought at the outset. Already in 1978, the foundation of the atoll had been so thoroughly perforated along the south coast, that the CEP people had fallen into the habit of jokingly referring to Moruroa as a Swiss cheese. The most sensible solution would, of course, have been to move the testing to France. Instead, the Chief of Staff, General Méry, came out especially to Tahiti to hold something labelled a 'press conference'. In fact, the invited local journalists were only allowed to listen to a series of questions, prepared by the CEP press officer in advance and read to the equally prepared general by a reporter from the government-controlled radio and TV station. The questions and answers were all recorded on tape, typed out in a government office, and then distributed to the three local newspapers which published them verbatim. Under these circumstances, it is not surprising that no embarassing questions were asked.

The message General Méry conveyed in this laborious manner was that Moruroa was still the perfect place for making underground tests, 'provided that the whole available area was used in a rational and efficient manner'. It took another general, Claude Dubost, who flew in from Moruroa some weeks later, to translate this last utterance into a more intelligible, but hardly more intelligent, policy statement. The gist of it was that the tests were henceforth to be made *in the centre* of the island, under the 40-50 metre deep lagoon. The only hitch with this, we were told, was that several huge oil drilling platforms, barges and derricks had to be transported half-way round the world, which would take some time. Until this new equipment had arrived and been installed, probably in 1980, the Swiss cheese area was to be used for another dozen or so big explosions.

As this decision to move the testing operations from the edge to the centre of the lagoon might have been construed as an admission of past mistakes, the CEP made a special effort in June 1978 to present it to the world as a proof of their great foresight and wisdom. The means chosen consisted of inviting a dozen French Conservative and/or Catholic newspaper editors to send out their most trusted men to Moruroa, to report on the great work being done there for the defence of France and the free world.

The resulting publicity was in several instances much more informative than they wished for, as there appeared several extremely critical accounts of the lax safety standards. But in order to avoid the accusation of being prejudiced against the CEP, by quoting too eagerly from these sources, we shall go to the other extreme and reproduce here the most positive and appreciative account, written by the extremely well-disposed correspondent of the state-owned *Agence France Presse*. This is the full text of this highly official version, distributed to the whole French press, and to most leading foreign newspapers:

Moruroa, 4 July 1978

The rock foundation of Moruroa will shake again in a few days. A delegation from the Atomic Energy Commission has recently taken up residence among the 3 000 men and twelve women, who live permanently on this Polynesian atoll, and their task is to supervise the final preparations for the next underground tests. The head of the nuclear testing programme, General Claude Dubost, has come out especially from Paris to order the key to be turned, which will release a mighty thunderbolt, fortunately encapsuled in the rock.

Since 1976, the French government has not supplied any information about the tests, whereas up to 1975, a warning to ships was broadcast well in advance of each test, not to approach Moruroa. In consequence of which, the governments in the Pacific rim countries, as well as the Polynesian Autonomists, were able to voice their protests right away. The veil of secrecy that since then has surrounded all nuclear activities was nevertheless drawn aside recently, when about a dozen journalists were allowed to visit Moruroa at the invitation of the Armed Forces.

As Mr Chatoux, who is in charge of the testing programme at Moruroa put it, the CEP differs from an ordinary laboratory of nuclear physics only inasmuch as it is located in a rather unusual place: a stretch of coral reef, fifty kilometres long and 300 metres wide, encircling a lagoon whose greatest depth does not exceed 50 metres. While the residential quarters with its swaying palm trees resembles a holiday camp (although everybody works sixty hours a week), the rest of the coral reef with its many derricks looks rather like an oil field. The reason is, of course, that the personnel is busily drilling shafts for making undergound tests. The depth of these shafts varies between 550 and 1 100 metres, depending on the size of the bombs. For instance, the required depth for a 100 kilotonne bomb is 700 metres. It costs about two million French francs to drill a shaft, which is only a small portion of the total costs for each test which amounts to 35 million. This is nevertheless only one-seventh of what a test costs the first year, and only half of what an atmospheric test costs.

The nuclear charge is placed in a white steel tube, roughly ten metres long and one metre in diameter. The rest of the space is filled with instruments capable of recording what happens during an explosion every nano-second (one milliardth of a second). The tube is transported in a horizontal position on a 28-wheeled trailer from the assembly plant to the shaft, usually only a few kilometres away. It is then raised to a vertical position and lowered into the water-filled shaft with the help of cables, terminating at a recording device on the surface. When the tube has reached the bottom, the shaft is filled with cement which encases the cables, and covered with a concrete lid.

The bomb is detonated from a blockhouse, and the energy released by the explosion produces a shock wave with a strength of well-above one hundred megabar, or one million times the barometric pressure at sea level, whose speed is twenty to thirty kilometres per second. The shock wave generates such enormous heat that the basalt rock melts and, at the centre of the explosion, is even vaporised. All around, the rock is crushed and fractured, while on the surface the level ground bulges and then falls back, leaving a depression.

In the small fraction of a second, the underground cavity formed in this manner is immediately filled with molten rock, which encapsules nearly 90 per cent of all radioactive substances. As the steam trapped in the combustion chamber cools and condenses, the pressure is lowered, which prevents iodine and rare gases from escaping. On the surface, the only signs that a bomb has been detonated are a light earthquake and ripples travelling across the lagoon waters. One hour later, when the lower region where the blast occurred is 'stabilised', the technicians are already at work at 'zero point', right above the combustion chamber.

'Our aim is twofold', explained Mr Chatoux, the man in charge of the experiments. 'The first is to gain more basic knowledge, and the second is to test new weapons, such as multiple warheads for the M 4 missiles,

248

which our submarines will be equipped with in 1980. The range of our experiments is unlimited, and this explains why the yields vary greatly from below one kilotonne and up to 150 kilotonnes. Incidentally, the aim of the small detonations is to find out what happens when a bomb blows up by accident. But we also study the destructive impact of big bombs, without neglecting to also develop a neutron bomb. But the decision whether neutron bombs should be mass-produced or not, belongs, of course, to the government. We learn something new every day, and we have therefore no intentions of cutting down on the number of tests.

General Dubost agreed, adding:

For technical reasons, the tests must go on forever, because when we invent a new weapon, the enemy will develop some defensive arms. If we stopped the tests, our nuclear striking force would quickly be outmoded and lose its value as a deterrent. By switching over to lagoon tests, Moruroa will serve us for many more years to come, and then we can continue our testing programme at Fangataufa. The only thing we have to fear, therefore, is that the local politicians will become too troublesome and stop us, before we have finished off these two atolls. But then, it is a fact that last year the CEP and the armed forces spent 507 million French francs in Polynesia, which represents 17 per cent of the local GNP. So perhaps even when Polynesia becomes independent, its leaders will hesitate to cut off this important source of revenue. Especially as there are no longer any serious health hazards, since we went underground. But just to be on the safe side, the AEC has already made a survey of other sites suitable for underground tests which exist both in France and in some other oceans.

49 UNFORESEEN FALLOUT DAMAGE

None of the political leaders felt reassured by this declaration. And their mood became outright nasty, when they learnt through foreign news agencies on 30 November 1978 that the New Zealand Seismological Observatory had just recorded a 5.9 explosion on the Richter scale (corresponding to a low kilotonne bomb) with its epicentre at Moruroa. It so happened that they all converged on Papeete at this time – the seasoned elderly statesmen in order to participate in the ordinary budget session of the Territorial Assembly; and the young, unexperienced members of the *Ia Mana* party to hold their second annual convention.

The Speaker of the House, John Teariki, fired the first shots by proclaiming in his inaugural address:

The achievement of independence is part of an irresistible historical process. The only question therefore is whether it will arrive in a concerted, intelligent manner, after careful preparations, or not. In my opinion, we can easily avoid the troubles and chaos, which some claim will accompany our access to independence.

Vice-president Francis Sanford chimed in with the commonsense statement that: 'to ask for independence is not a crime, but simply a right guaranteed by the French constitution.'

In an even more exuberant mood, the *Ia Mana* convention delegates decided to immediately start preparing the future by establishing working relations with other political parties in independent Pacific countries, able to counsel and guide them. In another resolution, the convention with one voice simply asked the CEP bombers to pack up forthwith and go home.

The Territorial Assembly was a little more polite, when it expressed it opposition to the bombers' new plans in the following resolution, tabled by Teariki and unanimously adopted by the assemblymen:

The director of the nuclear test programme, General Dubost has declared that the CEP is planning to detonate atomic bombs in the centre of Moruroa, under the lagoon.

The decision seriously worries me. Already at the time when the decision was taken to make tests along the rim of the atoll, there was a serious risk of contamination of the lagoon waters through seepage.

This risk will surely increase with the new method of carrying out the tests, especially if or when an accident occurs.

A local newspaper mentions that depressions, each one about 80 centimetres deep, mark the sites of the previous underground explosions made in the rim of the atoll. At the same time we learn that, with the new techniques to be employed, more powerful bombs can be tested than in the past.

If this is so, similar but more extensive damage will be done to the atoll under the bottom of the lagoon, and the hole drilled through the coral will then unavoidably be filled with water.

Therefore I think that we should let the CEP and the Minister of Defence know how worried we and the whole population are and request them to supply us with more ample information.

Whereas in the past all similar protests and requests had always been quietly buried in the bottom drawer of some ministerial desk in Paris, these new attacks were too bold and far-reaching to be ignored. What particularly bothered the French government was the *Ia mana* threat to get help from other Pacific governments and political movements. To most cabinet ministers in Paris, this almost amounted to treason. The Prime Minister Raymond Barre decided to intervene personally. His admonition took the unprecedented form of an 'answer' from the tribune of the French National Assembly to a question that he had permitted his new deputy Gaston Flosse to ask right in the middle of a national debate.

What Flosse sought to discover, in a remarkably insidious formulation, was 'whether the government was determined to maintain the existing bonds between France and Polynesia, as defined by the 1977 statute, or rather was ready to let the territory gradually slide towards independence, although everybody knows this will mean economic ruin?' Of course Barre thought independence totally unwarranted and expressed his firm belief that the territory would remain French forever.

This was a clear signal for the local Gaullists and the French-controlled mass media in Tahiti to launch a vigorous campaign against independence, describing it as the surest path to 'economic suicide'. As often before, Fiji was specifically mentioned as proof that independence equals abject poverty and racial strife. The reason for this great animosity towards Fiji was of course the Fiji government's mild protests against French nuclear tests and its frequent support of UN resolutions in favour of complete decolonisation. The stand of the Fiji government had been condemned as intolerable meddling in internal French affairs.

Very conveniently this time, Ratu Sir Kamisese Mara had offered an excellent pretext for a new attack, by reaffirming in a parliamentary debate on 6 December his government's policies. Barely a week later, the Prime Minister of Fiji happened to stop over for a few hours in Tahiti on his way to an ECM meeting in Brussels. He was effusively greeted at the airport by Teariki and Sanford carrying flower leis, and by a crowd of inquisitive reporters armed with notebooks and tape recorders. Since the French High Commissioner was still the official head of state and therefore required by protocol to do so, he too showed up at the airport and acted as Ratu Mara's host during his stay. In these circumstances everybody expected a polite 'no comment' in reply to the many nasty questions prepared by the newspapermen. But it turned out that Ratu Mara was perfectly willing to repeat his recent statements. He even had the gall to add that Fiji and Papua New Guinea were fine examples of successful decolonisation, thanks to the positive attitude and generous assistance of their former colonial masters.

The ruckus had now reached such proportions that Minister for French Overseas Territories, Paul Dijoud, flew in from New Caledonia. In a succession of meetings with local politicians and government officials, he told everybody to go back to square one and henceforth play the game strictly in accordance with the rules laid down by the French government. To make French intentions crystal clear, a commando of gendarmes prevented a group of demonstrators from displaying a banner at the airport, when Dijoud stepped off the plane. The offensive text of the confiscated banner read: 'INDÉPENDANCE – FRONT DE LIBÉRATION DE LA POLYNÉSIE'.

At the same time, the High Commissioner replied indirectly to the *Ia mana* leaders, who had thought that they had something to learn from the independent nations in the Pacific – he pointed out the sad fact that 'in all these scattered Pacific islands, as a rule, only a few privileged individuals profit from their independence, which is more apparent than real, as they completely lack economic resources, whereas French Polynesia alone is flourishing'.

It was now left only for the Minister for Defence, Charles

Hernu, to kill the equally ill-founded notion that nuclear tests are harmful for human beings. His demonstration took the form of the following good news, distributed by the *Agence France Presse:*

NO RADIOACTIVITY IN THE SOUTH PACIFIC

Accordingly to an official New Zealand document, no traces of radioactivity emanating from the French nuclear tests at Moruroa have been detected in the South Pacific since the CEP went underground in 1976. This document consists of the annual report for 1977 of the National Radiation Laboratory in Christchurch which, incidentally, has never been very friendly towards France. It shows that practically no particles of the most dangerous radioactive substances produced by such tests (i.e. strontium 90 and caesium 197) can be found today in an area comprising Fiji, Tonga, Samoa, Rarotonga, Aitutaki and Pitcairn, where six New Zealand monitoring stations exist. The average fallout of strontium 90 during the year 1977 amounted to less than 0.1 millicuries per square kilometre . . . This latest new document thus repeats the conclusions found in the previous report on the situation in 1976. They furnish fresh evidence, although none was needed, that our tests are indeed harmless for the populations, not only of French Polynesia but of the whole South Pacific region.

This interpretation of the New Zealand report was of course in no way supported by the facts and figures contained in it. To begin with, the monitoring undertaken in the western Pacific by the National Radiation Laboratory 'stations' (actually, weathermen working on a part-time basis) was limited to the gathering of air samples, which obviously did not show the amount of radioactive leakage into the sea water around Moruroa. Furthermore, one must ask of what use and interest it is to calculate, as the French ministry had done, the average amount of radioactive fallout per square kilometre of the Pacific Ocean from the pre-1975 tests? Especially as the New Zealand National Radiation Laboratory reports clearly indicate the irregular and highly localised pattern of the radioactive fallout which actually occurred after each test during the 1966-75 period.

Last but not least, it was downright innacurate to include the British colony of Pitcairn in the list of Pacific weather stations supplying radiation data to the Christchurch laboratory, as the French Ministry had done, presumably in order to foster the reassuring impression that scientific observers were at work in the immediate vicinity of Moruroa. As anybody can find out (from its published annual reports or by writing to its director), the New Zealand National Radiation Laboratory has never had any monitoring station at, or received any samples from, Pitcairn.

We expected the director of the Christchurch Laboratory, Mr Hugh Atkinson, to lodge a strong protest against the deliberate misrepresentation of its published data by the French Ministry for Defence. But all in vain, and this passive complicity very soon emboldened various spokesmen for the French government to declare the falsehood that the New Zealand National Radiation Laboratory had proved that the French underground tests are totally harmless.

50 COLONIAL JUSTICE ON TRIAL

After having been twice postponed, the trial of the *Toto Tupuna* gang finally got underway in Papeete in January 1979; and right from the beginning the target of the most serious accusations was the whole rotten colonial justice. The main credit for this unexpected turn of events goes to the friends and families of Charlie Ching, who had managed to scrape together enough money to hire several first-rate French metropolitan lawyers willing and able to speak up and denounce all the denials of justice and irregularities which had been overlooked or condoned in the past by all local lawyers. To begin with this had the salutary effect of obliging the French government to despatch to Tahiti, at the last moment, a new presiding judge who was presented as being extremely 'liberal'. What this meant, in the event, was that he did his best, as all judges should, to give everybody a fair hearing.

Ever since their arrest, the *Toto Tupuna* commando members had not only admitted but almost boasted of their deeds. Therefore the only really suspenseful aspect of the trial was provided by the public prosecutor's attempts to implicate Charlie Ching in the bomb attack and murder. The public prosecutor was evidently determined to secure a life sentence for the gang leader, as he insisted on styling him. However, he was unable to muster a single witness to support the charge that Charlie Ching had organised the bomb attack and murder. Marcel Tahutini, the self-confessed murderer of Jean d'Anglejean, went a step further and accused the French police of trying to persuade him to bear false witness against Ching. The betrayal was to be rewarded by an extremely lenient sentence. In his final speech, the public prosecutor dropped this charge altogether and maintained only the very vague one of 'consorting with proven criminals'.

When their turn came, the defence lawyers devoted their final addresses wholly to the wider issue of who was ultimately responsible for the mounting tide of violence and crime in Tahiti. They all pointed the finger at the government in Paris, which had consistently refused to let French Polynesia follow the road of all other Pacific peoples towards self-rule and independence. Even worse, they claimed that there was a deliberate policy of flooding the islands with French settlers from France and from former

African colonies to make the islands 'safe' for the continuation of nuclear tests.

Another more insidious French policy denounced by the defence lawyers was the systematic destruction of the Polynesian culture and personality, with the help of French-language schools, powerful government-controlled mass media, and compulsory military training programmes. For every Polynesian on a decent income, ten lived in slums. Therefore, the lawyers argued, it was not surprising that many young Polynesians did not see any alternative to armed revolt. One of the defence lawyers, who happened to be born in Algeria, drew a telling parallel between the Tahitian situation and the total blindness shown in Algeria by the French authorities and settlers who, almost to the bitter end, saw the Arab freedom fighters as nothing but criminals and bandits. The defence lawyers also pointed to unjust aspects of the colonial system as demonstrated by court proceedings. For example, the jury was composed of four persons only, instead of nine as in France. The four would obviously have much less chance of imposing their views on the three presiding judges than would the larger number. The defence counsel also pointed to the injustice of French-language skills being required of jurors, a requirement which unavoidably made it very difficult for accused persons, who were mostly Polynesians, to get a fair hearing.

In their final salvoes, the defence lawyers enumerated a long series of irregularities committed during the preparations for the trial. They especially singled out the disappearance of many documents; and brutal interrogations carried out not – as the law prescribes – by examining magistrates, but by various police officers. One of these police officers, who made the mistake of being present in the courtroom, was promptly pointed out by his victim. On other occasions, the interrogators had made the accused sign depositions in French that did not correspond to their statements in Tahitian. In a surprise move, the lawyers also brought to the witness box one of the ringleaders of the January 1978 prison riot, Tauhiro, who had an even more gruesome tale to tell. Two officers from the French 'thought police', *Renseignements Généraux*, had promised him parole if he killed Charlie Ching, who happened to be in the cell next to his own. Tauhiro cheerfully gave the names of the officers concerned.

Last but not least there had been a serious denial of justice in that, during the first six months of their detention, the accused were not assisted by the defence counsel at all. It appears that the justice department had actually appointed several local lawyers to perform this task, as the law prescribes in the case of 'paupers'. But the lawyers concerned had never found time to visit their clients. This was the main reason why the relatives and friends of Charlie Ching and the *Toto Tupuna* members eventually set about raising the necessary funds to call in metropolitan lawyers.

This transformation of the court, from a place convened to judge a few common criminals into a political forum, made a strong impression on the jury, and they took three and a half hours to reach their verdict. When it was finally read to a hushed audience – made up mainly of government officials, French gendarmes and plainclothes police flown in from Paris for the occasion – it was considerably more lenient than the death penalties and life sentences for which the local newspapers had long been clamouring. Marcel Tahutini, who fired the fatal shot, and his brother Jonas, who was captain of the *Toto Tupuna* group, were sentenced to 20 years apiece, while the other three members got off with 18, 10, and 5 years.

On the other hand, it can be argued that the sentence of 10 years meted out to Charlie Ching was less warranted, as he had been found innocent of the main charges of having personally organised and directed the bomb attack and the murder, and the only accusation maintained was that he had consorted with known criminals. There seemed to be grounds for quashing the verdicts and ordering a retrial – at least everybody expected the sentenced men to remain in custody in Tahiti until the decision of the appeals court had been made. However, in a surprise move four days later, the prisoners were taken out of their cells, bundled into a military plane at Faaa airport, flown to the atoll of Hao (the army base in the Tuamotu group) and transferred to another plane which immediately took off for France via the French West Indies.

Shortly afterwards, it was the turn of the ringleaders of the prison riot to enter the box of the accused in the Papeete court house. To identify as fully as possible with their own people, they wore Tahitian-style *pareu* loincloths. On their chests and arms were various tattoo marks, testifying to the strong contemporary revival of this traditional art form. Throughout the trial they all echoed the accusations of Charlie Ching and his *Toto Tupuna* 'liberation army' that France was poisoning the whole population with its nuclear tests and maintaining an old-fashioned colonial rule against the will of the Polynesian people. Since a warder had been brutally killed, heavy sentences were meted out at the end of the exhausting three-day trial: a life term for Tauhiro, 12-20 years for six of his co-defendants, and 5 years for the eighth conspirator.

51 NO PRESIDENT LIKE GISCARD

All these anti-colonial and anti-nuclear stirrings among the Polynesian people resulted in very bad publicity in Australia, New Zealand and other Pacific countries. High Commissioner Paul Cousseran therefore decided to make a goodwill tour of the biggest and most influential of these nations, Australia, 9–22 April 1979, 'in order to clear up certain misunderstandings'. Since he spoke no English, the Australian government obligingly provided him with an interpreter. The most embarrassing of these misunderstandings, from the French point of view, was the widespread notion that radioactivity might be harmful to human beings.

However, the timing was rather unfortunate, inasmuch as the Harrisburg Three Mile reactor accident on 29 March had reinforced this notion, which since then has been further strengthened by the more recent revelations about the dire consequences of the British desert tests at Maralinga in Australia in the 1950s.

Having probably some doubts as to the Australians' gullibility and willingness to accept the *Agence France Presse* story of how the Christchurch radiation laboratory had completely exonerated the French bombers, the High Commissioner resorted to offering an even less convincing 'proof'. What he told his audiences everywhere was that the 1 500 Polynesian workers employed at Moruroa were not in the least worried about any radiation risks, which they would have been, if there were any. There was, of course, another, and more likely explanation for this happy-go-lucky attitude of the Polynesians working at Moruroa (who by the way were only 700) that Cousseran never mentioned – and that was their total ignorance of all nuclear health hazards.

Cousseran also claimed that he was in the fortunate position of being able to estimate with accuracy the existing health hazards at Moruroa: they were ten times smaller than those suffered by the Americans and Russians at their test sites in Nevada and Siberia. As for the idea that radioactive fallout from the tests at Moruroa could have anything to do with the high incidence of fish poisoning in French Polynesia, the High Commissioner declared that it was so preposterous that it made him laugh.

On his return to Tahiti, a much more formidable task awaited the High Commissioner – the planning of the official visit in July of the president of the French Republic, Giscard d'Estaing, and his wife Anne-Aymone. Giscard had been preceded by a man whom the Polynesian leaders had hoped never to see again: the former Minister for the Interior, Michel Poniatowski. Although out of office, he still worked behind the scenes as the president's number one fixer and trouble shooter. The reason for the president's sudden appearance was a most futile event. It had been decided in Paris that the Polynesians were to participate in the election for the European parliament. Not even in France did this election capture the interest of the voters, who morever were utterly confused by the numerous disparate lists, containing the names of not less than 243 mostly unknown candidates.

Nevertheless, for the local parties, this election provided a welcome opportunity to gauge their popularity and thus better enable them to prepare for the next, more meaningful, territorial election. The outcome showed that the Autonomists, who supported the presidential list, had lost some ground. This was in spite of (or perhaps, because of) the many public endorsements they had recently received, from both Poniatowski and the Minister of Overseas Territories Paul Dijoud, who 'just happened' to be travelling through the Pacific at election time. The Autonomists received 40.8 per cent of the vote; compared to 44.7 per cent for Flosse's *Tahoeraa* party, which had favoured Chirac's list, while Mitterand's list, supported only by *Ia mana*, polled a mere 10.2 per cent. Although the result had not been fully up to expectations, the Autonomists had every reason to expect the president to reward them for their loyalty in some tangible manner.

They had to wait until the end of the two-day presidential visit, 19–20 July 1979, during which time Giscard remained terribly stiff and formal and spoke only in elegant platitudes. As for his message, it was the same old one, which his ministers had ceaselessly hammered home in more blunt terms: forget about independence, do not make any fuss over the bomb, and in exchange France will richly reward you. He even mentioned the exact amount of economic aid coming the Polynesians' way, and when the local politicians added up the figures, the sum stood at the quite satisfying mark of 1 100 million francs ($A10 000 000).

His message was preached with even greater firmness by the

squads of gendarmes and anti-riot police flown out from Paris for the occasion. The greatest troublemakers were the *Ia mana* party leaders who, even the day before the presidential couple arrived, began painting anti-colonial and anti-bomb slogans on banners, which they planned to display in public. However, when they drove home that same evening, they were stopped by some policemen who examined the banners and told them that the slogans were offensive, whereby they confiscated all of them. Yet they had only stated the political programme of the party in very measured terms such as: '150 YEARS OF COLONIAL RULE IS ENOUGH', and 'MAKE THE NUCLEAR TESTS IN THE ELYSEE PALACE GARDENS'.

Luckily, the authors had time to start all over again, and thus could march the following morning with their freshly painted banners under their arms to the de Gaulle memorial on the Papeete waterfront, where President Giscard was to lay a wreath. They reached the already crowded site half-an-hour before the president. Almost at once a police car drove up and out stepped an officer. The police officer contacted the High Commissioner on his car radio. The High Commissioner's advice was so loud that everybody heard it: all demonstrators were to be taken straight to gaol before the president appeared on the scene. The police officer invoked the law. The *Ia mana* party secretary Jacqui Drollet immediately asked him which law or regulation forbade a citizen from standing in a public place to demonstrate his disapproval of the policies pursued by the government. The officer was, of course, unable to quote any precise law, and therefore decided to tackle without further delay the task he was better equipped for: he beckoned a squad of about forty police and the drivers of two big vans to fetch the *Ia mana* party members! They were driven to the police station, where 10 were packed into a two-man cell, while the remaining 14 were locked up in a slightly more spacious one. There was only standing room in the cells and the heat was almost suffocating.

The wives of the demonstrators had not been taken into custody. They immediately phoned the head of the justice department, who seemed surprised by this new detention which he declared to be illegal. The wives told him that they were all going to Place Tarahoi, with their children, at the time when the president was to deliver his key speech. They planned to heckle him until their husbands were released. Since 36 journalists and radio and TV reporters had come out from France to cover the presidential visit, such a possibility appeared so distasteful in ruling circles that the prisoners were set free.

In the meantime, without seeing the irony of it all, President Giscard had placed a wreath at the foot of the monument honouring the great freedom fighter and decoloniser, de Gaulle. He then moved on the Place Tarahoi in the centre of Papeete, to make the key speech of his tour at a much-advertised 'mass meeting'. Although a national holiday had been declared, so as to allow the whole population of Tahiti to attend, only about 500 people had cared to do so, half of whom at least were government officials, French plain-clothed policemen and curious tourists. Giscard's address, delivered with the usual inhuman perfection, again spelt out the numerous pecuniary advantages of belonging to the great French Republic whose glorious motto was 'liberty, equality and fraternity'.

The ones most enthralled by this noble speech were the founder of yet another pro-independence party, Tetua Mai, and his wife Ina, who were sitting on the lawn in front of the presidential tribune. Well in advance, they had told everybody who cared to listen of their plans – to deliver a petition to the president, outlining a number of reforms they wished him to undertake. The speech was hardly over, however, when a gang of plain-clothes policemen who had been watching them all the while, pounced upon them and carried them off to a police van.

A thorough search of their persons was rewarded with nothing more than the discovery of a copy of a typed letter, which they had sent to the president through the regular mail one month earlier, asking for an appointment. Since this was hardly a criminal or subversive act, Tetua was charged with the rather improbable offense of having stolen the watch of one of the police inspectors who had searched him. In the end, however, Tetua and Ina were received by a member of Giscard's entourage, who did his best to cajole them.

52 TAKEN FOR A RIDE

Giscard flew off to Moruroa on 21 July without his wife, Anne-Aymone, who we must assume was seen as a security risk. Everybody expected a particularly impressive presidential explosion to be recorded by the New Zealand Seismological Observatory the following day. It did not occur, however, until three days after President Giscard's safe arrival home in Paris, and it appeared strangely oversized, for the reading was 6.3 on the Richter scale, corresponding to a blast in the 150–200 kilotonne range. What had gone wrong?

The first explanation was supplied by the French socialist CFDT trade union, to which most of the technicians employed at Moruroa belong. In a short statement distributed to the French mass media, it revealed that two separate accidents had occurred within a time span of two weeks. The first one took place on 6 July, when a surface explosion had killed two technicians and badly injured four more. The second one happened on 25 July, when a tidal wave had swept over the southern part of the atoll and injured two French technicians and four Polynesian workers. The trade union bulletin ended with a pious hope that the accidents would prompt the CEP and CEA bosses at Moruroa to tighten the notoriously lax safety standards.

While the CEP kept silent, the Atomic Energy Commission responded with a communiqué of its own, saying that the first accident occurred during a chemical experiment, and that the second was caused by a natural phenomenon. However regrettable they were, they should not therefore be used as a pretext for criticising the nuclear test programme, which was proceeding without a hitch, in perfectly safe conditions.

A reporter from the Papeete television and radio station managed to locate the director of the whole French military nuclear research programme, General Dubost, who somewhat surprisingly had just retired. The general was much less talkative than during the 1978 press visit to Moruroa, and had nothing to say at all about the first accident. Nor did he explain why he had retired or been retired. On the other hand, he was very eager to establish the truth about the second accident, at which he had been personally present. This is his very succinct account:

'On 25 July, several hours after a bomb had been detonated on the south coast of Moruroa, I was supervising some routine work on a nearby islet, when suddenly a tidal wave washed over the whole reef. It turned over several vehicles, containing about a dozen men. They were all injured, but most of them very slightly.'

'What produced this freak wave, do you think?' asked the reporter.

'I have not the slightest idea,' answered the general. 'Many have speculated about the cause, but none of the answers offered so far is satisfactory; so everybody keeps speculating.'

Less than a week later, the Parisian left-leaning daily *Le Matin* published a fuller and more plausible version of the accidents. Its two leading reporters, Jean Darriault and Jean-Charles Rosier, had obtained extremely detailed information from some of the injured Moruroa technicians under treatment in a military hospital in Paris, to whom they had gained access by pretending that they were relatives. Not knowing whether they would ever recuperate or even survive, the injured men had no hesitation about telling what they knew, and *Le Matin* printed their story on 8 August.

The most sensational revelation was that Moruroa had for some years been used not only for underground tests but also for detonation experiments. These were carried out in concrete bunkers on the surface of the atoll, resulting each time in the release of unknown quantities of the most lethal of all radioactive substances, plutonium, with a half-life of 24 000 years.

The bunkers had usually been sealed and abandoned at the end of each experiment. But, 'for economy reasons', it was decided early in July 1979 to decontaminate and re-use the latest chamber built on the coral rim. The inside walls were plastered with paper drenched in acetone, which supposedly would dissolve the plutonium released by the detonation device. Special filters were installed in all openings in the walls, to 'capture' the plutonium before it escaped into the air.

The experiment took place according to schedule on 6 July. What happened next must be attributed largely to faulty instructions and human error. Six 'decontaminators' entered the bunker soon after the experiment. One of them decided, or had orders, to enlarge a hole in a metal plate. The boring machine he used for this purpose caused a spark which ignited the gas still filling the chamber. The first man in the team was killed instantly by the intense heat (1500–1800°C). Another had his chest crushed by a door thrown off its hinges by the blast and died soon afterwards. The remaining four were all badly burnt. Both dead and injured were immediately flown to Paris. Subsequently, a team of forty 'decontaminators' arrived with orders to undertake the hopeless task of cleaning up the whole atoll which, by now, had received an unknown amount of radioactive fallout from the plutonium cloud emerging from the death chamber.

The second accident, which took place on 25 July was, like the Harrisburg disaster, exactly the sort of thing that all technicians had sworn could never happen. As the 150–200 kilotonne bomb (to be exploded for the greater glory of France and its president) was being lowered down the shaft drilled in the southern portion of the coral ring a few days before Giscard's visit, it got stuck before it reached the bottom. Unable to dislodge it in time, the test directors waited until 25 July when they decided to detonate it anyway.

As a result of this misplaced blast, an enormous chunk of the outer wall was pried loose and fell out about three hours later, producing a tidal wave which spread throughout the Tuamotus. The greatest damage occurred on the nearby atoll of Marutea, where a Frenchman runs a pearl farm.

The CEA-CEP directors stuck to their guns and repeated their previous version of the events. The following French press report was reproduced by the mass media all around the world on 10 August:

ATOLL BLAST ABSOLVED

The French Atomic Energy Commission has denied any connection between last month's nuclear device test at Moruroa atoll and the tidal wave which hit the island shortly afterwards. Two people were injured by the wave on July 26, about two hours after the explosion. The blast was picked up on seismographs in New Zealand.

According to the French newspaper *Le Matin*, the test did not go according to plan. The newspaper said yesterday that, as the device was being lowered into its 800 metre deep shaft, it became stuck half way down. Because this device could not be moved, the newspaper said, it was detonated where it was.

However, a spokesman for the Atomic Energy Commission dismissed *Le Matin's* claim as 'fantastic'. He denied that anything had gone wrong with the test and said such an explosion could not cause a tidal wave. These waves were common in the area, said the spokesman.

The Atomic Energy Commission has also revealed that accidents at the Moruroa testing site killed two people last month and injured four others. However, it said, the accidents were 'non-nuclear'.

The thirty members of the Territorial Assembly were still waiting for a more informative reply to their request of 6 December 1978 to be told the truth about Moruroa. Defence Minister Yves Bourges had blandly assuranced them that the tests were totally harmless. So it was with a vengeance that they now put on their agenda 'the problem of the obvious lack of satisfactory safety standards at Moruroa'. The rather agitated debate took place on 17 August and led to the adoption by the house – once more unanimously – of a resolution whose key section read:

All previous official, reassuring statements have been flatly contradicted by the two accidents which occurred at Moruroa on 6 and 25 July.

Consequently, we cannot accept that human lives are being sacrificed, because the technicians are unable to control the testing. For this reason we ask the highest authorities of the French Republic to suspend further tests, so as to permit:

(1) The setting up right away of a local committee of inquest, having as its main task to receive depositions from Polynesian workmen and to investigate the circumstances surrounding the accidents that occurred on Moruroa during the month of July.

(2) The dispatch to Tahiti of a team of civilian, impartial French and foreign radiobiologists. It is our wish that these scientists be allowed to visit all islands in French Polynesia, in order to carry out all technical and medical investigations and to take all samples they deem necessary. We request moreover the establishment of a permanent radiation laboratory here, likewise staffed by impartial and competent professional men.

If no satisfactory answer to these above-mentioned requests, and/or to those made by this committee of inquest, have been received within a month, we the elected representatives of the territory reserve the right to take appropriate actions.

It was signed by the presidents of the three parliamentary groups: Pierre Hunter, for *Pupu Here Aia*; Joel Buillard, for *Ea Api*; and Jacques Teuira, for *Tahoeraa Huiraatira*.

As the French government saw it, the situation could easily get out of hand if the assemblymen's inclination to take the matter into their own hands was not checked at once. The High Commissioner was therefore instructed to inform them that, in compliance with their request for a thorough investigation of the radiation problems at Moruroa, 'a group of internationally known scientific experts' was coming to French Polynesia. Moreover, the Territorial Assembly would be allowed to send a number of their own members to Moruroa to investigate the circumstances surrounding the accidents, as they had expressed a wish to do. On their return from Moruroa, the 'internationally known scientific experts' were empowered to testify before the house – but behind closed doors, of course, in order to protect vital French defence secrets.

A few days later, the High Commissioner submitted the names of the 'internationally known scientific experts'. They were all French and consisted of one of the bosses of the CEA bomb unit; two of his closest collaborators; and two university professors of geology and physics, who had never been to the South Seas before. There was also the director of the French National Radiation Laboratory, Pierre Pellerin, which looked fine on paper. Unfortunately, his laboratory had never been allowed to undertake any field work whatsoever in French Polynesia (a most surprising fact, that had always been strongly criticised by local political and civic leaders), and the only data on radiation and cancer available to him were therefore those concocted by the army doctors in the pay of the CEP. This was certainly a strange and totally inadequate way of responding to the assemblymen's demand for a health survey to be undertaken by impartial medical doctors and independent radiation experts.

As soon as these six government experts on the wrong subjects disembarked in Tahiti from the military plane which flew them out from Paris, they were bundled into another airplane bound for Moruroa, together with five assemblymen and two government councillors. On their arrival at Moruroa at noon on 24 September, they were all taken for a ride again – literally and figuratively speaking – by an army helicopter, circling the atoll in less than an hour, whereupon they had to sit through an elementary course in geology. The day ended more pleasantly with a fine French meal. The following morning there were more dreary lectures until it was time to fly back to Tahiti. The time spent at Moruroa by these two groups was therefore a mere twenty-four hours. The 'internationally known experts' had brought no scientific equipment and had thus been unable to make any pertinent observations.

As for the Polynesian assemblymen and councillors, who gave an account of their flying trip in a special report which we have used here, the only difference was that they at least tried to gather some information about the two accidents. They learned, for instance, that not less than twenty-eight Polynesian workmen had been involved in the rescue operations following the accident of 6 July. But when they asked the camp commander to let them talk to them, he could only produce one man, who declared that he belonged to the fire brigade, which arrived very late on the scene. He volunteered the not particularly useful information that there was no water in their tank.

They ran into the same problem when they asked to be shown the medical records for the personnel. According to the CEP doctors, these records proved that nobody had ever been contaminated at Moruroa – however, their demand was turned down 'for security reasons'. Their only successful quest concerned the tidal wave accident, which everyone remembered and without the slightest hesitation attributed to the detonation, three hours earlier, of a bomb too large jammed in the shaft too near the surface.

Confronted with these findings by the Assembly and the local press, the six members of the French team grudgingly admitted, before they flew home to France, that the official CEP-CEA version of the 25 July accident was a lie. Well, they did not really use this ugly word, but talked in more elegant and measured terms about 'the exaggerated discretion, natural to officials accustomed to work in sensitive areas covered by military secrecy'. As for the 6 July accident, for the same reason, all they could say was that 'the conflagration had been caused by unknown and uncontrolled factors'.

53 FLOSSE'S U-TURN

The great haste with which the French authorities had swept the embarrassing bomb accidents under the carpet can be easily explained. From 6 to 12 October 1979, Papeete was to be the location of the Nineteenth South Pacific Commission Conference, with participating delegates coming from all of the independent nations, plus the three foreign powers with possessions in the Pacific – the United States of America, Great Britain and France. Public fuss over security problems at Moruroa would therefore have fuelled the strong resentment that existed against the French tests in the region.

Even with this issue conveniently out of the way before the opening of the conference, there remained another serious risk of political contagion – that is, the delegates from already independent nations might establish close contacts with the local freedom fighters. The deterrent tactics devised by the French High Commissioner consisted of drawing up such a full programme of feasts, shows, dinners, cocktail parties and other extracurricular activities that there would be no time left for the delegates to meet the local pro-independence leaders, who were of course not on the list of *persona grata* invited to these government-sponsored social events.

Undaunted, the five pro-independence parties organised a dinner meeting of their own, and to the fury of the French High Commissioner, several dozen of the conference delegates left his reception at the Residency that evening in order to attend. Five foreign correspondents covering the conference were also present and later reported, among other things, that several of the invited guests had made speeches strongly endorsing the pro-independence position. For instance, the deputy prime minister of Papua New Guinea, Ebia Olewale, said:

You must stand together, because those people who govern you are very clever and will try to divide you in order to rule you. They play off one group against another. I am speaking from experience, because I and many other Papua New Guinean leaders have gone through all the stages of decolonisation that will confront you. Remember that you are not alone. We are with you.

Deputy Chief Minister of the not yet fully independent New Hebrides, George Kalkoa, agreed in these terms:

We have pushed France and the UK for the past seven years and are now about to achieve independence. The Vanuaaku party will always be behind New Caledonia and French Polynesia in your struggle for independence.

To undo this harm, the High Commissioner persuaded the vice-president of the local government council, Francis Sanford, to receive the foreign press and explain that the territory was not quite ready for independence yet. The editor of the *Pacific Islands Magazine*, Stuart Inder, quoted Sanford as having stated tongue in cheek:

Immediate independence is not what French Polynesia wants. What we have got is genuine self-government – the right to run our own internal affairs, to use our own language officially, to fly our own flag, and that is enough for now. The rest will come.

Most of Francis Sanford's coalition partners, starting with John Teariki, were considerably more impatient and had already on several occasions denounced the 1977 statute as 'a glossy new wrapper concealing the same old-fashioned colonial rule'. To everybody's surprise, their ranks were suddenly swelled on 7 March 1980 by the conservative, pro-French, Gaullist deputy Gaston Flosse, who convened the local press to the *Tahoeraa* headquarters to announce a complete political U-turn. His party had just decided to ask the French government to replace the hollow 1977 statute with a new one, enabling French Polynesia to become at long last a truly self-governing territory!

The most surprising thing was the thoroughness and secrecy with which Flosse had acted. Not only had he prepared, with the help of his staff of 'technical advisers' (practically all young local men with university degrees), a detailed draft for a new statute, but he had also made a quick trip to Paris to have it tabled in the French parliament.

One of its key provisions conferred wide powers on a cabinet, made up of ministers in charge of departments and headed by a premier. The novelty resided, of course, not in the system itself (which is common to all democratic countries), but in its application to a French overseas territory.

Equally important were the policies in the economic field, which would give Polynesia complete freedom to trade with any countries she likes, to handle international air traffic and landing rights, to exploit freely her own maritime resources, and to open the islands to foreign investors. In his comments, Flosse said openly that it was both natural and desirable to strengthen Polynesia's economic ties and increase her trade with the other Pacific countries, specifically America, Australia, New Zealand and Japan. This represented a complete break with the colonial-type economic policy which had always tied the territory firmly to the mother country 20 000 kilometres away.

What Flosse was aiming at in the first place was thus economic independence, although he had in the past often warned that the realisation of this goal, always given high priority on the Autonomist programme, would put the Polynesian people on the slippery road to *political* independence. When reminded of this declaration, Flosse maintained with convincing sincerity that he was still in favour of a continued close association with France.

The ones most embarrassed by Flosse's unexpected U-turn were naturally the old Autonomists, who now had been overtaken – not only on their left, but also on their right. The only valid criticism they could formulate, however, was that Flosse had stolen their idea for purely opportunistic motives, in order to attract their voters to his own party.

For the Minister of Overseas Territories, Paul Dijoud, this sudden about turn was sheer treason, as Flosse had always enjoyed favours and protection from all French ministers, including himself. How for instance, had he become a deputy, if it was not as a result of a clever gerrymandering performed by his Parisian friends? What angered Dijoud particularly was that at the time when the old Autonomists were eventually behaving like lambs, Flosse began charging about like a wild ram, bleating Autonomist slogans.

In a terse communiqué, Dijoud let it be known that any further modification of the 1977 statute was out of the question. Why?

Because its latent potentials have not yet been fully exploited by the vice-president and his councillors. If they want more power, they can obtain it within the existing statutory framework. It is of course a gradual process, which probably will take years and years to implement.

What Dijoud did not say was that this 'gradual process' could last forever, or at least as long as the French government needed Moruroa as an experimental site for its nuclear testing programme, which was almost the same thing. The only possibility that this period of testing would be shortened lay in the sudden, cataclysmic disappearance of the battered atoll into the depth of the ocean. This short notice, which appeared in *La Dépêche de Tahiti* on 15 March 1980, seemed to indicate that such an eventuality was not completely excluded:

MORUROA SUPER BANG

Many rumours are circulating about the next test which will take place during the impending visit by the Minister for Defence Yvon Bourges. According to one rumour, the planned blast is of such magnitude that the personnel will have to be evacuated before the bomb is detonated. The officials will watch the test from an airplane.

It seems that portions of the atoll have sunk so much that there are hollows between one and two metres deep which are now being filled with concrete.

The CEP has denied these rumours in these terms: 'We do not detonate any big bombs, as our aim is the opposite, that is, to make them as small as possible. As for the sinking of certain portions of the atoll, it is solely due to the effect of wave action.'

The Minister for Defence, Yvon Bourges, was not the only VIP to be effusively welcomed to Tahiti at this time by High Commissioner Paul Cousseran. The Chilean dictator Augusto Pinochet also flew in on 21 March to recuperate from the blow his prestige had suffered. (Half way to the Philippines, a cable from his colleague Ferdinand Marcos suddenly called off his planned state visit for unspecified political reasons.) Both guests were lavishly entertained at the Residency and then headed east, Pinochet passing above Moruroa high in the skies, and Yvon Bourges disembarking there to watch a fifty kilotonne blast which, of course, pierced another big hole in the flank of the atoll. By then, however, an oil derrick and several barges had arrived from France, and the first drillings under the lagoon were well under way.

54 TROPICAL VIOLENCE

The commotion created by Flosse's bold change of mind and the even more audacious turn of events at Moruroa were soon overshadowed, however, by the public uproar caused by the first gangster-style kidnapping in the history of Tahiti, which took place on 27 March 1980. The unfortunate victim was the 26-year-old son of French Polynesia's wealthiest businessman, Jean Bréaud, whose holdings comprise the *Banque de Tahiti*, the Citroen-Fiat car agency, the 5 000-acre Atimaono plantation, the Tahiti-Petroles oil distributing company (a big export-import firm), and much real estate. His son Olivier, equally gifted in business deals, had for some years been his business partner and general manager. The kidnappers promptly phoned and asked for a $2 000 000 ransom to be paid in the United States of America – but never rang again to give further instructions.

The High Commissioner went on the air to declare that it was a highly professional job performed by experienced overseas gangsters, who had in all probability already left Tahiti with their victim on a yacht. Less than twenty-four hours later this explanation was proved quite incorrect, when the gendarmes apprehended two French-born businessmen, Yves Le Goff and Daniel Chellé, who had been established in the colony for several years. After one night's interrogation, they broke down and confessed that they had kidnapped Olivier Bréaud because they needed the ransom money to avoid bankruptcy.

The speed with which they had been caught was due to the amateurish manner in which they had acted and the incredible blunders they had made. As soon as the big police hunt began they became so scared that they gave up all thoughts of obtaining a ransom, and beat their poor victim to death in the most barbarous manner with iron bars because, they said, he was cursing and insulting them. They then mutilated and burned the body to make it unrecognisable, but hid it under a few boughs in a ravine, right in the middle of the plush Lotus residential area where they lived. Having accomplished all of these gruesome deeds with the ready assistance of their wives, they all four went to a night club and enjoyed a good evening.

Though Le Goff and Chellé had proved to be very inept

273

kidnappers, it soon became known that they had had a very heavy criminal record before they had migrated to Tahiti to begin a new life. While Chellé had 'only' been sentenced for theft and robbery, Le Goff had murdered his mother-in-law in cold blood, a crime for which he had spent eight years in a French prison. They were also guilty of numerous fraudulent bankruptcies, which barred them from further business activities in France – this was the main reason why they had gone overseas.

In Tahiti, Vice-president Francis Sanford's government had welcomed the two criminals as bona fide investors. Their initial business activities in the colony had certainly not been above reproach. They had, for instance, run a brothel, disguised as a massage parlour, until it was closed by the police. The French authorities had failed to warn the too gullible local government that the men were convicted criminals. When they decided to start a textile mill (without any previous experience in this field), they were therefore quickly granted a $400 000 loan, with exemption from payment of custom duties on the imported machinery. To top it all, the local government promised to pay the salaries of the whole workforce of fity men and women during the first six months of operation! During a post-murder inspection of the corrugated iron shed which these men had grandly baptised 'The Textile Mill', it was discovered that only three of the forty looms functioned, because they were all part of a batch of condemned material bought from a French scrap iron dealer.

Of course, the question everybody in Tahiti asked after these revelations was why and how these convicted criminals had been let into the country. Restrictive measures were suggested, so as to prevent a repetition of similar tragedies. The two deputies, Gaston Flosse and Jean Juventin, blamed the French immigration police for laxity and negligence, and tabled a bill in the French parliament which, if adopted, would make it compulsory for all Frenchmen residing in the islands who had criminal records to report to the police once a month. Highly embarrassed, Minister Paul Dijoud vetoed the proposed measure, branding it 'discriminatory' and an 'infringement of civil liberties', though the only sufferers would have been the crooks who deliberately discriminated against innocent citizens by infringing on their civil liberties.

A more efficient and radical solution was proposed by the leader of the new Polynesian Liberation Front, Oscar Temaru, who publicly chided all other political leaders for lacking the courage to confront the problem squarely. His message was:

Our problem is not simply a matter of stopping the French criminals and crooks from settling in our islands. They form only a small portion of the total number of French immigrants who, since the bomb tests began, have been pouring into Tahiti at the rate of a thousand a year.

The French want to continue these deadly tests and they plan to grab all the wealth our ocean contains. This is why it is the deliberate policy of the Paris government to swamp the country with French settlers. If we don't stop them now, we shall soon be a minority in our own country. This is what has already happened in New Caledonia. Our only salvation is therefore to achieve independence as fast as possible.

For weeks and months, the newspapers were full of lurid accounts of Olivier Bréaud's brutal killing and the murderers' sex orgies, attended by what seemed to be the cream of the local establishment. The murderers were lucky that so many VIP's were involved, because they pulled strings that delayed the trial for such a long time that the death penalty was abandoned before they were eventually brought to justice, and they thus escaped with life sentences.

In these circumstances, it was not so surprising that very little was said or written in the colony about a much more worrying threat looming up on the horizon. This was the so-called *El Niño* meteorological phenomenon, causing the temperature of the surface waters between the Marquesas and the Tuamotu islands to rise to more than 30°C, which meant that this area had become a dangerous breeding ground for cyclones.

Until then, cyclones – which are extremely common in the western region of the Pacific – had been rare in islands of French Polynesia. In fact, no atolls in the Tuamotu archipelago had suffered any serious cyclone damage since the beginning of the century. For this reason, when a cyclone began forming at the end of November 1980 in the vicinity of the Marquesas islands, the precursory signs were not recognised as such by the inhabitants in the atolls to the south. The meteorological service also failed to forecast this – they only spoke of a 'tropical depression'. Nor did the path followed by the rapidly developing cyclone cause much apprehension, for it seemed to avoid most of the big, inhabited islands, with one exception – Moruroa – which was hit on 28 November. As always, the CEP was very discrete and saw to it that the weathermen spoke only vaguely of 'a disaster zone comprising Tureia, Tematangi and adjacent islands'. But, as everybody in the colony knew, these 'adjacent islands' were Moruroa and Fangataufa.

Gradually, Polynesian workmen returning from Moruroa were able to confirm that the island had been hit by a wind of hurricane force, and that huge waves had washed over the atoll rim and wrecked a great number of buildings. Luckily for the 3 000 men and twelve women living on the atoll, twenty-three 4.5 metre-high refuge platforms had been built during the sixteen month interval since the shock waves caused by the awry bomb accident in July 1979, and all the 'islanders' had managed to crawl up on them in time. As if this flooding had not been enough, the personnel were also drenched by 100 inches of rain during their 24 hour stay on the platforms.

This predictable but unannounced disaster had occurred only three days after the tenth bomb in the 1980 test series had been detonated. Its yield was a paltry 2-5 kilotonnes which made it highly probable that it was another tactical neutron bomb. The green light was given for the eleventh and last blast for the season on 3 December. Its yield was estimated at 30 kilotonnes by the New Zealand seismological station in Rarotonga. It was in all likelihood a warhead for use on a strategic missile.

Three months later, the Moruroa camp commander was again taken by surprise. A cyclone which came into being in the remote Cook islands did not travel south and peter out at colder latitudes, as such cyclones usually do, but instead veered suddenly east towards Moruroa. At the same time, it gradually increased speed until it reached full hurricane force on 11 March 1981. This time the CEP directors saw to it that no news leaked out to the press.

Try as hard as they might to hide what had happened, it was nevertheless now obvious to any thinking person that the recurrence of cyclones in the ocean area where Moruroa and Fangataufa were situated, added to the previously well-known drawbacks (such as the porous and brittle character of the subsoil), definitely demonstrated what we and other critics had been saying right from the beginning – that an atoll is the worst possible place for making underground tests.

276

55 TOPSY-TURVY ELECTIONS

At the time, nobody in Tahiti paid much attention to the new cyclone danger, because of the impending French presidential elections, which occupied all thoughts and energies. The two main contenders were, as in 1974, the leader of the socialist party, François Mitterand, and the incumbent conservative president, Giscard d'Estaing. Teariki, Sanford and all other old Autonomist leaders had regularly supported Mitterand in the past, because of his firm opposition to the French nuclear striking force. He had frequently condemned this as being both inefficient and ruinous. But the socialists had gradually changed their stand in the late 1970s and were now, with some reservations, in favour of it, which meant that they accepted as a corollary that the tests must go on at Moruroa. Thus, the main motivation the Polynesian Autonomists had had for supporting Mitterand and the socialist party no longer existed in 1981.

The French High Commissioner was not missing an opportunity to remind the Autonomists of this fact and to urge them to switch their allegiance to Giscard, arguing that the incumbent president was a sure winner and that it would be more rewarding for them to be on the winning side. Of course, they were not expecting Giscard to change the nuclear policies he had been pursuing in true Gaullist tradition during his 1974–81 term of office. But, as he had shown by his acts, he was a true liberal and was willing, the High Commissioner told them confidentially, to give them even more power than Flosse had dared to ask for in his recent bid for a new statute. This clever suggestion sounded like sweet music to the Autonomists, who were becoming increasingly annoyed by Gaston Flosse's unabashed insistence that he was the only true Autonomist in the territory.

President Giscard also remembered his Polynesian friends at the right moment and invited them to Paris for a friendly chat. They sent their toughest man, John Teariki, who came back with fast-talking Paul Dijoud at his elbow. Teariki, therefore, was unable to get in a word as long as the minister remained in Tahiti, which was more than a week. The main theme the minister elaborated on was how valuable it still was (and he used figures to support this) for the Polynesians to have such excellent relations with an understanding and well-disposed president of Giscard's caliber. And yet there were some miserable fools (*douloureux débiles*) who wanted independence, not realising the economic disasters and abject poverty which would immediately follow, as proved by recent events in another Pacific territory which had previously enjoyed French assistance, Dijoud added as a philosophical afterthought. It was obvious that his inability in 1980 to keep the lid on the New Hebridean situation still rankled him.

However, hardly had Dijoud's plane vanished beyond the horizon than John Teariki summoned the local press to make a statement. This was in striking contrast to his usual reserve, so everybody sensed that he must have had something particularly important to say. As most observers of the political scene had guessed in advance, it concerned his recent talks with Giscard. In a low-key speech, Teariki revealed that President Giscard had now generously promised to implement the reform that his Minister for Overseas Territories and Departments had up till then constantly vetoed and ridiculed – that is, giving more power to the Polynesian people by placing the local government in the hands of an elected premier assisted by other cabinet ministers, each one at the head of his own department. In other words, the Autonomists had recovered the main plank in their election platform, which had been surreptitiously stolen from them by Gaston Flosse.

A few days after Teariki's exciting revelations, his arch-rival Gaston Flosse, who was in his second month of a whirlwind campaign in favour of the Gaullist RPR presidential candidate, Jacques Chirac, called a press conference. Denouncing Giscard's promise as a cheap last-minute electoral trick, he chided Teariki for being gullible and asserted that 'verbal promises without witnesses are absolutely worthless in politics, even when the person making them happens to be the president of the republic'.

The task of carrying the Mitterand banner was left to the only local party with a socialist programme, *Ia mana te nunaa*. It could be said that they held the banner higher and waved it with greater fervour than was warranted by Mitterand's public statements – they repeated endlessly that they were for independence and against the nuclear tests.

After the first round on 26 April, which eliminated eight of the ten candidates, only one thing was certain: the three Polynesian parties had preserved their traditional relative strengths. The candidate supported by the Autonomists, Giscard d'Estaing, got

51.4 per cent of the votes; Flosse's candidate, Chirac, 35.9 per cent; and the *Ia mana te nunaa* candidate, Mitterand, 8.32 per cent.

During the second round, the pro-Giscard forces adopted the scare tactics of their metropolitan patron who, like his predecessors de Gaulle and Pompidou, tried – without much success – to persuade voters that the communists would be masters of France if Mitterand won. At the level of local affairs, they propagated the idea that a victory for the crypto-communists led by Mitterand would lead to the cancellation of all pensions and welfare payments, the sacking of thousands of civil servants, and the abolition, as in Russia, of private property!

With this sort of propaganda being spread through the islands, it was little wonder that Giscard won handsomely in the second round. However, a sufficient number of supporters of Flosse and Teariki-Sanford voted for Mitterand to treble his first-round vote: he scored 11 357 votes in the second round, as against 37 414 for Giscard.

Of course, all voters in French Polynesia might as well have stayed home, as they were totally unable to influence the outcome of a national election of this type, for the reason that their 48 000 votes, as the colonial system prescribed, were lumped together with the thirty million votes cast in metropolitan France. In France, Mitterand beat Giscard by about one million votes.

Barely a month later, Mitterand called a general election, in the hope that the groundswell of support he had enjoyed in the presidential election would deliver to his party the majority in the National Assembly, which was required to carry out his mildly socialistic programme of reforms. Unfortunately, there was no time to remedy the injustice committed by the gerrymandering of the electoral map in 1978. Gaston Flosse thus enjoyed the advantage of running again in a constituency that had been tailor-made for him by Giscard and his men.

The only significant departure from previous electoral practices was the allocation of campaign time on television and radio for all candidates. This probably doesn't sound terribly revolutionary to most citizens of democratic countries, but in Tahiti – where the French government has always banned its political opponents from the strictly controlled and censored television and radio programmes – it was a most welcome breath of fresh air.

The leaders of the small pro-independence parties grasped this opportunity most eagerly. In the past, they had always been hampered by lack of funds to travel to the outer islands, as the candidates of the big parties were able to do quite regularly. The time allotted to each candidate was not more than seven minutes, but this was compensated for by the new ruling which allowed speakers to speak in Tahitian, if they wished to. At close of nominations, no fewer than eight candidates favouring independence had entered the lists. Needless to say, they were all opposed to the continuation of nuclear tests in French Polynesia.

On election day there was an unusually high percentage of abstentions – about 40% in both constituencies – which must be ascribed to a general 'battle fatigue' after two months of political campaigning. In the eastern constituency, for the reasons outlined, Gaston Flosse had an easy first round win with a 56 per cent vote, a little better than in 1978. In the western constituency too, the incumbent deputy Jean Juventin stood again, but ran into a few snags in the first round, because another leader in the Autonomist camp decided to run as an independent. But in the second round he again beat his *Tahoeraa* rival to the finish, by a 51.5 per cent to 48.5 per cent vote.

The combined percentage of 'miserable fools' (as Dijoud described them) who voted for candidates advocating independence was surprisingly high in both constituencies – 20.41 per cent in the western and 19.77 per cent in the eastern. The biggest vote-getters among them were the *Ia mana* candidates, Jacqui Drollet and Peni Atger. Yet they enjoyed no support from their 'big brothers' in Paris, because they were in favour of independence and even worse were opposed to the nuclear tests. In other words, they were totally opposed to the two important points in the French socialist programme.

In France, the election resulted in a landslide victory for the socialist party, assuring it of an absolute majority in the National Assembly. Among the 112 Gaullist and Giscardian deputies who lost their seats was the former Minister for Overseas Territories, Paul Dijoud, whom nobody has ever heard about since then. As the two re-elected deputies for French Polynesia, Flosse and Juventin, had both waged a furious campaign against Mitterand in the presidential election, they found themselves in a difficult position in the parliament of being treated as non-entities by the new ruling party.

56 NO SECRETS HERE

Let us go back one month, however, to the end of May, when the first socialist government was formed. (Most ministers were reconfirmed in power after the legislative elections in June/July.) To everybody's delight in the Pacific, the first decision the new government took was to suspend the nuclear tests at Moruroa. The official explanation was that Mitterand and his Minister for Defence, Charles Hernu, wanted to review carefully the existing military programmes and policies they had inherited from the previous regime.

As the usually very well-informed French newspaper *Le Monde* told the story, Hernu was particularly concerned about the slack security at Moruroa. But according to the same source, he had been immediately reassured by the CEA directors and the CEP admirals and generals that all rumours about radioactive pollution and structural damage to the atoll were lies propagated by fanatic 'greens', whose true colour was red. So after having completed his 'review' in five days, simply by accepting the assurance of the bombers that there were no problems at all at Moruroa, on 2 June 1981, with Mitterand's approval he decided to go ahead with the tests as scheduled. This meant three explosions in quick succession during the month of July.

It seemed nevertheless that Hernu still harboured some doubts, for it had by then been announced that he was soon coming out to inspect Moruroa in person. When he did arrive on 31 July, it was hard to believe that the suave gentleman in the dark double-breasted suit was indeed a member of the new socialist government, swept to power on a radical programme of far-reaching social and economic reforms.

Except for the fact that he sported a thin beard, he looked exactly like the numerous Gaullist ministers who had preceded him. The local reception committee, too, seemed very familiar – it consisted of the same old guard of politicians and businessmen who had always prospered under the existing colonial and capitalist system. Incidentally, less than two months before most of them had ardently supported Chirac and Giscard in the presidential elections. But here they were on the tarmac again completely unabashed by their about-turn. As for the dancers, musicians and beauty queens – supposedly symbolising the friendly *aroha* spirit of the islands – they smiled as happily as they always do when they are paid well for their services.

Not unexpectedly, the new Defence Minister also spoke like his Gaullist predecessors, although in a somewhat more rambling and befuddled manner. Thus, at a press conference held the same evening at the Residency, he lost no time in announcing that the nuclear tests were to continue. At Moruroa. Indefinitely.

When a reporter asked whether there was any truth in the persistent rumour that the Kerguelen islands in the Indian Ocean were being considered as a more suitable testing ground than the much battered atoll, Hernu literally exploded, declaring that the rumour was so silly that it was not worth answering. 'Everybody is perfectly happy with Moruroa,' he added. 'Even the Polynesian people?' asked an incredulous reporter. Hernu took a deep breath and made an even more incredible statement:

The people of Polynesia have already expressed their approval in what amounts virtually to a popular referendum, for since I took over as Defence Minister, I have received thousands of letters from French Polynesia, all in favour of continued nuclear testing at Moruroa.

Of course this was impossible to believe. We publicly challenged Hernu in the local newspapers to produce these pro-nuclear letters, or at least provide some more information about this unique 'mail-order referendum'. Were the letter writers really all Polynesians? Or were they perhaps mainly French expatriates, making a lot of money out of the bomb? Or were they simply reactionary Frenchmen back home, who equate honour and glory with the bomb? The only answer Hernu cared to furnish was extremely evasive. He claimed that letters received by his ministry were 'confidential documents'.

The exact number of neutron bombs exploded at Moruroa was likewise a top secret. But as far as security problems were concerned, Hernu swore that the new socialist government was going to make a complete break with the despicable hush-up policies of the previous conservative regimes:

The press must be informed about security problems. If there is an accident, it is better to let the truth be known than to let all sorts of rumours spread. Nothing must be hidden that affects the health of the population. When New Zealand and Australia ask us for information about these problems, we shall supply it.

Hernu thereupon flew off to Moruroa on 1 August and spent three days there, during which time a 20 kilotonne bomb was detonated. As usual, this information came from the New Zealand Seismological Observatory. One year later, the French Defence Ministry unintentionally told the full story in a so-called 'position' paper: it was a neutron bomb that had been detonated on this occasion.

Nobody in Tahiti had expected Hernu to reveal any military secrets. But most of the political leaders had hoped for at least some sort of reply to their demand, made in the Territorial Assembly exactly two years previously, for a thorough investigation of the 1979 accidents at Moruroa and for a health survey of the whole population by impartial medical doctors. They were sorely disappointed; for, on his return to Tahiti from Moruroa, Hernu behaved no better than had his predecessors. That is, accompanied by his charming wife, he basked in the sun, attended a native feast and did a little sightseeing, until it was time to fly back to Paris.

Was Mitterand's firm determination to keep Moruroa as a nuclear testing ground making him less inclined to apply to French Polynesia the emancipation policy for all French overseas territories that was part of socialist party policy? The man who should have known the answer to this question was, of course, Dijoud's successor, Henri Emmanuelli, who arrived only a week after Hernu's departure as a passenger on a regular flight from Fiji. He, too, had the polished look of all his Gaullist predecessors. He was clasped to the bosom of the same old-guard reception committee, by now even more warmly pro-socialist – after all, his ministry had the ultimate say in all money matters affecting French Polynesia.

It soon became obvious that the minister's very sensible attitude was: I shall wait and see (or more to the point – I shall see the sights first and then wait for the outcome of the territorial elections to be held in May 1982). Consequently, Emmanuelli undertook a gruelling but perfectly futile trip that in six days took him around Tahiti and then to the Leeward and the Tuamotu islands, with stops at schools, dispensaries, town halls, museums, solar installations, factories, slums, markets and hotels. The only noticeable innovation was the absence of the popular 'flower girls' who, during ministerial visits in the past, used to embellish most official receptions, and who, to tell the sad truth, often tempted elderly and portly civil servants and politicians to behave in a most undignified fashion.

Throughout his ordeal, Emmanuelli kept smiling in the most engaging manner and rarely talked for more than five minutes at a time, in a pleasant but uninteresting manner. Not even on the last day of his stay, when he made his only full-length political speech in the packed Territorial Assembly (behind a socialist-red bouquet of roses, thoughtfully provided by the House), did he have much to say. His greatest achievement was that he almost scared some of the hosts out of their wits by casually suggesting that it was time to introduce income tax, so they didn't have to go on forever begging the mother country for money. But what his many speeches came down to in the end was a vague promise to examine 'what reforms might be needed to make the 1977 statute conform better to the wishes of the Polynesian people, as expressed in a parliamentary manner'.

It was not until three months later that we eventually learned what had happened at Moruroa and in the French Defence Ministry during the year 1981. As in the case of the 1979 accident, the truth came out as a result of the sleuthing of a courageous Parisian journalist. Her name was Françoise Berger, and her main informants were French CFDT technicians employed at Moruroa who feared for their health and their lives and therefore disregarded their secrecy pledge. The following excerpts from the article published in the independent newspaper *Libération* on 6 November 1981 contain their most important revelations and accusations:

For the past ten years the north coast of Moruroa has been thoroughly contaminated by the deliberate release of plutonium. This has been done as a sort of security excercise to train the personnel in procedures to be followed in the event of an aircraft accident. The most tangible effect was the spilling out on the atoll and beyond it into the ocean, over several kilogrammes of plutonium. To prevent the plutonium from being blown by the wind off the surface of the atoll it was 'fixed' with tar. The idea was that eventually everything, tar as well as plutonium, would be removed. This, however, has not been done.

In 1979, a bomb explosion in the southern portion of the coral ring blasted out a piece of the atoll's underlying crater. This produced a spectacular tidal wave which carried away some shelters. As a precaution for the future, a seismograph was installed and connected with a whistle which was supposed to warn the 'islanders' if a similar accident occurred during or after some future nuclear blast. At the same time, platforms resting on stilts and equipped with handrails were built for the use of personnel during tests, and as a refuge from possible tidal waves. Each platform accommodates 500 people.

Then, on 11 March 1981, the greatest disaster yet occurred. It was caused by a cyclone more violent than those which usually rage in this region, where the wind can swing full circle in the course of a single day. It had been the practice over a number of years to store all sorts of radioactive waste – metal scrap, wood, resin plastic bags, clothes, and so on – in a huge heap on the north coast of the atoll. This dump eventually covered 30 000 square metres. As long as the atoll was fairly high above sea level, waves broke against the reef and did not reach the massive pile of garbage. But, during the March 1981 hurricane, heavy seas swept the garbage into the lagoon, where it was not long in reaching first the southern and then the eastern side of the atoll, the site of the living quarters. The plutonium-impregnated tar was torn off the reef, and spread all over the atoll. An accident of precisely this kind had, incidentally, been foreseen some time before by a visiting expert from the Atomic Energy Commission.

The base commander, General Rouyer, reported the March disaster to the then Defence Minister Yvon Bourges, telling him that the personnel were in danger of contaminaton. Nothing happened. Two months later, however, following the change of government in France, the same report was shown to the new Defence Minister, Charles Hernu. He suspended the tests very briefly and then announced that they were to be resumed. During all this time, swimming in the lagoon in front of the living quarters area was permitted. If the swimmers swallowed a mouthful of plutonium-spiced water, they knew nothing about it – at least not right away, as no health checks were being made outside the forbidden zones. Swimming was considered moreover to be good for the morale.

At the beginning of July 1981, a ten-man delegation of civilian technicians at Moruroa sought and was granted an interview with Charles Hernu in Paris. The minister declared that he was unaware of this grave problem – and he was, of course, later told that the Russians, or perhaps some West Indians, were pulling strings behind the scenes in the hope of bringing French nuclear testing to a halt. The minister then decided to visit Moruroa, stepping ashore there on 1 August. A few days earlier a general clean-up had been undertaken in order to remove the traces of the scars left by the 11 March hurricane. But it so happened that another storm hit the atoll on the eve of the ministerial visit, revealing once again the full extent of the pollution. A dinner was held for the minister during his visit. In the course of a speech at the dinner, the local CFDT leader harangued Hernu on the matter of living conditions. In the course of his remarks he used the familiar form of address *tu* (instead of the formal *vous*), no doubt on the grounds that he and the minister were socialist party comrades. The minister turned crimson and told the insolent fellow to shut up.

At the end of his stay Hernu decided: (1) to clean up the atoll, a job the military brass undertook to accomplish in three months, and (2) to reorganise the security system. General Rouyer and the civilian director of the protection service, Jean-Marie Lavie, kept their jobs. But two engineers – one military, one civilian – and ten minor officials were posted elsewhere.

Despite the promise made by the camp commander to clean up the atoll quickly, it was twice as contaminated on 31 October than on 31 July. Actually, it was a totally impossible undertaking, because the plutonium, which has a half-life of 24 400 years, had deeply impregnated the coral ring. That is, the portion of the stuff that had not been washed into the ocean.

These revelations created a sensation, and a great number of French and foreign newspapers and magazines published prominently-displayed stories under such headlines as 'Moruroa is sinking', 'Moruroa, the unstable volcano', 'N-waste from French tests swept into the sea' and 'Moruroa men throw their own bomb'. In a speech in the National Assembly on 9 December 1981, Hernu eventually conceded the correctness of this report and promised 'to remedy the situation'.

57 SEAFARERS, FOUND AND LOST

Locally, the Territorial Assembly was, as usual, the centre of the storm of protest that broke out. With a singular lack of originality, Hernu could not think up any response other than to invite a delegation of assemblymen to make a meaningless flying visit to Moruroa 'to see for themselves that there are no radiation dangers'. The tour was to be conducted by no less than the commander of the French nuclear submarine fleet, Admiral Pieri, who was already on his way to Tahiti. The assemblymen, who had been taken for a similar tour only two years earlier, refused the invitation and reminded the minister that they were still waiting for the long overdue report about 'the presidential accident' on 25 July 1979, and for the arrival of a team of impartial doctors to undertake the promised health survey.

The assemblymen had been emboldened to take this tougher stand by the anti-nuclear protest cruise of the Greenpeace yacht *Vega*, which had left Mexico at the end of October and reached Moruroa in early December 1981. On board was the veteran protester David McTaggart, who ten years earlier had spearheaded the shipborne attack against the French base, which did more than anything else to stop atmospheric testing at Moruroa for good. History thus seemed to be repeating itself, but there was an important difference. With the test now being made underground, the presence of a protest vessel in the waters around Moruroa did not hold them up any longer, as had been the case in 1972 and 1973, when it was impossible to explode a bomb above ground without exposing the protesters to lethal radiation. This is why the French military high command in those days often resorted to piratical seizure in international waters.

Greenpeace president McTaggart had adapted his tactics for this new 1981 cruise in an appropriate manner by embarking with a man whom the French marines would hesitate to lay their hands on. This key person looked exactly like the other long-haired and bearded crew members – Chris Robinson from Australia, Lloyd Anderson from the USA and Tony Marriner from the UK. But he was the politically astute leader of the French ecological movement, Brice Lalonde, the veteran of the 1973 sea battle off Moruroa (where he had arrived on the vessel *Fri*), who had continued ever since to wage a valiant fight against the proliferation of nuclear power plants in France. He acted to such good effect that he became eventually, at the age of thirty-five, the candidate for the French ecological movement in the May 1981 presidential poll. In the first round of the election he secured 3.9 per cent of the total vote, or 1 126 254 votes. It was largely due to the support of Brice's voters in the second round that François Mitterand became president. The ecologists were thus holding the balance of power in a good number of French constituencies during all future elections.

The goal of the cruise was to elicit a firm commitment from President Mitterand that all nuclear tests at Moruroa would be suspended, until the whole disarmament problem came up for discussion at the special United Nations conference on the subject in May 1982. Mitterand again demonstrated what a consummate politician he is by sending a most graciously-worded message, saying that he was most strongly in favour of general disarmament, and that Brice Lalonde was 'welcome to come back to Moruroa at a later date to make a personal examination of the flora and fauna in the region of the testing site'.

Brice replied that he considered the message 'an excellent starting point for further discussions', and that he was 'much interested in taking an active part in the study of the radioactive pollution in French Polynesia'.

Not a word was said on either side about the proposed moratorium, even though at the very moment of the exchange of these polite messages, the New Zealand Seismological Observatory announced that on 5 and 8 December 1981, two more bombs had been exploded at Moruroa. As we learned later, these were the first explosions made in the centre of the atoll, in shafts drilled with the help of an oil derrick mounted on a barge anchored in the lagoon.

By then the *Vega* had been at sea for forty days, and her provisions were almost exhausted. No invitation to land at Moruroa had been received. On the contrary, the French navy ship *Hippopotame* kept circling the yacht in the most threatening manner, obviously bent on provoking an 'accident'. Wisely, David and Brice set sail for Tahiti, tailed closely by the *Hippopotame*.

The yacht docked in Papeete harbour on 16 December 1981. The timing was perfect, for the Territorial Assembly was in session, and the members were still outraged by the many horror stories they had read recently about the cyclone accidents at Moruroa. Gaston Flosse was the most vocal, and he tabled a motion embodying the main requests formulated in the motion adopted by the Territorial Assembly, after the July 1979 accidents, for an independent investigation and a health survey of the whole population.

During the debate on this motion, which took place on 21 December, the traditionally anti-nuclear Autonomists criticized Flosse for having been so slow to see the light. They proposed to co-sponsor the motion, as it simply rephrased one of the main points in their own party programme. Some of them even suggested that Flosse's dramatic reversal was purely opportunistic, given that a territorial election was only five months away.

Flosse and other members of his party replied that they had changed their minds after the recent revelations of the frightening spread of radioactive pollution at Moruroa. To show that they intended to remain in the forefront of the anti-nuclear battle, the Autonomist assemblymen, after having voted in favour of the motion, tacked on an amendment. This requested the French government to suspend all testing at Moruroa, until an international team of radiation experts and medical doctors had completed their investigations.

As another and more visible expression of their anti-nuclear and anti-colonial policies, the Autonomists decided to unveil, two weeks before the territorial election, the four-metre high, three million franc monument. This honoured the old freedom fighter Pouvanaa a Oopa, and had been under construction for some time. 10 May had been chosen for the inauguration, as Pouvanaa was born on that day in 1895. Flosse, in his turn, decried the decision as a propaganda stunt, designed to help the Autonomists win the 23 May election. In addition, strong criticism was levelled by all camps at the monument itself, which consisted of a stela of imported French stone, topped by a perfectly hideous bust by a French sculptor, who got the commission because he was a close friend of the late High Commissioner, Charles Schmitt.

The protests directed at the banality and ugliness of the monument were nothing, however, compared to the angry outbursts of Pouvanaa's son David and nephew Charlie Ching when they saw the inscription engraved on two marble plaques at the foot of the monument. Although the text was twenty-three lines long, its anonymous author (probably one of the numerous

French expatriates employed by the local government) had absolutely nothing to say about Pouvanaa's life-long struggle for independence and his strong condemnation of the nuclear tests at Moruroa. Instead, it was blandly suggested that he had become a hero of the Polynesian people because he had persuaded the French administration to employ more natives, increase welfare handouts, and return some land to its rightful owners.

The territorial election which was held on 23 May 1982, five years after the colony supposedly obtained internal self-government, clearly showed that there had only been one significant change – the voters had by then become accustomed to blaming Francis Sanford's puppet government for all wrongs, forgetting that the strings were still being pulled by the powerful French High Commissioner.

During the election campaign, Vice-president Sanford vowed: 'Our canoe is caught in a raging storm. But we have faced other tempests in the past, and we shall pull through this one, too, and eventually reach our destination.' It is with great sadness that we must record, in a similar metaphorical vein, that instead of reaching harbour safely, the Autonomist's double canoe broke asunder.

Expressed in the European language of figures, this means that 60 000 of the 85 000 registered voters who went to the polls to elect thirty assemblymen (out of 398 candidates) cast enough votes – 15.8 per cent of the total – for Teariki's *Pupu here aia* party to return him and his five companions. On the other hand, the voters demonstrated their strong disapproval of Francis Sanford's leadership by giving his party only a pitiful 2 929 votes. The magnitude of the defeat is more clearly brought out if the *Ea api* vote is expressed as a percentage of the total number of votes cast: 4.4 per cent. This gave a seat in the assembly only to the bearer of the first name on the *Ea api* list, Francis Sanford. Up to then, his party had occupied seven seats. Another notable victim of this election was the last Frenchman to siege in the Territorial Assembly, Frantz Vanizette. For twenty years he had been regularly elected, with the help of his friends Teariki and Sanford, because of his fine grasp of parliamentary procedure and his excellent contacts in the ministries in Paris.

So much for the losers. Let us now move on to the winners: Foremost among them was Gaston Flosse and his *Tahoeraa Huiraatira* party, affiliated with the French RPR Gaullist party and therefore the natural choice of the 10 000 expatriate voters.

With 17 787 votes, or 29.3 per cent of the total, it won thirteen assembly seats, a gain of four, but still three seats short of an absolute majority.

The progress made by the *Ia mana* party, which previously was not represented in the assembly, was equally impressive, although it lagged far behind *Tahoeraa* in absolute figures. Its achievement in winning three seats crowned years of hard, slogging work by its young and dedicated members among the most destitute and miserable Polynesians. They would have won a fourth seat if everybody in favour of independence had voted for them, instead of spreading out about 2 000 votes on eight other pro-independence candidates. These did not include Charlie Ching who, although he had been granted amnesty in 1981 by the new president of France, François Mitterand, was still deprived of some of his civil rights – for example, that of running for a political office. His stand-in was far below him in popular appeal and rhetorical skills, and as a consequence, the *Taata Tahiti Tiama* party polled only 726 votes.

Francis Sanford's crushing defeat must above all be ascribed to the burdens and limitations of the 1977 statute. To begin with, he had to cope with an endless succession of ceremonial tasks: cutting gaily coloured ribbons at the opening of new schools, bridges and roads, crowning beauty queens, entertaining French ministers and their wives, and eating, eating, eating, as the guest of honour at banquets organized by the hundreds of clubs and associations that exist in the territory.

When it came to important policy planning and government business, however, his powers were pitifully restricted – not only by statutory regulations, but also by the fact that he had to depend for the execution of his decisions mainly on French expatriate officials, who were more inclined to listen to the High Commissioner than to him. Even worse, the few supposedly independent collaborators the statute allowed him to choose were either pompous pseudo-intellectuals, greedy fortune-hunters or worthless hangers-on, who produced a series of wild schemes which invariably collapsed – if they ever got off the ground at all.

What finally sealed Sanford's fate was the defection, less than two months before the election, of his own party secretary. 'Sheriff' Vernaudon managed to persuade enough *Ea api* members to follow his example, and with the help of these renegades he formed a new party, *Aia api*. To top it all, after winning three seats, Vernaudon allied himself with Sanford's arch-rival, Gaston Flosse, who thereby gained a precarious majority in the assembly. As the last bitter pill for Francis Sanford to swallow, Vernaudon was rewarded for his switch of allegiance with the post of Speaker of the house.

58 EXPLORATORY MISSIONS

Two more assemblymen, elected on independent lists concerned with local issues, decided to support the *Tahoeraa-Aia api* coalition on a tentative basis, in the hope of being richly rewarded with budget allocations and public works for their constituencies. As a result Flosse was easily elected to the coveted post of vice-president of the executive government council, or to use a more comprehensible language for English readers, to the post of premier or prime minister of the local government. To fill the other six cabinet posts, he chose the ablest young technocrats from the upper crust of his party, who had proven their worth during the long uphill power struggle towards the glorious summit they had at long last reached.

Incidentally, the debates of the new assembly were considerably livened up by the three *Ia mana* MPs, who true to their popular image of angry young men, immediately insisted on using the Tahitian language. They were quickly joined by the six returned *Pupu here aia* assemblymen. The only member who felt incumbent upon him to defend the French honour was the part-European representative for a Tuamotuan constituency, Napoleon Spitz. But he, too, soon met his Waterloo, as the House took the unprecedented step of allowing the debates to be held in the language of the country.

This provoked the ire of the parliamentary reporters employed by the French language dailies (still the only ones in the territory), who threatened to stay away from the Territorial Assembly until a simultaneous translation system was installed. The incorrigible *Ia mana* newcomers gleefully suggested a cheaper and more efficient solution: that the editors hire journalists who understand Tahitian.

The first act of the new vice-president was to fly off to Paris together with his most valuable allies – that is, the maverick speaker of the house, 'Sheriff' Vernaudon, and the majestic Napoleon Spitz. The vice-president to press the old Autonomist demands – which he had made his – for full internal self-government, and for an impartial investigation into the radiation and health problems. On their return, a long communiqué was published, which made it clear that they had met with the same categorical refusal encountered by all previous Polynesian delegations on similar errands. This was still applied because the French military policy had not changed one iota since the socialists took over the reins of government.

The only thing the Minister for Overseas Territories could promise Flosse and company was the setting up of a mixed Commission, entrusted with the task of examining 'the possibility of making statutory adjustments on the local level'. As an example of such an adjustment, he hinted that he might be willing to confer on the members of the Government Council the rank of cabinet ministers – provided that their departments continued to be run by expatriate Frenchmen, taking orders from the High Commissioner.

The Minister for Defence, Charles Hernu, had begun by offering his 'personal guarantee' that the tests were harmless – an assurance that evoked more hilarity than relief among his visitors – whereupon he made them speechless with an offer which was described thus by Flosse, after his return home:

A scientific team, conducted by the Government Commissary Haroun Tazieff will be sent out to Polynesia, and the members will be allowed to undertake all studies and checks they wish in the geological and radiobiological fields. The members of this team will present to the elected representatives of the Polynesian people the results of their investigations. The dispatch of this group of experts thus meets the demands expressed in a motion tabled in the Territorial Assembly concerning the possible health hazards resulting from the nuclear tests at Moruroa.

Haroun Tazieff seemed to be a good choice. He is a world-famous volcanologist and Moruroa rests, like all other atolls, on a supposedly extinct underwater volcano. Even more important, he had already been to Moruroa in 1975 at the request of Giscard d'Estaing, when the first trial borings were made. His advice on that occasion was to forget about Moruroa and make the underground tests in the Massif Central mountains in France. Displeased with this sensible advice, Giscard's government never consulted him again and forged ahead with its huge testing programme – at Moruroa. After the socialist takeover in 1981, Tazieff had been appointed Commissary for the Prevention of Natural Disasters. So it seemed a not too far-fetched idea to send him out now in the company of competent experts to study the man-made disasters in French Polynesia.

Sad to say, the composition of this scientific team, made public shortly afterwards, immediately gave a lie to Hernu's promise. What the Territorial Assembly had asked for, both in 1979 and 1981, was the dispatch of a team of medical doctors to do a health survey. In place of this, Hernu supplied a seven-man team, composed of highly-placed CEA officials (three of whom had already participated in the previous 'study visit' in 1979), and a few university professors of geology and zoology. As for Brice Lalonde, he had turned down the invitation kindly extended to him. Or that was what Haroun Tazieff told us, when the team arrived in Tahiti in June 1982. He should have added that Brice Lalonde's refusal had been motivated by the obvious futility of making another quick jaunt to Moruroa.

After having spent forty-eight hours with this team at the atoll, Haroun Tazieff admitted that it was a rather hurried visit, but that it had nevertheless fullfilled its purpose which was to prepare the ground for a complete and thorough investigation. A written statement distributed to the press ended on the following promising note: 'Concrete proposals for further field work will be made within the next months, and no security or environmental problems will be excluded.'

We had to wait a whole year before anything was heard again from Commissary Tazieff, and all he had to say then was that the promised, thorough investigation of Moruroa was definitely off. At the same time, however, he lifted the veil of secrecy that had up to then surrounded his 1982 visit to Moruroa in a semi-confidential report, just enough to give some tantalizing glimpses of the strange goings-on there. We managed to get hold of a copy and were most forcefully struck by the insurmountable difficulties the team had faced to obtain relevant and reliable information. The team members attributed this sorry state of affairs to the absence of a scientific director at Moruroa to coordinate the researchers in keeping with an overall plan. Each group of technicians had acted on its own, or rather on orders from their military chiefs, and their studies too often either overlapped or left huge gaps.

For example, one of the team members, a marine biologist by profession, pointed out in this report that nobody had bothered to map the ocean currents sweeping past the atoll. Consequently, it was far from certain that the samples of plankton and fish which were occasionally taken by the army technicians could, in fact, reveal anything about the seepage risks.

Tazieff himself made an even more shocking disclosure. When

he began looking into the serious problem of venting (radioactive releases into the atmosphere from underground explosions), he discovered that the military observers had consistently installed their monitoring equipment too far from the bomb shaft and too late after the explosion, which made all their data useless and misleading. This particularly angered another member, the director of the CNRS National Laboratory for the Study of Low Level Radiation, Professor Gérard Lambert, who became convinced 'that certain gaseous fission products like krypton and xenon are capable of rising eventually to the surface of the atoll'.

Tazieff's men had brought their own monitoring instruments and were invited to use them for checking any venting that occurred during a nuclear test made especially for their benefit on 27 June 1982. Unfortunately the yield of the bomb detonated on this occasion was the smallest ever, less than one kilotonne, and nothing could therefore be learnt about the risks entailed during the normal test programme, when bombs of ten to one hundred bigger yields are exploded.

The army technicians did not know much more when questioned about the leakage of radioactive matter, which must have occurred on several occasions, when the outer wall of the atoll was pierced far below the waterline by accidental explosions. Tazieff estimates that the 25 July 1979 accident alone pried loose one million cubic metres of coral and rock. Yet no attempt had been made to ascertain the exact number and the size of all these gaping holes in the side of the atoll, with the help of a bathyscaphe.

The situation was identical when the team asked for information about the slow seepage risks. The official French line has always been that all radioactive elements are trapped in the cavity produced by the bomb explosion, and that the subsoil of Moruroa is so watertight that no seepage into the ocean occurs at all. Well, it turned out that the army technicians had never taken any water samples from the bottom of the bomb shafts. Professor Lambert comments severely:

I regret that no researches have been undertaken in view of tracing the existence in the ground water and the subsoil of radioactive elements – that is, researches which would have made it possible to verify how watertight the base of the atoll is.

As to the anguishing problem of what had become of the heap of plutonium and the mountain of nuclear waste, described in fearsome detail by the CFDT 1981 report, Tazieff and his men had nothing to say about it, for the very simple reason that they were never allowed to visit the contaminated zone on the north coast.

59 TRAGIC HIT PARADE

The fact that the team headed by Haroun Tazieff was forbidden to visit the north coast of Moruroa could only mean one thing: that the 1980 and 1981 cyclones had not washed away all the nuclear waste that had been dumped there over a period of fifteen years. The final cleanup was undertaken not by the CEP personnel, as planned, but by a series of new cyclones, which devastated our islands between January and May 1983.

The first one, called Nano, swept down through the eastern half of the Tuamotus and hit with amazing precision the only important target in the area, the huge military base at Hao. This also has an airstrip of international dimensions, allowing the CEP to maintain a flight service with France via Martinique in the French West Indies. The damage done there by the cyclone Nano was tremendous. Continuing in a southerly direction, Nano next steamrolled over Moruroa, where the 3 000 men and 12 women again had to climb up on the refugee platforms to escape the combined onslaught of the wind and the sea.

While Nano followed a beautifully curved path from north to south, the next cyclone, dubbed Orama, behaved in a completely erratic manner. After having moved slowly towards Tahiti for four days, it suddenly changed its direction and veered off due east through the Tuamotus. Everyone expected Orama eventually to peter out in the empty vastness of the ocean. It did exactly the opposite: it stopped dead in its tracks, then quickly returned to the scenes of its earlier crimes in the centre of the Tuamotu group, flattening the few houses still left standing from its first assault. Then, on 23 February, it set out for Tahiti. Or so it seemed. But it soon changed course once again, taking off at increasing speed in a south-easterly direction passing eventually over Moruroa.

Vice-president Gaston Flosse flew off immediately to the Tuamotus to assure the dispirited islanders that they would be receiving relief money and loans to rebuild their houses. The estimated cost was a staggering 2 500 million francs ($A24 000 000), in addition to the 700 million Nano had already cost. Flosse, of course, counted on France to provide most of the money 'out of a sense of national solidarity', while reaping some political kudos for himself. Other politicians launched their own

298

charitable relief programmes – always making sure that a press photographer was on hand to snap pictures.

This ostentatious solicitude on the part of the local politicians no doubt had something to do with the imminence of the municipal elections, which occur only every six years. These elections are held in two rounds. That is, if one list of candidates obtains 50 per cent of the votes in the first round, that's the end of it. But if no list secures so high a percentage, a second round must be held.

At the beginning of March, chaos still reigned in the Tuamotus, where voters and electoral rolls had been scattered far and wide by Nano and Orama. Elections in seven of the communes in the group were postponed. But in the rest of French Polynesia almost 60 000 of the 85 000 registered voters went to the polls on 6 March. As usual, the main issues were down-to-earth matters such as garbage disposal, sewerage, water and electrical supplies, school and sport facilities, roads, crime and medical care.

The campaign for the second round was barely under way, when the weather station announced the almost unbelievable news that a third cyclone, Reva, was heading for Leeward Island from the north. Being by now accustomed to the capricious ways of the new 1983 generation of cyclones, we were all holding our breath in Tahiti. Although the very worst did not happen, we were nevertheless pretty close to total disaster on Saturday 12 March, when Reva passed 100 kilometres northeast of Tahiti. Altogether, more than 1 000 houses were either destroyed, unroofed or damaged in other ways. This added at least another 2 000 million francs ($A19 000 000) to the disaster bill. If the cyclone had been just a little bit slower, the assault on Tahiti would have occurred on election day and prevented the voters from reaching the polling stations. As it was, when election day dawned, Reva was already on its way, believe it or not, to Moruroa!

Despite all these previous experiences, we were not prepared when the fourth cyclone, Veena, hit Tahiti on the night of 11-12 April. One reason was the general feeling that all cyclone dangers must be over. Another reason was that both the High Commissioner and the head of the local government, Gaston Flosse – as well as our senator and two deputies, plus an assortment of party leaders – had flown off to Paris a few days earlier to take part in a meeting of the mixed commission devoted to the long overdue statutory reforms. So at this critical moment,

299

there was simply nobody in charge of the territory.

Flosse, who was at the Elysée Palace with President Mitterand at the very moment Veena started veering off towards Tahiti, asked for immediate French aid. He even managed to return on the first relief plane loaded with tarpaulins, chainsaws, nails, water purification tablets and army rations. The other political leaders followed within a day or two, and by the end of the week the Minister for Overseas Territories, Georges Lemoine, and the Commissary for the Prevention of Natural Disasters, Haroun Tazieff, also flew in.

By then the count of houses destroyed or damaged by Veena stood at 6 000. As the previous cyclones had destroyed about 4 000 houses in the Leeward and Tuamotu islands, the grand total was now 10 000. With an estimated average value of about 1 000 000 francs ($A9 800) per house, the staggering sum of 10 000 million ($A98 000 000) would be required to rebuild them. To repair damaged roads, power lines, schools, town halls and other public buildings would cost another 5 000 million. A French journalist overheard and was pleased to quote Tazieff saying that this sudden financial plight of the colony would have at least one beneficial side-effect: that of making the Polynesian leaders a little more humble and less inclined to make impatient noises about such matters as nuclear testing and independence.

Less than a week after this disaster, it was rumoured in Tahiti that yet another cyclone was on its way. The meteorological station eventually confirmed that this was so, but at the same time pointed out that it was located about 1 300 kilometres east of the Marquesas, and was therefore most unlikely to reach any island in French Polynesia. However, as the days passed, the new cyclone (first named Whisky, and then William) travelled in an unusually straight line in a south-western direction, until it reached, unbelievably, Moruroa! But unlike cyclones Nano, Orama and Reva, William did not score a direct hit, which explains how two days later a sufficient number of drenched atoll dwellers were fit enough to explode the biggest bomb in the 1983 test series. As usual, Paris kept silent about the blast, whose yield was put at 70 kilotonnes by the Wellington Seismological Observatory.

An equally impenetrable silence met all anxious enquiries in Papeete about what had happened during all these cyclones to the remaining heaps of nuclear waste stored in metal drums and plastic bags, which must still have existed at the beginning of the year in the dumping area on the north coast of Moruroa. Even the talkative Haroun Tazieff, interviewed during his stay in Tahiti, could not find a word to say about this important problem. Our guess is that the lethal stuff was swept little by little into the ocean, where it drifted about for some time, until it sank or was washed up on the shores of some other islands.

After all the damage done by these six cyclones between 1980 and 1983, Moruroa's unsuitability for underground testing was even more obvious. The best, if not ideal, solution from a purely technical point of view, would have been to transfer the whole nuclear test base to France. It would have had the additional advantage of reducing considerably the high costs, resulting above all from the necessity of having to transport material and personnel half way round the world, from France to the Pacific.

So why didn't the French government choose this alternative? The often repeated official explanation is, in the words of the French ambassador in Australia, Monsieur J. B. Merrimée (spoken during a recent meeting of the Australian Institute of International Affairs), that: 'if testing were conducted in France, the tremors from underground explosions would damage historic buildings and churches'. This is, of course, patent nonsense. As can be easily ascertained, there exist in France many heaths and mountainous regions, which have a firm geological structure and are totally devoid of historic buildings and churches.

Even better, the French Ministry for Defence owns dozens of large tank and artillery training grounds, which could be turned over to the CEP bombers without any red tape and at no cost. We especially recommend the following five, which are all larger than Moruroa:

Canjuers	34 600 hectares
Suippes	14 800 "
Mailly	12 000 "
Mourmelon	11 700 "
Larzac	10 000 "

Last but not least, there is the 35 000 hectare Albion plateau in Southern France, where only a small fraction – eighteen – of the originally planned missile silos have been and will ever be dug, and where there is consequently plenty of space for drilling nuclear test pits.

Everything in 1983 was therefore in favour of transferring the tests to France – except French public opinion, which was as scared of the tests as ever, and still greatly preferred them to be made in somebody else's backyard. For this and no other reason, instead of ordering the CEP bombers to go home, the French government told them to stay and fortify Moruroa!

When trying to carry out these instructions, the CEP admirals and generals reached back to the pre-war military strategy in France for inspiration, when her defence rested on the famous Maginot Line. Their latter day version of it, costing an estimated 450 million francs, consisted of building a four metre high and two metre thick concrete wall along both the sea and the lagoon shores of Moruroa. Comparisons with the ill-fated Maginot Line are the more justified, as there is on the north side of the atoll a four kilometre wide pass, through which future hurricane-lashed waves can enter and attack the CEP installations from the flank, as easily as the German troops did, when they invaded France in 1940. . .

60 AN UNHEALTHY SITUATION

The conservative French presidents – de Gaulle, Pompidou and Giscard – reacted to criticism of the nuclear tests at Moruroa by wrapping themselves in a cloak of haughty silence. As we have seen, the socialist government of President Mitterand, which took over the reins of power in May 1981, declared from the start, through the mouth of the Minister for Defence Charles Hernu, its willingness to explain and inform neighbouring nations what it was doing in the Pacific.

Actually, it took the socialists two years to come good on this promise, for it was not until May 1983 that the French embassies in the Pacific region began distributing statistical information about a touchy subject: the incidence of cancer in French Polynesia, which up to then had been a closely-guarded secret. These were the official figures supplied by the territorial health department, run by French army doctors:

CASES OF CANCER IN FRENCH POLYNESIA
(POPULATION 160 000)

LOCALISATION	YEARS				
	1977	1978	1979	1980	1981
Lung	3	6	2	13	15
Skin	13	11	15	—	—
Uterus	8	12	17	11	14
Breast	5	10	14	6	—
Ear-Nose-Throat	7	6	5	—	11
Liver	2	1	2	4	8
Gall-duct	2	1	—	—	—
Parotid	2	—	—	—	—
Ganglion (undetermined)	6	—	6	—	—
Digestive tract	2	11	9	—	6
Male genital	2	—	3	—	—
Urinary	1	2	1	3	4
Eyes	1	1	—	—	—
Bone	1	1	1	2	1
Nervous system	1	—	—	—	—
Thyroid	2	1	1	—	1
Ovaries	—	1	4	3	—

LOCALISATION	YEARS				
	1977	1978	1979	1980	1981
Hydatiform mole	—	—	1	—	—
Stomach	—	—	—	2	—
Intestines	—	—	—	2	—
Abdomen	—	—	—	2	—
Blood	—	—	—	7	8
Mediastinum	—	—	—	1	—
Brain	—	—	—	1	2
Undetermined	4	1	4	—	—
Generalised	—	—	—	1	—
Sacrum-coccyx area	—	—	—	—	1
TOTAL	62	65	85	58	71

This table was supplemented by a second one, listing the number of patients evacuated overseas for treatment:

Year	Total number	Cancer cases	To France and Caledonia	To New Zealand	To the U.S.A.
1975	54	22	11	11	—
1976	66	18	5	12	—
1977	92	26	10	16	—
1978	102	43	13	30	—
1979	123	57	18	39	—
1980	188	80	42	38	—
1981	257	75	43	32	—
1982 (prov.)	263	70	49	13	2

These tables were accompanied by the following comments:

The main conclusion to be drawn from the statistics is that the number of cancer cases in Polynesia, while subject as elsewhere to variations, is *in no way higher than in other areas*. It is in fact *significantly lower than in some places*, being on the average 50 per 100 000, compared with 106 in Australia, 175 in metropolitan France, and 264 in New Zealand.

(1) Total figures. For recent years they are as follows:
1977:62, 1978:65, 1979:85, 1980:58, 1981:71.

The fluctuations in numbers is a direct result of the limited size of the population concerned (160 000), and is a normal statistical phenomenon.
(2) Types of cancers. Cancers affecting organs which are the most radio-sensitive – thyroid, blood cells – do not occur more frequently than other types of cancers, and have shown no significant variations.

On the other hand, cases of cancer linked with tobacco and alcohol – lungs, upper respiratory tract, and digestive tract – are very much on the increase, and this is a cause of great concern to the authorities. Tobacco appears to be the major issue, since 75 per cent of all Polynesians are smokers, and tobacco consumption increased by 150 per cent between 1961 and 1979, while population rose by only 50 per cent.

Skin cancer occurrences appear to be no more numerous than would be expected in a climate such as prevails in Polynesia.

(3) Persons evacuated for medical reasons. It should be noted that these figures obviously do not coincide with the figures for cancer cases. The same person may be evacuated for treatment overseas, twice or more in the course of a year, and this in any case may not be required in the year in which cancer has been diagnosed.

The number of persons evacuated for medical reasons has been increasing. But all evacuees are not necessarily cancer cases. In 1982, for example, the latter were 70 out of a total of 263 persons sent overseas for medical treatment, the remainder being victims of heart disease, or cases requiring major surgery. Some are sent to metropolitan France, others to the United States or New Zealand. The reason for this is that the small population in French Polynesia has not made it possible to provide the islands with the complete range of medical facilities to be found in larger communities.

At the same time, increasing efforts are going into the early detection of cancer cases. This, coupled with a substantial rise in life expectancy, which brings a larger segment of the population into the potential cancer age groups, explains that there has been an increase in the numbers of persons evacuated.

The decision to evacuate patients is made on purely medical and/or personal grounds, and no attempt is made, contrary to certain allegations, to hide the fact since statistics on the matter, herewith provided, are readily available.

We immediately replied in several regional newspapers and magazines in the following terms:

A recent communiqué distributed by the French embassies in the region claims that the number of cancer cases in French Polynesia is lower than in all other Pacific countries. In support of this bold statement, a table of statistics headed 'Cases of Cancer in French Polynesia' is presented. The figures given are: 62 in 1977, 65 in 1978, 85 in 1979, 58 in 1980, and 71 in 1981, which represents an incidence of about 50 cases per 100 000 population. This compares very favourably indeed with the averages for Australia (106), France (175), and New Zealand (264). Wonderful, if it were true.

Actually, these statistics do *not* show the *total* number of cancer cases in

305

French Polynesia (as the heading would have us believe). They show only the number of cases treated in the Mamao government hospital, and one small private hospital in Papeete. Conspicuously lacking are data concerning cancer patients treated by:

—The 80 doctors in private practice who have no obligation to provide information on such matters.

—The Polynesian healers and various quacks.

—The special hospital for military and civilian personnel on Moruroa, where *all* data are top secret.

—The doctors in France, who are consulted by former servicemen discharged after serving in French Polynesia for shorter or longer periods. A parallel with this last category is provided by the belated discovery in the United States and Australia that servicemen present during nuclear testing in Nevada and at Maralinga were contaminated to such an extent that they got cancer.

—Finally, there are large numbers of people living in remote islands of French Polynesia where there are no doctors at all, and who consequently die from all sorts of diseases, including cancer, without receiving any medical treatment at all.

Yet, in the French embassy statement, a glaringly incomplete collection of figures is compared with the overwhelmingly more comprehensive and reliable cancer statistics kept by countries like Australia, France and New Zealand, and the totally unwarranted conclusion is drawn that the rate in French Polynesia is much lower.

This is an unabashed attempt to deceive the governments and peoples of the South Pacific, no more and no less.

It should also be noted that it was precisely because of the absence of reliable health statistics in French Polynesia that the World Health Organisation in 1981 pressed the local health authorities to start a cancer register on the internationally approved model. It is still in the developmental stages.

The document distributed by the French embassies in the Pacific also claims that the most common type of cancer in French Polynesia is lung cancer, due to heavy smoking. Once again, the statistics are reassuring only because they are so outrageously incomplete. For example, in the cancer file which we have compiled ourselves in an extremely haphazard manner, because it contains simply the cases that happened to come to our notice, we have for each and every one of the years 1977-81 many more patients than those listed in the official statistics, who have contracted such typically radiation induced diseases as leukemia thyroid cancer and brain tumour!

Last but not least it is stated in the French document that reliable statistics on the number of cancer patients treated overseas are readily available, which definitely is not the case. If we take, for instance, the New Zealand figure of 13 for 1982, in the second table, it represents in fact solely the number of cancer patients sent there *by the territorial health department*, thus leaving out the much greater number of people who paid out of their own pocket for their trip and treatment in New Zealand. Although this country is the destination of most Polynesian cancer victims who can afford a trip abroad, others also go, on their own initiative, to Hawaii, the United States and France.

The only valid conclusion to be drawn from the official French figures concerns the gradual reduction of cancer patients despatched by the territorial health department to New Zealand (39 in 1979 as against 13 in 1982), and the simultaneous increase in the number sent for treatment in military hospitals in France (18 in 1979 as against 49 in 1982). The explanation for this is obviously the inquisitive nature of the New Zealand press, which has no counterpart in metropolitan France.

Instead of trying to refute our criticism, the civilian and military authorities in French Polynesia have now reverted to their former policy of putting a secrecy stamp on all local health statistics.

61 TOWARDS A REFERENDUM?

The release of these health statistics to the press, in May 1983, was part and parcel of a larger French propaganda drive, whose principal actor, or we can almost say star performer, was presidential advisor Regis Debray. At the same time, he made an extended tour of the Pacific to explain to the various governments in the region the unfortunately too often misunderstood French defence policies. The reason why Debray had been chosen for this delicate mission was, of course, his solid reputation for being a genuinely peace-loving 'dove' and 'radical' left-winger devoid of all militaristic leanings. Therefore expectations were high in Paris that his soft-voiced pleadings in favour of nuclear testing and a go-slow decolonisation in the Pacific would go down better than the usual blunt pronouncements by a long succession of French cabinet ministers, high commissioners and ambassadors to the effect that Moruroa, Tahiti, New Caledonia and so on are all integral parts of France and that it is nobody else's business what she does in her own country.

Debray's trump card during his 1983 Pacific propaganda jaunt was to extend an official invitation from President Mitterand to all Pacific Forum governments to send scientific observers to Moruroa. The Forum nations, whose leaders met in Canberra, Australia, in August, decided to accept the French invitation. This prompted the New Zealand and Australian branches of International Physicians for Prevention of Nuclear War to write to their respective governments, urging the inclusion of some medical doctors in the team. The greatest and most tragic cases of contamination, they argued, were not found among the personnel at Moruroa (who after all had voluntarily accepted these radiation risks and moreover were examined regularly by army doctors), but among the inhabitants of all other islands in French Polynesia, who had been involuntarily exposed to the radioactive fallout from the atmospheric tests and long since absorbed this into their bodies. This was precisely what the Territorial Assembly had been fearing and protesting against for fifteen years. Therefore, simply to let a few 'observers' spend a couple of days at Moruroa under strict French supervision would not serve any purpose whatsoever. On the other hand, the doctors concluded, it was high time to undertake a thorough health survey of the whole population.

The two governments immediately transmitted this request to Paris, where it was turned down with even greater alacrity. Incredibly enough, the New Zealand and Australian prime ministers Muldoon and Fraser swallowed this rebuff, and went ahead with the preconceived plan to dispatch the wrong sort of experts to the wrong place. To be more specific, the team consisted of the director of the New Zealand National Radiation Laboratory, Mr Hugh Atkinson; his closest collaborator; plus three Australian specialists on the protecton of the environment, who were instructed to make a quick four day 'inspection' of Moruroa, on conditions to be dictated on their arrival by the French base commander.

In the meantime, however, the Polynesian political and religious leaders, who had been blocked and sidetracked for years in the same arrogant manner by French government officials, discovered to their delight that they had been joined by several new powerful allies. To begin with, the assembly of the World Council of Churches, which met in Vancouver, Canada 25 July –10 August 1983, adopted a strongly-worded resolution, condemning the tests at Moruroa and demanding a rapid decolonisation of the last French possessions in the Pacific.

As usual, Mitterand and his ministers treated the protesting Polynesian pastors with the benevolent indulgence that parents show towards young children not yet able to understand the grim realities of the cruel adult world. Shortly afterwards, however, the nuclear and colonial policies of the French socialist government were suddenly attacked from within, and it had every reason to take this 'fifth column' as seriously as it did.

It all started in Canberra, during the South Pacific Forum meeting in August 1983, and the 'traitors' were, of course, once more the *Ia mana enfants terribles*, who took the unheard of initiative of travelling to Canberra to establish contact and working relations with their natural allies, the political leaders of the other Pacific nations which had already gained independence. The mightiest and longest independent of these nations, Australia, was represented by the chairman of its international committee, Chris Schacht, who hatched an idea which appealed greatly to the Tahitian delegation. Why not put the problem of the French refusal to decolonise and demilitarise before the next meeting of the Socialist International to be held on 21–27

309

November in Brussels? The suggestion was accepted without delay by its steering committee, and an invitation extended to the *Ia mana* party to send its secretary-general, Jacqui Drollet, to Brussels to plead its cause.

He was only too happy to make the trip, and both spoke and distributed a four page pamphlet to the 120 delegates present from thirty countries. The pamphlet told the story of how General de Gaulle, 'when France was chased out of Algeria by the victorious patriots of that country, forcibly installed in our Polynesian islands the nuclear testing centre to which his own people had refused house room in France'. The leaflet ended with a call to all socialist comrades gathered in Brussels for joint action, either to persuade or to force President Mitterand to hold a referendum in French Polynesia on the nuclear testing issue.

Scared by this unexpected and unwelcome intrusion into their hitherto secluded club, the French delegates were so furious that they treated their Polynesian brother almost as an outlaw and rebel. On the other hand, a sufficient number of delegates from other countries were so impressed that the problem of French nuclear testing in the Pacific was placed on the agenda of the next meeting of the Socialist International in Copenhagen in April 1984.

True to his usual defiant form, on his return to Papeete, Jacqui Drollet held a press conference to publicise this victory for his party. He also announced that an association of 'progressive' political parties in the Pacific region was likely to occur soon. It might have been pure coincidence, but when the older and larger nationalist party, *Pupu Here Aia*, held its annual convention a few days later, anti-nuclear feeling was running more than usually high. It could almost be interpreted as a last homage to the life-long party leader, John Teariki, who had been killed two months earlier in a tractor accident on his farm.

Some delegates spoke in favour of a referendum, others wanted the tests stopped immediately, and the latter faction eventually won the day. Because independence had been the main goal of the party for so long, fewer speakers felt obliged to speak to the resolution calling for the creation of an independent Polynesian state, with some sort of commonwealth ties with France, which was adopted unanimously. The choice of Teariki's successor did not create much controversy, and the man selected by acclamation was old faithful Jean Juventin, who had been re-elected mayor of Papeete the previous year with an increased majority.

The idea of holding a popular referendum to let the Polynesian people decide whether they wanted the nuclear tests to continue or not steadily gained ground among local political leaders and was at the core of the anti-bomb demonstration held in Papeete on 25 February 1984. The date chosen was as near as possible to 1 March, or Bikini Day.

At the end of the impressive 2 000-strong procession marched the new *Pupu Here Aia* party leader and Papeete Mayor, Jean Juventin; the secretary-general of the *Ia mana* party, Jacqui Drollet; and the presidents of the ecological association *Ia ora te natura*; and the local branch of the Women's International League for Peace and Freedom.

During the meeting in Tarahoi park, which followed the march, the speeches were interspersed in Tahitian fashion with rousing anti-nuclear songs to traditional tunes. The main speech was delivered by the secretary of the *Ia mana* party, Jacqui Drollet, who dwelt mostly on the tragic, belated colonisation which the establishment of nuclear testing bases had led to:

The Polynesian land, our *fenua maohi*, has been defiled by man's apocalyptic folly, and not only has Moruroa been polluted by the fallout engendered by this monstrous undertaking, but the whole social, economic and cultural fabric of our Polynesian society has at the same time been destroyed.

We have heard much about the wonderful prosperity and progress allegedly resulting from this industry of death. But if we look back on what has happened during the past twenty years, we must ask these questions:

Does it really represent progress to have all these vast slums here in Tahiti, inhabited by Polynesian immigrants from the other islands? And what has happened to the 10 000 Polynesians employed on all sorts of heavy construction work by the CEP during the first years? Today 7 700 of them have been laid off and are unemployed.

And those Polynesians who were able to buy a car in the early days, do they still have it today? And the Polynesians who sold their land in the CEP heydays, are they wealthier today?

The speaker ended on this sad note:

Our land has changed hands, we have sold it for a dream.

Our power of decision has been taken from us, and all we have got in exchange are a few social welfare benefits.

Our society has become tough, cruel, merciless, and we are dominated by a new desire to make individual profits.

To continue along this road is sheer nuclear prostitution.

The petition, addressed to President Mitterand, was in the end proposed, and of course also adopted by a show of hands. This reminded Jacqui Drollet of what candidate Mitterand had said during a visit to Tahiti long before he was elected to the highest office of the Republic. These are the main points of Drollet's response:

In 1975 you told us people of Polynesia in a speech in the Town Hall here in Papeete that, if you were elected president of the Republic, we should be consulted and our choice respected. Today, Mr President, we should like to remind you of this promise to let us freely choose our destiny.

In 1962 General de Gaulle had decided for us, against our will, to install here in French Polynesia the nuclear testing centre, which had been functioning in the Sahara up until the independence of Algeria. In other words, it was transferred to the other end of the world, to our islands, because no French leader wanted it in his own country.

We ask you today, Mr President, to repair this injustice by consulting in a democratic manner the Polynesian people, whether the tests should be allowed to continue or not. This request is supported by practically all political parties in our country.

When the organising committee entered the government compound to have this petition transmitted in the proper manner to President Mitterand, it was met (just like in the pre-Mitterand days) by an underling who explained that the High Commissioner suffered from a temporary indisposition, which unfortunately made it impossible for him to appear in person.

Also in accordance with a long government tradition to suppress all adverse news, the RFO radio and television announcers barely mentioned in the subsequent newscasts that there had been a protest march and, of course, said absolutely nothing about the embarassing contents of the speech and the petition. On the other hand, exactly as during the pre-socialist regimes, the French police filmed all protesters as they marched by, so as to be able to keep a better tab on their activities in the future.

62 NO END IN SIGHT

As agreed upon in Brussels, the colonial problem of French-nuclear Polynesia was again on the agenda for the 1984 meeting of the Socialist International in Copenhagen, 24-26 April. The Australian delegation – Gough Whitlam, Kate Moore and Don Grimes – made a well-argued, detailed submission to the special Disarmament Advisory Committee. Their main points were:

France's testing programme at Moruroa rests on two main considerations.

First, its colonialist position in the Pacific. The territory which France utilises as its testing site is part of French 'dominion' territory. It is far removed from metropolitan France, where it is clear that such a testing programme would be unacceptable to both French and European publics.

It is of fundamental importance when considering France's testing programme at Moruroa to recognise that it relies upon the maintenance of its control of the islands and people involved. The position may be different if this were not the case.

The French nuclear testing programme has ensured that the worst features of European colonisation have been inflicted upon the Polynesian people.

Severe economic and social dislocation has been created by the presence of over 10 000 French military and technical personnel involved in the nuclear testing programme. The continuance of the nuclear testing programme ensures that this economic and social imperialism will further erode the Polynesian culture and social fabric.

The capital city, Papeete, has significant urban slums which were created by the French authorities recruiting labour from outlying islands to construct the military and technical facilities for the nuclear testing programme. However, now that the construction phase has been completed, this labour has been left unemployed and forced to live in dreadful slum conditions on the outskirts of Papeete, despite promises that they would be repatriated to their original islands.

Second, its testing programme is a product of the structures for the defence of France developed under the de Gaulle Government and maintained by successive French governments, irrespective of their political colouration.

That notion of the defence of France posits the need for an *independent* French nuclear deterrent force. De Gaulle's decisions to remove France

313

from the military structures of NATO were a part of the definition of this doctrine of independence.

While France argues that its nuclear forces contribute to Western defence, French nuclear doctrine is such that the clear purpose of its *independent* deterrent is to rescue France alone, even in a situation where overall Western defence was jeopardised if not defeated.

While such a national aspiration may be understandable, especially given France's recent history, this policy is essentially an extreme nationalist one and it underlines the speciousness of France's claim that the purpose of its deterrent is to contribute to Western defence arrangements. This has bearing on East/West arms control negotiations, a point which is discussed further below.

It is of great significance that virtually without exception, member governments of the Socialist International have agreed on the urgent need to stop the nuclear arms race and nuclear testing.

France has rarely been governed by such a fraternal party. But it is today. It is a matter of deep concern that the present socialist government of France has maintained the Gaullist policies of nuclear weapons and nuclear weapons testing. By taking advantage of a continuing colonialist position in the South Pacific, this means that the fraternal government of France is behaving in a way that is contrary to two principles thoroughly endorsed by the Socialist International – the right of self-determination of all people, and the urgent need for nuclear disarmament and an end to nuclear testing.

The opposition to the French policies and practices was so strong that in the end the French delegation threatened to bow out of the International if the attacks were carried further. So the attacks were carried no further – on this occasion.

The wholly inaccurate version the French press gave of what had happened during this meeting inspired the local French-language newspaper *Les Nouvelles* to the following scathing attack on the main culprit – the Australian Labor Party:

THE SOCIALIST INTERNATIONAL CONDEMNS THE DECEIT SHOWN BY AUSTRALIA

Although a rare occurrence, the Socialist International is capable of *momentarily putting aside demagogy*. This happened recently in Copenhagen, when it rudely rejected an Australian proposal, made by the former Prime Minister Gough Whitlam, who criticised in the most violent terms the policies pursued by France in the Pacific. On this occasion, the secretary of the French socialist party, Lionel Jospin, threw his whole weight into the battle to make it clear to the comrades from Canberra that they interfered in problems which were none of their business. Gough Whitlam, who after having been Prime Minister has now become ambassador to the UNESCO, disregarded all diplomatic niceties when denouncing, in his submission, 'the French nuclear tests and colonial rule in the Pacific'.

This champion of Australian expansionism ignores completely the use of circumlocutions and euphemisms. Nor does he care to observe the rules which should be respected among neighbours. This incident can therefore not be passed over lightly. It confirms the aggressive character of the Australian policy towards France. What do the Australian leaders want? Is it to place the whole Pacific under their guardianship and boot out the last European nation?

Fortunately for the beleaguered French government, it could now reap the benefits of the clever manoeuvre mounted half a year earlier. As will be recalled, a group of five scientists from Australia, New Zealand and Papua New Guinea had been dispatched to Moruroa in October 1983 and had been taken on a whirlwind tour of the island of less than four days. On 20 December of that same year, long before they had even produced a first draft of the first chapter of their report, the visit was exploited in the most shameless manner by the Minister for Overseas Territories, Georges Lemoine, in an address to the National Assembly, which summed up the future findings of the distinguished foreign scientists in these succinct terms:

After thorough investigation of the Moruroa site, lasting eight days, and after having taken all the samples they needed and desired, the members of the team have admitted that France has adopted all necessary safeguards to assure that the tests are harmless. These are words uttered by scientists, whereas the opinions expressed by church ministers only have moral value. It can therefore be concluded that the tests at Moruroa are not dangerous.

Not one of the wildly applauding deputies asked when, where and to whom the members of the team had made the alleged statements. As for Mr Atkinson, he kept silent, as usual.

Six months later, on 8 July 1984, the 166-page report put together by Atkinson and his men was at last released. It was an exquisite study in futility, as can be seen by simply looking up the 'Diary of Events'. It shows that the team departed from Papeete for Moruroa at 1.30 p.m. on 25 October and returned from there at 4.45 on 29 October 1983, and therefore that the total time spent on the atoll was less than four days – not eight days, as Minister Lemoine pretended.

Even more revealing were the indications about the sort of 'studies' and 'investigations' carried out. The first day, 25 October, the team arrived so late at Moruroa that there was only time to listen to a few lectures in bad English about subjects such as 'The Nuclear Defence Concept' and 'The Role of the French Atomic Energy Commission'. The following day, 26 October, the weary travellers were offered, in the early morning, a ride around the atoll in a helicopter and a short walk in the residential area, only to be followed by a new round of dreary lectures which lasted until late into the night.

The morning of the third day was taken up by visits to various laboratories and decontamination centres until 3.30 p.m., when the team members carefully inspected an object which cannot have been entirely unfamiliar to them: a drilling rig of the sort used for all oil explorations. After dinner, they talked from 8.30 p.m. until presumably late into the night about 'the formation and structure of an atoll'.

The fourth day, 28 October, was quite exceptionally devoted to sample taking from 1.00 p.m. The fifth day, 29 October, the team members visited an abandoned sealed underground test site in the morning, before catching the plane back to Tahiti for a few more days of courtesy visits, luncheons, dinners and discussions.

Incidentally, when browsing through the official French documents reproduced as appendices, one is struck by the lack of such an essential piece of information as a complete list of all the nuclear tests made so far at Moruroa and Fangataufa, with the precise time, yield, etc. It is not good enough, as the case now is, to have to depend on incomplete data supplied by the New Zealand Seismological Observatory.

Even with all these extracurricular activities, it seems to us that the five-man team should still have been able to obtain at least *some* useful information about two particularly serious types of nuclear pollution which have demonstrably occurred.

The first is, of course, the possible venting, seepage and leakage into the air and the ocean. The best way to ascertain these risks would, of course, have been for the team to observe an actual test of the usual 10-70 kilotonne yield. Mr Atkinson does not say in his report whether he asked his hosts in advance to detonate a bomb for their benefit, but the fact is that this was not done. Nor did the

CEP put at their disposal any diving apparatus capable of taking them down to depths of 600-1000 metres, where the explosions are made, although a fully-equipped French submarine for this type of underwater researches was cruising in eastern Polynesian waters at the time of their visit. Therefore nothing could be learnt about the venting, seepage and leakage, and the three chapters of the Atkinson report devoted to these problems only contain surmises.

Then there is the pollution problem which had figured prominently in all leading newspapers and magazines throughout the world in November and December 1981. This did not require any special equipment and effort to report on. In fact, it could have been done during an hour-long inspection of the north coast of Moruroa, for at the root of this problem were the huge amounts of radioactive waste – including between ten and twenty kilogrammes of plutonium – which had been dumped there between the airstrip and the pass.

As Mr Atkinson tells the story, when he asked for permission to visit this incongruously called 'safety trial area' – fifteen minutes distant by car from the residential area where the team stayed – he was told that it was completely out of the question, due to the many 'military secrets' there which had to be protected. Disappointed though they might be, the investigators were not even permitted to collect specimens of coral from the lagoon. In the published report, these major restrictions were dismissed in the following, totally unconcerned manner: 'As the Mission was not permitted to sample sediments from the lagoon, nor take any types of sample from the safety trial area, this avenue of verification was denied.' Instead of protesting in the strongest possible way – that is, by flying straight back home, the team spent the day taking surface samples of the ocean water which, sure enough, was not terribly contaminated, as the last very small bomb blast had taken place three months earlier at a depth of 800 metres!

If Mr Atkinson and his companions had limited their remarks to such subjects as radiation, venting, leakage and waste disposal, on which they were more or less experts, our only criticism would be that they had not contributed any new information or insight. Unfortunately, the authors also included a section on 'Cancer Incidence and Statistics for French Polynesia', a subject totally outside their competence. They were obviously unaware that the data they reproduced – which were supplied by the French army doctor, with the rank of a general, who ran the territorial health department – represented only *a small portion* of the actual cases of cancer in French Polynesia, as we have demonstrated in a previous chapter.

Why Mr Atkinson did not turn over these health statistics to some medical colleagues in New Zealand or Australia for a critical analysis is beyond our comprehension. This blunder was, of course, immediately exploited by the Minister for Defence, Charles Hernu, who on 10 July 1984 claimed in a press release that the main findings of 'the distinguished foreign scientists, who had made a thorough, independent investigation at Moruroa, were that the tests are totally harmless for the health of the Polynesians and the other peoples living in the Pacific'.

If we are to judge by newspaper cuttings received so far from other Pacific countries, many politicians and journalists have, quite understandably, made the mistake of taking these concocted statistics at their face value. Whereas most people here in French Polynesia have, of course, seen through this sinister propaganda trick of first feeding the unsuspecting scientists with phoney data and then quoting them as their own, genuine findings.

For this very reason, the Evangelical Church (to which the majority of Polynesians belong), again confirmed in August 1984, during its annual Synod, its firm opposition to the nuclear tests, and once more declared itself in favour of a referendum. This demand was reiterated with even greater insistence by the annual convention of Flosse's *Tahoeraa* party, held on 1 September. This was actually a much more important event than the promulgation one week later of the long heralded new statute. This new statute turned out to be only a muddled rewrite of the totally inadequate 1977 statute.

So far, the reaction of the French government to the request for a referendum on the nuclear testing issue has not been very promising. All it has done has been to send out to Tahiti, in October 1984, one of the new French admirals, Yves Leenhardt. Leenhardt happens to be a Protestant, and during his previous two-year term of duty in French Polynesia he was a faithful church-goer. At Admiral Leenhardt's insistence, half-a-dozen dignitaries of the Evangelical Church consented to participate in a trip to Moruroa, during which they were lectured to about the urgency of defending the free, Christian world against the godless communists – something that can, of course, only be done with the help of nuclear weapons of the sort tested at Moruroa. The whole scheme backfired, however, for when the CEP issued a bulletin afterwards saying that 'the anxiety hitherto felt by the church leaders about the nuclear tests had now been laid to rest', the Evangelical Church replied with its own communiqué, reaffirming that it is still 'totally opposed to the pursuit of French nuclear tests at Moruroa and that it has already written three times to President Mitterand asking him to stop them'.

Will there ever be any other more positive, or at least more explicitly formulated reply from Paris to this general clamour for a referendum? The answer is, of course, no. As this account of the post-war history of French Polynesia shows, the sad truth is that the French government, whatever its political hue may be, always acts, in the first place, in its own interest. And unfortunately, it is in their interest to continue the nuclear tests at Moruroa and Fangataufa.

EPILOGUE

The Real 'Underwatergate' Scandal

On previous visits to Europe, the only news items on the Pacific we had seen had been short notices, rarely more than five lines, announcing in a matter-of-fact manner the detonation of yet another nuclear device at Moruroa. It was therefore an unusual experience, during our most recent European trip, to find major European newspapers, day after day, giving front page treatment to events taking place in Moruroa, Papeete, Auckland, Wellington and Canberra.

The sinking of the *Rainbow Warrior* had precipitated this interest. As the facts were revealed, the story developed into a major French 'Underwatergate' scandal, with serious national and international repercussions – especially after the main focus had shifted from the incredibly amateurish and clumsy manner in which the French not-so-secret agents did their job, to the question of who in France's political hierarchy issued the fatal orders.

At the time of writing, President Mitterand, Prime Minister Fabius and the sacked Defence Minister Hernu are still blaming each other for having ordered military combat divers to 'neutralize' the Greenpeace protest flotilla. They are probably all equally guilty, although the only thing certain is that the undercover, underwater agents interpreted this ambiguous instruction exactly as the French gendarmes did in New Caledonia when they 'neutralized' the Kanak FLNKS leader Eloi Machoro by shooting him in cold blood. One also wonders about the real worth of the promise repeatedly made by Mitterand and Fabius to punish the men guilty of this 'criminal and absurd act', when the only individuals interrogated so far by the military police are the undercover agents who, in order to embarrass the government, leaked the true story to the press.

There is also much concern and fuss in the French media about the fate of the Turenge couple, imprisoned in New Zealand, whom both the government and public opinion in France see as valiant soldiers who deserve to be decorated, because 'all they did was obey orders'. As for the Greenpeace activists, there is a general agreement in France that they are wittingly or unwittingly working for the Russians – with American funds!

On the other hand, we cannot find in the metre-high pile of newspaper cuttings that we have collected about the various aspects of this tragicomic affair, one single reference to the problems, sufferings and aspirations of the people most deeply involved, the Polynesians, in whose islands 120 nuclear bombs have been detonated during the short period of twenty years. When reading all these articles, it is almost as if the 118 islands of French Polynesia were uninhabited, except perhaps for the few lovely hula girls who welcome French officials.

President Mitterand's much touted pilgrimage to Moruroa just after the *Rainbow Warrior* bombing was a splendid illustration of this long-established French policy of considering the Polynesian people as a *quantité négligeable*. Not once did he even consider making a detour to Tahiti, where he risked facing Polynesian political leaders clamouring for independence – they now represent more than 50 per cent of the electorate – and condemning the nuclear tests. On the latter issue, the Synod of the Evangelical Church, to which 80 per cent of the Polynesians belong, has been writing to Mitterand for years, entreating him to stop the Moruroa madness. (The only reply so far is a short letter saying that he will stop when the Russians and Americans have done so.)

Mitterand might also have been reminded of the many bold promises he made while he was still in opposition – to grant all colonial peoples independence, to stop the murderous tests in the Pacific and to scrap 'the ruinous and strategically worthless *force de frappe*'.

The Territorial Assembly has long had on its agenda the setting up of a commission of medical doctors to make an impartial investigation of the health hazards resulting from the tests. The French Government has consistently blocked this move.

Last but not least, there has been a widespread opposition in Tahiti to the present uncontrolled and unlimited immigration of French settlers, as in New Caledonia. The swarm of French reporters accompanying Mitterand considered all these issues as strictly local, and consequently of no interest to their French readers and the world at large.

When on his return to Paris Mitterand addressed the French nation, he did not once depart from his main object and theme: that French Polynesia is an integral part of the French republic, and what his government does in the Pacific is no one else's business – least of all that of the Australians and New Zealanders.

There was also the usual praise for the Atkinson Report, which he claimed proved that nobody at Moruroa had ever been touched by any radioactive contamination. The only new twist in this homecoming speech was that Mitterand had decided to set up a French Cultural Institute in Tahiti for the benefit of uncouth foreigners in the Pacific region who, it was hoped, would acquire a more positive opinion of France and French culture.

The numerous French radio, TV and newspaper reporters who have been dispatched to the Pacific in the wake of the presidential trip, have continued to supply the popular demand for a good, true spy story in a never-ending succession of instalments, and have paid scant attention to native problems and politics. Well, a few of them have loudly praised the Polynesians in general terms, contrasting their friendliness and hospitality with the dourness and hostility of the Kanaks in New Caledonia, who they believe have been so unhappily misguided by a handful of agitators.

At the end of September 1985, the prestigious SOFRES institute organized a public opinion poll to find out what the French people thought of whole 'Underwatergate' scandal. None of the questions asked concerned the implications for the Polynesian people. The nearest the pollsters got was the following question: 'Are you in favour of or opposed to France continuing its underground testing in the Pacific?' Not less than 60 per cent approved, only 24 per cent were opposed and 16 per cent were without an opinion.

This represents a 'national consensus', we are told, which should be respected by all peoples in the Pacific. So far, no French politician or editorialist has cared to mention the embarrassing fact that political, civic and church leaders in French Polynesia have for years been asking the Paris government to organize a *local* referendum so as to allow the people most concerned, the islanders themselves, to decide the issue.

February 1986

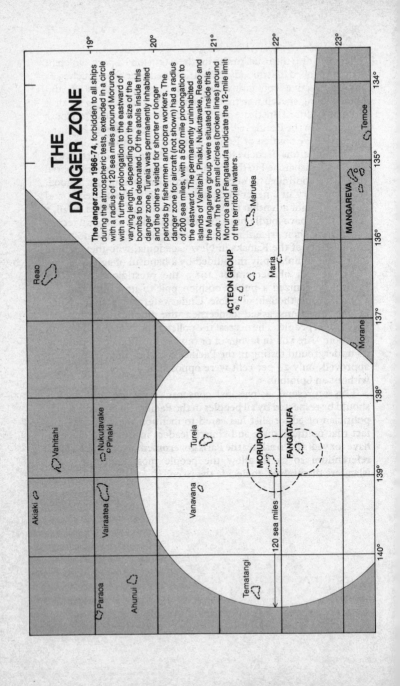

THE
DANGER ZONE

The danger zone 1966-74, forbidden to all ships during the atmospheric tests, extended in a circle with a radius of 120 sea miles around Moruroa, with a further prolongation to the eastward of varying length, depending on the size of the bombs to be detonated. Of the atolls inside this danger zone, Tureia was permanently inhabited and the others visited for shorter or longer periods by fishermen and copra workers. The danger zone for aircraft (not shown) had a radius of 200 sea miles, with a 500 mile prolongation to the eastward. The permanently uninhabited islands of Vahitahi, Pinaki, Nukutavake, Reao and the Mangareva group were situated inside this zone. The two small circles (broken lines) around Moruroa and Fangataufa indicate the 12-mile limit of the territorial waters.

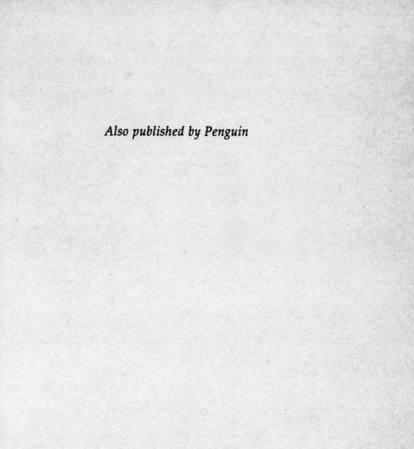

Also published by Penguin

THE WHITLAM GOVERNMENT
1972-1975

Gough Whitlam

**A frank and expansive book by a literate and visionary
statesman is a rarity. *The Whitlam Government* is such a rarity.**

Gough Whitlam's Government was a government of reform and
his account shows the Labor administration's concern for
Australia's place in a more just world; for the quality of
Australian life; for equality of opportunity for all Australians and
how these issues were elevated to the national agenda under his
leadership.

In this book Gough Whitlam not only draws a vivid portrait of
three memorable years in Australia's history. He paints a broad
and illuminating canvas of Australia as it was, as it has become
and as it yet might be.

THE ELECTRONIC ESTATE
New Communications Media and Australia

Trevor Barr

The traditional world of Australia's publishing broadcasting and communications institutions is undergoing substantial and rapid change.

Trevor Barr, in discussing the new technologies of change – the domestic satellite, videotex, cable television, electronic funds transfer, microcomputers – shows that they are not isolated innovations. They are inter-relating and combining to change our society.

The emergence of The Electronic Estate not only provides a challenge to the strategies of corporations and institutions – it issues an ultimatum to politicians. The new information society demands the formulation of policies that are broad, brave and bipartisan.